THE AMERICAN ECONOMY

ISSN 1554-4400

THE AMERICAN ECONOMY

Kim Masters Evans

INFORMATION PLUS® REFERENCE SERIES
Formerly Published by Information Plus, Wylie, Texas

GALE
CENGAGE Learning™

Detroit • New York • San Francisco • New Haven, Conn • Waterville, Maine • London

The American Economy

Kim Masters Evans

Paula Kepos, Series Editor

Project Editors: Elizabeth Manar, Kathleen
J. Edgar

Rights Acquisition and Management: Margaret
Abendroth, Jackie Jones

Composition: Evi Abou-El-Seoud, Mary Beth
Trimper

Manufacturing: Cynde Bishop

Product Management: Carol Nagel

For product information and technology assistance, contact us at
Gale Customer Support, 1-800-877-4253.
For permission to use material from this text or product,
submit all requests online at **www.cengage.com/permissions.**
Further permissions questions can be e-mailed to
permissionrequest@cengage.com

Cover photograph: Image copyright Karen Struthers, 2008. Used under license from Shutterstock.com.

Gale
27500 Drake Rd.
Farmington Hills, MI 48331-3535

ISBN-13: 978-0-7876-5103-9 (set)   ISBN-10: 0-7876-5103-6 (set)
ISBN-13: 978-1-4144-3368-4   ISBN-10: 1-4144-3368-9

ISSN 1554-4400

This title is also available as an e-book.
ISBN-13: 978-1-4144-5756-7 (set)
ISBN-10: 1-4144-5756-1 (set)
Contact your Gale sales representative for ordering information.

Printed in the United States of America
1 2 3 4 5 6 7 13 12 11 10 09

TABLE OF CONTENTS

economy. Major trade agreements, the International Monetary Fund and the World Bank, economic sanctions, and the increasing trend toward global free trade, or globalization, are also discussed in this chapter.

PREFACE

The American Economy is part of the *Information Plus Reference Series*. The purpose of each volume of the series is to present the latest facts on a topic of pressing concern in modern American life. These topics include today's most controversial and studied social issues: abortion, capital punishment, care for the elderly, crime, the environment, health care, immigration, minorities, national security, social welfare, women, youth, and many more. Even though this series is written especially for high school and undergraduate students, it is an excellent resource for anyone in need of factual information on current affairs.

By presenting the facts, it is the intention of Gale, a part of Cengage Learning, to provide its readers with everything they need to reach an informed opinion on current issues. To that end, there is a particular emphasis in this series on the presentation of scientific studies, surveys, and statistics. These data are generally presented in the form of tables, charts, and other graphics placed within the text of each book. Every graphic is directly referred to and carefully explained in the text. The source of each graphic is presented within the graphic itself. The data used in these graphics are drawn from the most reputable and reliable sources, in particular from the various branches of the U.S. government and from major independent polling organizations. Every effort has been made to secure the most recent information available. Readers should bear in mind that many major studies take years to conduct, and that additional years often pass before the data from these studies are made available to the public. Therefore, in many cases the most recent information available in 2009 is dated from 2006 or 2007. Older statistics are sometimes presented as well, if they are of particular interest and no more-recent information exists.

Even though statistics are a major focus of the *Information Plus Reference Series*, they are by no means its only content. Each book also presents the widely held positions and important ideas that shape how the book's subject is discussed in the United States. These positions are explained in detail and, where possible, in the words of their proponents. Some of the other material to be found in these books includes historical background, descriptions of major events related to the subject, relevant laws and court cases, and examples of how these issues play out in American life. Some books also feature primary documents, or have pro and con debate sections giving the words and opinions of prominent Americans on both sides of a controversial topic. All material is presented in an even-handed and unbiased manner; readers will never be encouraged to accept one view of an issue over another.

HOW TO USE THIS BOOK

The U.S. economy in the twenty-first century is enormous and is extremely complicated. Workers, employers large and small, consumers, the equities markets, the U.S. government, and the world economy are constantly interacting with each other to affect the U.S. economy and, through it, each other. The U.S. economy produces and consumes raw materials, services, manufactured goods, and intellectual property in vast amounts. This book describes the size and scope of the U.S. economy, explains how it functions, and examines some of the challenges it faces, such as inflation, government regulation, offshoring, and corporate scandals.

The American Economy consists of ten chapters and three appendixes. Each of the chapters is devoted to a particular aspect of the U.S economy. For a summary of the information covered in each chapter, please see the synopses provided in the Table of Contents at the front of the book. Chapters generally begin with an overview of the basic facts and background information on the chapter's topic, then proceed to examine subtopics of particular interest. For example, Chapter 8: Wealth in the United States begins by detailing the components of wealth: net worth (assets and liabilities) and personal income. Next, the chapter addresses poverty in the United States by providing statistics of the poverty rate and the working poor. Wealth distribution within the United States is given particular attention, and two types of tools that are used in determining this distribution—Gini coefficients and concentration rates—are explained. The chapter then moves on to a description of wealth demographics in the United States, including race, financial assets, and nonfinancial assets. The chapter concludes by discussing whether or not wealth inequality is harmful to the U.S. economy. Readers can find their way through a chapter by looking for the section and subsection headings, which are clearly set off from the text. Or, they can refer to the book's extensive index, if they already know what they are looking for.

Statistical Information

The tables and figures featured throughout *The American Economy* will be of particular use to readers in learning about this topic. These tables and figures represent an extensive collection of the most recent and valuable statistics on the U.S. economy—for example, graphics in this book cover the spending habits of the typical consumer, employment in manufacturing and service industries, the gross domestic product, the trade deficit, and consumer debt levels. Gale, a part of Cengage Learning, believes that making this information available to readers is the most important way to fulfill the goal of this book: to help readers understand the issues and controversies surrounding the U.S. economy and reach their own conclusions.

Each table or figure has a unique identifier appearing above it, for ease of identification and reference. Titles for the tables and figures explain their purpose. At the end of each table or figure, the original source of the data is provided.

To help readers understand these often complicated statistics, all tables and figures are explained in the text. References in the text direct readers to the relevant statistics. Furthermore, the contents of all tables and figures are fully indexed. Please see the opening section of the index at the back of this volume for a description of how to find tables and figures within it.

Appendixes

Besides the main body text and images, *The American Economy* has three appendixes. The first is the Important Names and Addresses directory. Here readers will find contact information for a number of government and private organizations that can provide further information on aspects of the U.S. economy. The second appendix is the Resources section, which can also assist readers in conducting their own research. In this section, the author and editors of *The American Economy* describe some of the sources that were most useful during the compilation of this book. The final appendix is the detailed index.

ADVISORY BOARD CONTRIBUTIONS

The staff of Information Plus would like to extend its heartfelt appreciation to the Information Plus Advisory Board. This dedicated group of media professionals provides feedback on the series on an ongoing basis. Their comments allow the editorial staff who work on the project to continually make the series better and more user-friendly. Our top priorities are to produce the highest-quality and most useful books possible, and the Advisory Board's contributions to this process are invaluable.

The members of the Information Plus Advisory Board are:

- Kathleen R. Bonn, Librarian, Newbury Park High School, Newbury Park, California

- Madelyn Garner, Librarian, San Jacinto College–North Campus, Houston, Texas

- Anne Oxenrider, Media Specialist, Dundee High School, Dundee, Michigan

- Charles R. Rodgers, Director of Libraries, Pasco-Hernando Community College, Dade City, Florida

- James N. Zitzelsberger, Library Media Department Chairman, Oshkosh West High School, Oshkosh, Wisconsin

COMMENTS AND SUGGESTIONS

The editors of the *Information Plus Reference Series* welcome your feedback on *The American Economy*. Please direct all correspondence to:

Editors
Information Plus Reference Series
27500 Drake Rd.
Farmington Hills, MI 48331-3535

CHAPTER 1
THE U.S. ECONOMY: HISTORICAL OVERVIEW

It is not what we have that will make us a great nation;
it is the way in which we use it.

—Theodore Roosevelt, 1886

The workings of the U.S. economy are complex and often mysterious, even to economists. At its simplest, the economy runs on three major sectors: consumers, businesses, and government. (See Figure 1.1.) Consumers earn money and exchange much of it for goods and services from businesses. These businesses use the money to produce more goods and services and to pay wages to their employees. Both consumers and businesses fund the government sector, which spends and transfers money back into the system. The banking system plays a crucial role in the economy by providing the means for all sectors to save and borrow money. Finally, there are the stock markets, which allow consumers to invest their money in the nation's businesses—an enterprise that further fuels economic growth for all sectors. Thus, the U.S. economy is a circular system based on interdependent relationships in which massive amounts of money change hands. The historical developments that produced this system are important to understand, because they provide key information about what has made the U.S. economy such a powerful force in the world.

DEFINING THE U.S. ECONOMY

The term *market economy* describes an economy in which the forces of supply and demand dictate the way in which goods and resources are allocated and what prices will be set. The opposite of a market economy is a *planned economy*, in which the government determines what will be produced and what prices will be charged. In a market economy, producers anticipate what products the market will be interested in and at what price, and they make decisions about what products they will bring to market and how these products will be produced and priced. Market economies foster competition among businesses,

which typically leads to lower prices and is generally considered beneficial for both workers and consumers. By contrast, a planned economy is directed by a central government that has a far greater degree of influence over prices and production, as well as a tighter regulation of industries and manufacturing procedures. The United States has a *mixed economy*, which combines aspects of a market economy with some central planning and control to create a system with a high degree of market freedom along with regulatory agencies and social programs that promote the public welfare.

This mixed economy did not develop overnight. It has evolved over more than two centuries and has been shaped by American experiences at various times with hardship, war, peace, and prosperity.

HISTORICAL TRENDS
Colonial Times

When European colonists first came to the New World, they found a vast expanse of land inhabited by Native Americans. Many of the first colonies were business ventures called charter companies that were financed by wealthy English businessmen and landowners. The colonies were granted limited economic and political rights by the king of England. After profits proved to be disappointing, many of the investors turned over the companies to the colonists themselves. These actions were to have far-reaching consequences on the shape of the United States. Christopher Conte and Albert R. Karr note in *The U.S. Economy: A Brief History* (2007, http://usinfo.state.gov/products/pubs/oecon/chap3.htm) that "the colonists were left to build their own lives, their own communities, and their own economy."

At first, the colonists were preoccupied with merely surviving. Eventually, they engaged in commerce with Europe by exploiting the natural resources of their new homeland. The main agricultural products of the colonies were tobacco, wheat, rye, barley, rice, and indigo plant.

FIGURE 1.1

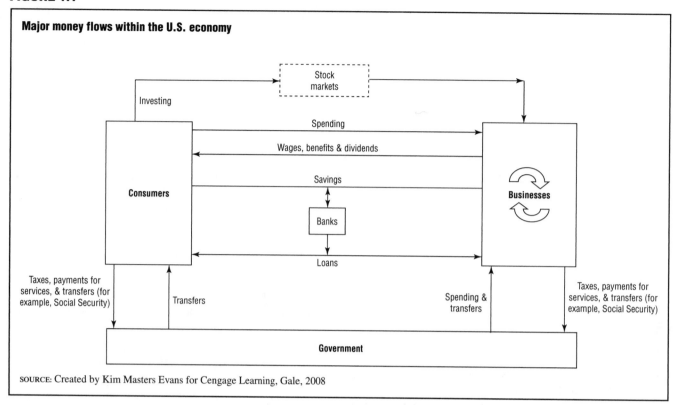

Major money flows within the U.S. economy

SOURCE: Created by Kim Masters Evans for Cengage Learning, Gale, 2008

Other important exports were animal furs, products from fish and whales, and timber. Shipbuilding became a major industry in New England.

Political and Industrial Revolution

Frustrated with the political and economic interference of England, the colonists banded together to forge a new nation: the United States of America. The push for independence from Britain, which culminated in the Revolutionary War (1775–1783), was driven by economic and political motivations, including the desire for greater self-governance and tax relief.

In 1776 a book was published in England that would have long-reaching effects on the new United States. The Scottish philosopher Adam Smith (1723–1790) wrote *An Inquiry into the Nature and Causes of the Wealth of Nations*. The book was remarkable for many reasons. It discussed economic principles in a common sense, non-mathematical manner and argued that the forces of supply and demand affect prices and wages. It criticized the restrictions and regulations common in European countries, and it advocated free and open trade within and between countries and the abolishment of wage and price controls. Smith believed that an "invisible hand" was guiding workers seeking to better their private finances, which in turn helped nations achieve prosperity. In other words, people who work hard for their own gain unconsciously contribute to national wealth. The principles of a competitive marketplace with little gov-

ernment interference were adopted by the new United States and dominated the nation's economic policy for more than a century.

During the late 1700s Britain and the newly formed United States underwent a major social and economic change from agriculture to industry. The Industrial Revolution saw the introduction of the steam engine, the cotton gin, and other machines capable of increasing production while decreasing human labor. Farming, in particular, became much less labor intensive, freeing up people to pursue other forms of employment. Over the next century the United States changed from an agrarian-based nation to one in which the majority of income was generated by manufacturing, trade, and business providing services to consumers. (See Figure 1.2.)

The 1800s: Expansion and Civil War

The 1800s were a period of enormous growth for the United States in terms of territory, population, and economic might. The Northeast developed thriving industries, and cities swelled with hundreds of thousands of European immigrants. Even though the South remained largely rural and agricultural, mechanical innovations, such as the cotton gin, changed the region's focus. Cotton became a major crop and was exported to textile mills in the North and overseas. Much of the economic success of the South was based on the use of slave labor.

Deep divisions arose between factions in the North and South on the morality of slavery and associated

FIGURE 1.2

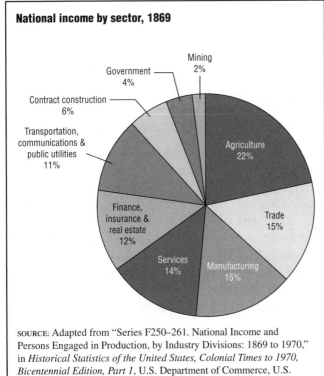

National income by sector, 1869

- Mining 2%
- Government 4%
- Contract construction 6%
- Transportation, communications & public utilities 11%
- Finance, insurance & real estate 12%
- Services 14%
- Manufacturing 15%
- Trade 15%
- Agriculture 22%

SOURCE: Adapted from "Series F250–261. National Income and Persons Engaged in Production, by Industry Divisions: 1869 to 1970," in *Historical Statistics of the United States, Colonial Times to 1970, Bicentennial Edition, Part 1*, U.S. Department of Commerce, U.S. Census Bureau, September 1975, http://www2.census.gov/prod2/statcomp/documents/CT1970p1-07.pdf (accessed April 3, 2008)

political and economic issues, which led to the devastating American Civil War in 1861. By the time the war ended in 1865, the factories of the Northeast had become extremely important in fueling the U.S. economy.

The Gilded Age

In 1873 the American author Mark Twain (1835–1910) cowrote with his neighbor Charles Dudley Warner (1829–1900) the novel *The Gilded Age*, which describes an American society in which unscrupulous businessmen and corrupt politicians pursue quick fortunes at the expense of the common people. Indeed, the decades following the Civil War were characterized by scandals involving high-level politicians making money from crooked business deals and by an unprecedented boom in business. The resulting social atmosphere was one of decadence among the upper classes contrasted with poverty and labor unrest among the lower classes.

The U.S. government had a hands-off approach to business regulation, a tactic described by the French term *laissez faire* (leave alone or "do as you please"). It was generally believed that the government should not interfere in economic affairs but should instead allow supply and demand and competition to operate unfettered, resulting in a free market.

The gilded age is notable for a growth in corporations. A corporation is a legally defined entity that may receive financial support from many investors but is treated as an individual under the law. A corporation is granted a state charter including specific rights, privileges, and liabilities. This type of business organization became popular in the late 1800s. It allowed people to invest in businesses without taking on all the responsibilities and risks of being a business owner. State charters limited the liability of individual investors, who were paid dividends in proportion to their share of investment in the corporation.

Some corporations grew through mergers or by buying out the companies of their competitors. Then they developed a business structure called a trust, in which the component companies were managed by a small group of people called a board of trustees. These corporations controlled nearly all the business in their respective industries, a condition known as monopolization. The public feared that trusts squelched competition that helped keep prices in check. In 1890 Congress passed the Sherman Antitrust Act. Its stated purpose was "to protect trade and commerce against unlawful restraints and monopolies." However, due to court challenges, the law was not successfully applied until the early 1900s.

Panics and Depressions

In economic terms a panic is a widespread occurrence of public anxiety about financial affairs. People lose confidence in banks and investments and want to hold onto their money instead of spending it. This can lead to a severe downturn, or depression, in the economic condition of a nation. The U.S. economy suffered from panics and depressions even during the booming growth of the 1800s and early 1900s. Economists argue about the exact definitions of panics and depressions, but in general it is agreed that panics and/or economic downturns occurred in the United States in 1819, 1837, 1857, 1869, 1873, 1893, and 1907.

The crises were triggered by a variety of factors. Common problems included too much borrowing and speculation by investors and poor oversight of banks by the federal government. Speculation is the buying of assets on the hope that they will greatly increase in value in the future. During the 1800s many speculators borrowed money from banks to buy land. Huge demand caused land prices to increase dramatically, often above what the land was actually worth in the market. Poorly regulated banks extended too much credit to speculators and to each other. When a large bank failed, there was a domino effect through the industry, which caused other banks and businesses to fail.

A panic or depression results in a downward economic spiral in which individuals and businesses are afraid to make new investments. People rush to pull their money from banks. As panic spreads, banks demand that borrowers pay back money, but borrowers may lack the funds to do so. Consumers are reluctant to spend money, which negatively affects businesses. Demand for products goes down, and prices must be lowered to move merchandise off of shelves. This means less profit for business owners. Businesses lay off employees to cut costs and do not hire new employees. As more people become unemployed or fearful about their jobs, there is even less spending in the marketplace, which leads to more business cutbacks and so forth. The cycle continues until some compelling change takes place to nudge the economy back into a positive direction.

The Twentieth Century Begins

The early twentieth century was a time of social and political change in the United States. Public disgust at the corruption and greed of the gilded age encouraged the movement called progressivism. Progressives promoted civic responsibility, worker's rights, consumer protection, political and tax reform, "trust busting," and strong government action to achieve social improvements. The progressive era greatly affected the U.S. economy because of its focus on improving working conditions for average Americans. Successes for the progressives included child labor restrictions, improved working conditions in factories, compensation funds for injured workers, a growth surge in labor unions, federal regulation of food and drug industries, and the formation of the Federal Trade Commission to oversee business practices.

Some people viewed the progressive movement as an attack on capitalism and a prelude to socialism. The U.S. economy was first described as "capitalist" by the German economist Karl Marx (1818–1883), who used the term to describe an economy in which a small group of people control the capital, or money available for investment, and, by extension, control the power within the economy. A common criticism of capitalism was that it favored profits over the well-being of workers. Marx advocated a socialist system in which wealth and property were not held by a few individuals but were equally distributed among all workers under a heavily planned economy. The socialist movement gained some momentum during the progressive era, thanks in large part to its ties to organized labor. In *The Tyranny of Change: America in the Progressive Era, 1890–1920* (2000), John Whiteclay Chambers II states that during the 1912 presidential election the socialist candidate Eugene V. Debs (1885–1926) garnered more than nine hundred thousand votes—around 6% of the popular vote. However, socialism soon faded as a serious challenge to U.S. capitalism.

Despite its laissez-faire attitude, the federal government took two actions in 1913 that were to have long-lasting effects on the U.S. economy:

- Establishment of the Federal Reserve System to serve as the nation's central bank, furnish currency, and supervise banking

- Ratification of the Sixteenth Amendment to the U.S. Constitution authorizing the collection of income taxes

World War I and Inflation

World War I erupted in Europe in August 1914. The United States entered the conflict in April 1917 and was engaged until the war ended in November 1918. Even though the nation spent only nineteen months at war, the U.S. economy underwent major changes during this period.

It is sometimes said that "war is good for the economy" because, during a major war, the federal government spends large amounts of money on weapons and machinery through contracts with private industries. These industries hire more employees, which reduces unemployment and puts more money into the hands of consumers to spend in the marketplace. This benefits other businesses not directly involved in the war effort. On the surface, these economic effects appear positive. However, major wars almost always result in high inflation rates.

Inflation is an economic condition in which the purchasing power of money goes down because of price increases in goods and services. For example, if a nation experiences an inflation rate of 3% in a year, an item that cost $1.00 at the beginning of the year will cost $1.03 at the end of the year. Inflation causes the "value" of a dollar to go down over the course of the year. In general, small increases in inflation occur over time in a healthy growing economy, because demand slightly outpaces supply. Economists consider an inflation rate of 3% or less a year to be tolerable. During a major war the supply and demand ratio becomes distorted. This occurs when the nation produces huge amounts of war goods and far fewer consumer goods, such as food, clothing, and cars. This lack of supply and anxiety about the future drive up the prices of consumer goods, making it difficult for people to afford things they need or want.

During World War I the federal government intervened in private industry to support war needs and exert some control over supply and demand dynamics. Agencies were created to oversee the production of war goods, food, fuel, and nonmilitary ships. Even though the government tried to impose some level of price control in the food and fuel industries, inflation still occurred. According to the U.S. Census Bureau, in *Historical Statistics of the United States, Colonial Times to 1970, Bicentennial Edition, Part 1* (September 1975, http://www2.census.gov/prod2/statcomp/documents/CT1970p1-07.pdf), the prices for many consumer goods nearly doubled between 1915 and 1920. Figure 1.3 shows the average annual inflation rate from 1914 through 1924. The inflation rate was unusually high from 1916 through 1920, peaking at 18% in 1918. Wartime inflation was particularly hard on nonworking citizens, such as the elderly and sick, because there were no large government programs in place at that time to assist needy people.

FIGURE 1.3

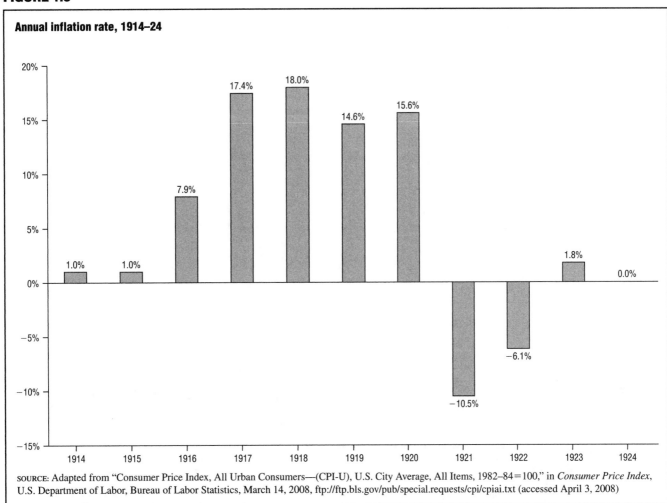

Annual inflation rate, 1914–24

SOURCE: Adapted from "Consumer Price Index, All Urban Consumers—(CPI-U), U.S. City Average, All Items, 1982–84=100," in *Consumer Price Index*, U.S. Department of Labor, Bureau of Labor Statistics, March 14, 2008, ftp://ftp.bls.gov/pub/special.requests/cpi/cpiai.txt (accessed April 3, 2008)

A lasting legacy of World War I was the assumption of large amounts of debt by the federal government to fund the war effort. Figure 1.4 shows the enormous differences that occurred between government revenues (receipts) and spending during the war years. In 1919 government spending peaked at nearly $18.5 billion; revenues for that year were just over $5 billion. The government made up the difference by borrowing money. One method used was the selling of Liberty bonds. Bonds are a type of financial asset—an IOU that promises to pay back at some future date the original purchase price plus interest.

The Roaring Twenties

The Roaring Twenties began with a whimper; there was a severe economic downturn in 1921. However, this crisis was followed by several years of robust economic growth. Mass production and the availability of electricity led to huge consumer demand for household appliances. Installment plans became a popular means for middle-class Americans to purchase expensive long-lasting (durable) goods such as refrigerators, washing machines, and automobiles.

Americans also began spending more money on entertainment. They bought radios and went in large numbers to see motion pictures and baseball games. For many people, the automobile became a necessity, rather than a luxury. Booming car sales boosted the petroleum and housing markets and allowed city dwellers to move to the suburbs.

The prosperity of the 1920s was not shared by all Americans. During World War I demand for agricultural goods had skyrocketed, particularly in Europe. Overoptimistic farmers borrowed heavily to pay for tractors and other farm equipment, only to see food prices plummet during the 1920s when supply outpaced demand. Financial problems in the agricultural industry directly affected many Americans. In addition, banks in rural areas were stressed by farmers who were unable to pay back loans. The agricultural crisis was accompanied by downturns in the coal mining and railroad industries that affected many workers.

In the late 1920s the stock market became a major factor in the U.S. economy. Investors were richly rewarded, as stocks increased dramatically in value. Many people took out loans from banks to pay for stock or purchased stock by "buying on margin." In this arrangement an

FIGURE 1.4

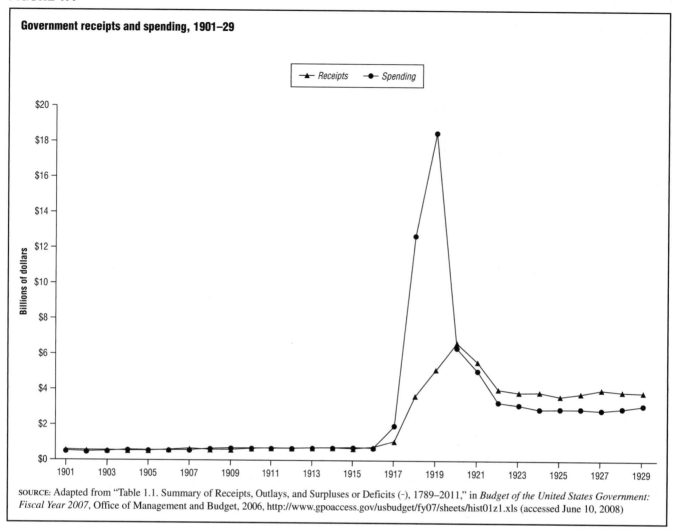

Government receipts and spending, 1901–29

SOURCE: Adapted from "Table 1.1. Summary of Receipts, Outlays, and Surpluses or Deficits (-), 1789–2011," in *Budget of the United States Government: Fiscal Year 2007*, Office of Management and Budget, 2006, http://www.gpoaccess.gov/usbudget/fy07/sheets/hist01z1.xls (accessed June 10, 2008)

investor would make a small down payment (as little as 10%) on a stock purchase. The remainder of the balance would be paid (in theory) by the future increase in the stock value. Buying on margin was widely practiced by optimistic investors of the time. In "The Crash and the Great Depression" (2000, http://us.history.wisc.edu/hist102/lectures/textonly/lecture18.html), Stanley K. Schultz and William P. Tishler of the University of Wisconsin state that "by 1929, much of the money that was invested in the stock market did not actually exist."

Black Tuesday—October 29, 1929

On October 29, 1929, the stock market crashed. For months, President Herbert Hoover (1874–1964) and other influential people had warned that there was too much speculation in the stock market and that stock prices were higher than the actual worth of the companies. In the fall of 1929 investors began to get nervous. On October 24, 1929, there was a selling frenzy as people tried to get rid of stocks they thought might be overvalued. The day was dubbed "Black Thursday." The following day the market

rebounded somewhat, and stock prices climbed back upward. However, this recovery was short lived.

On Tuesday, October 29, 1929, panic selling took place all day. Stock values dropped dramatically. The drawback to buying on margin was that if a stock value went down by a certain amount, the lender would make a margin call by asking the buyer for more cash up front. If the margin buyer could not pay, the lender sold the stock to recoup the money. As "Black Tuesday" progressed, desperate margin buyers paid lenders all their cash in savings in hopes of saving their stock for the expected recovery, but no recovery came. As stock values fell further, lenders demanded more money. By the end of the day, many margin buyers had lost their life savings and their stock. Those who managed to hold on to their stock found it was worth only a fraction of its former value.

According to Harold Bierman Jr. of Cornell University, in "The 1929 Stock Market Crash" (March 26, 2008, http://eh.net/encyclopedia/article/Bierman.Crash), the U.S. stock market lost 90% of its value between 1929 and 1932.

FIGURE 1.5

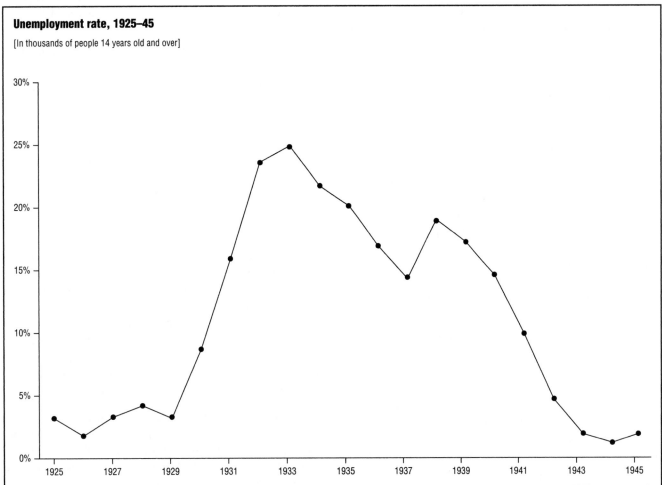

Unemployment rate, 1925–45

[In thousands of people 14 years old and over]

SOURCE: Adapted from "Series D85–86. Unemployment: 1890 to 1970," in *Historical Statistics of the United States, Colonial Times to 1970, Bicentennial Edition, Part 1*, U.S. Department of Commerce, U.S. Census Bureau, September 1975, http://www2.census.gov/prod2/statcomp/documents/CT1970p1-05 .pdf (accessed April 4, 2008)

The Great Depression

The U.S. economy suffered a devastating downturn following the stock market crash. The depression was so deep and lasted so long—more than a decade—that it is called the Great Depression.

Historically, economic depressions had been short downturns with limited consequences. They were temporary dips in an overall trend of American prosperity. The Great Depression was a completely different experience. It brought long-term unemployment and hardship to millions of people. The unemployment rate soared from 3.2% in 1929 to nearly 25% in 1933. (See Figure 1.5.) It remained more than 10% through the end of the 1930s. The public lost confidence in the stock market, the banking system, and big business.

Like all previous depressions, this one included a downward cycle in which businesses reduced spending and production and laid off employees. Unemployed workers and those fearful of losing their jobs cut back on spending, which forced businesses to lay off more people. The economy underwent

"deflation"—a condition where a lack of money among consumers depresses demand and pushes prices downward. Lower prices for agricultural and industrial goods hurt farmers and businesses, particularly those with high debt. Consumers also had assumed high levels of debt during the 1920s.

The Great Depression was aggravated by a crisis in the banking industry. Some banks had invested heavily in the stock market using their depositors' money or loaned large amounts of money to stock market investors. These banks failed after the crash, and the depositors lost their savings. Fear of further failures caused "bank runs," in which large numbers of depositors rushed to withdraw their money at the same time. This caused more bank failures, which perpetuated the cycle. In addition, some economists believe that the banking market became oversaturated during the 1920s with underfunded and loosely regulated banks that loaned money too easily. These institutions were already financially troubled before the crash and could not survive the stress.

The United States' Great Depression was felt worldwide, particularly in other industrialized countries. By the

1920s the United States played a major role in world commerce by exporting and importing large amounts of goods and investing money in foreign businesses. A prolonged downturn in U.S. production, spending, and investing, combined with the banking crisis, had international consequences. Europe, in particular, suffered financially as it struggled to recover from the devastation of World War I.

The New Deal

When the Great Depression began, the laissez-faire attitude still dominated political opinion. Some economists, including Andrew W. Mellon (1855–1937), who served as the secretary of the treasury from 1921 through 1932, advised President Hoover not to interfere. Mellon took the traditional viewpoint that supply and demand factors would eventually equilibrate and that the economy would recover on its own. Hoover was not convinced. He tried a variety of tax adjustments, asked industry not to cut wages, and pushed for public works projects. However, the depression only deepened.

By 1932 Americans were ready for a change in leadership. Franklin D. Roosevelt (1882–1945), the governor of New York, promised "a new deal" for the nation. He was elected in a landslide victory and developed a government that aggressively acted in economic affairs. The New Deal included a wide variety of programs intended to bring relief to suffering Americans, revive farming and business, and reform the stock market and banking industry. After more than seventy years, economists still argue about whether the New Deal was actually "a good deal" for the nation. They all agree, however, that it was a turning point in U.S. economic history.

Some New Deal programs did not survive court challenges. The National Industrial Recovery Act of 1933 encouraged companies within industries to form alliances and set prices and wages. The companies that participated were exempt from antitrust laws that ordinarily would have forbidden such collusion. In 1935 the U.S. Supreme Court ruled the law unconstitutional. The Agricultural Adjustment Act of 1933 paid farmers to reduce production. It was thought that lower supply would raise prices and improve the living conditions of farmers. In 1936 the Supreme Court invalidated parts of the act. However, the payment of farm subsidies became a permanent component of U.S. economic policy.

Other legacies of the New Deal era include:

- Federal Securities Act (1933)—regulated the selling of investment instruments (such as stock) to ensure that buyers are better educated about their purchases and to prevent fraudulent practices

- Glass-Steagall Banking Act (1933)—separated the commercial and investment banking industries and established the Federal Deposit Insurance Corporation to safeguard depositors' money

- Securities Exchange Act (1934)—regulated the stock exchanges and created the U.S. Securities and Exchange Commission

- National Labor Relations Act (1935)—guaranteed the right of employees in most private industries to organize, form labor unions, and bargain collectively with their employers; it also established the National Labor Relations Board

- Social Security Act (1935)—established a program to provide federal benefits to the elderly and assist the states in providing for "aged persons, blind persons, dependent and crippled children, maternal and child welfare, public health, and the administration of their unemployment compensation laws"

Government employment programs under the Public Works Administration, the Works Project Administration, and the Civilian Conservation Corps put people to work building roads, dams, bridges, airfields, and post offices and developing national parks for tourism. Robert J. Samuelson explains in "Great Depression" (2002, http://www.econlib.org/library/Enc/GreatDepression.html#biography) that as many as ten to twelve million Americans were employed in these programs at various times during the 1930s.

Perhaps the greatest legacy of Roosevelt's New Deal was the new role of the federal government as a manipulator of economic forces and a provider of benefits to the needy. This change in U.S. policy was seen as a wise and compassionate move by some people and as a dangerous shift toward socialism by others. In U.S. history the New Deal is considered the birth of "big government."

By 1940 the unemployment rate was 14.9%. (See Figure 1.5.) Even though the rate was down from a peak of 25% in 1933, it was still high by historical standards. Nearly a decade of New Deal programs had softened the hardship suffered by many Americans, but had not boosted the country out of the Great Depression. It was going to take a war to accomplish this task.

World War II

Even though the United States officially entered World War II in 1941, it had been gearing up its industries for war for more than a year. This experience at mobilization (converting civilian industries to produce military goods) proved to be invaluable. The federal government established a host of agencies to oversee wartime production, labor relations, and prices. Efforts were made to avoid the huge inflation increase that had occurred during World War I. Rationing (tight controls over how much of an item a person can use or consume in a certain amount of time) was instituted on some goods to prevent dramatic price increases. Overall, these efforts were successful. Figure 1.6 shows the annual rates of inflation experienced in the United States between 1940 and 1950. Inflation

FIGURE 1.6

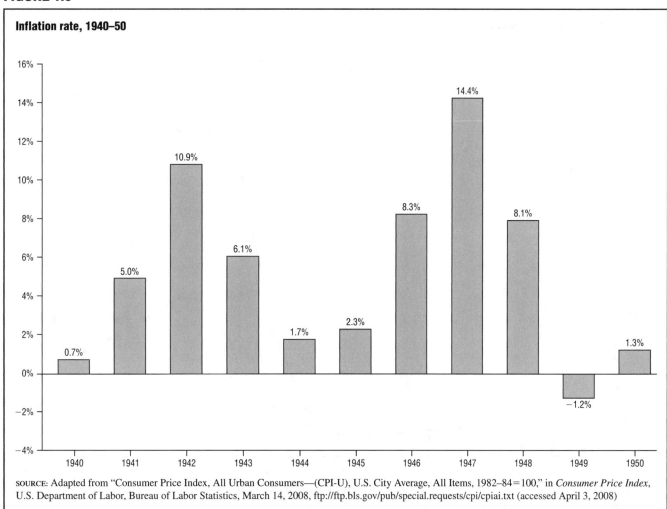

Inflation rate, 1940–50

SOURCE: Adapted from "Consumer Price Index, All Urban Consumers—(CPI-U), U.S. City Average, All Items, 1982–84=100," in *Consumer Price Index*, U.S. Department of Labor, Bureau of Labor Statistics, March 14, 2008, ftp://ftp.bls.gov/pub/special.requests/cpi/cpiai.txt (accessed April 3, 2008)

spiked during the early years of the war and immediately after but was not consistently high over the decade.

Businesses rushed to increase production and hire workers to produce the goods needed for the war effort. Unemployment dropped dramatically and wages went up, particularly for workers in low-skilled factory jobs. Laborers found themselves in high demand and joined labor unions in record numbers to consolidate their power and seek better working conditions.

World War II was an expensive endeavor for the United States. However, it was believed that the stakes were so high that the war had to be won at any cost. According to Figure 1.7, government spending during the war far outpaced revenues. By 1945 the government was spending around $90 billion per year and taking in revenues around half this amount. Once again, the difference was made up by borrowing.

Keynesian Economics

The Great Depression shook many peoples' beliefs in the laissez-faire approach to economics advocated by Smith in the eighteenth century. During the 1930s and 1940s different approaches to capitalism began to receive serious attention. One of the most famous economists of the time was John Maynard Keynes (1883–1946). Keynes was an English expert in the application of economic theory to real-world problems. He published several influential books, including *The Economic Consequences of the Peace* (1919) and the *General Theory of Employment, Interest, and Money* (1936). In the latter book, Keynes advocated strong government intervention in the economy as a remedy for the ongoing economic depression.

Politicians of the 1930s were not completely convinced by Keynes's arguments, particularly in regards to government spending. Maintaining a balanced federal budget was considered so sacred that the governments of Hoover and Roosevelt were reluctant to veer far from that precedent. However, following World War II it appeared obvious that huge government spending had helped fuel recovery from the Great Depression. Keynes's theories on capitalism, unemployment, and business cycles became highly regarded, and he is credited with inventing macroeconomics. This is a "big picture" approach that measures

FIGURE 1.7

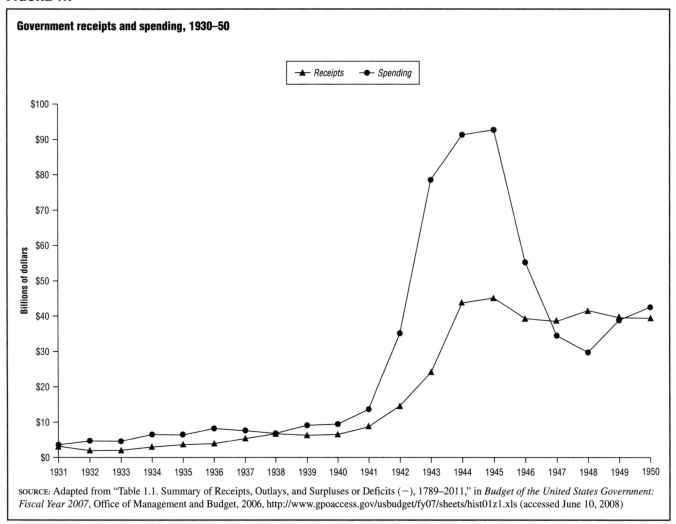

Government receipts and spending, 1930–50

Legend: ▲ Receipts ● Spending

SOURCE: Adapted from "Table 1.1. Summary of Receipts, Outlays, and Surpluses or Deficits (−), 1789–2011," in *Budget of the United States Government: Fiscal Year 2007*, Office of Management and Budget, 2006, http://www.gpoaccess.gov/usbudget/fy07/sheets/hist01z1.xls (accessed June 10, 2008)

broad trends in an economy, such as employment and inflation, and the way these trends interact. In contrast, microeconomics analyzes the economy on a smaller scale—for example, by studying the supply and demand factors at work in individual markets or industrial segments.

Keynesian economics became the operating principle of the U.S. government in the post–World War II era. Even though Keynes had his critics, and his methods have been revised over time, he is considered by many to be the father of the mixed economy system used in the United States to this day.

The National Income and Product Accounts

One innovation of the 1940s was the National Income and Product Accounts (NIPAs), which are compilations of national economic data. Before that time there was a lack of comprehensive macroeconomic data on the nation's inputs and outputs, such as labor and production of goods and services. This problem became apparent during the Great Depression, when the Hoover and Roosevelt admin-

istrations were forced to make decisions based on fragmented and incomplete data on the nation's financial condition. As a result, the federal government asked researchers at the National Bureau of Economic Research (NBER) at the University of New York to begin estimating national income (e.g., wages, profits, and rent). The NBER had been founded in 1920 as a private nonprofit organization dedicated to economic research.

During World War II the federal government began compiling another macroeconomic measure called the gross national product (GNP). The GNP is the amount in dollars of the value of final goods and services produced by Americans over a particular time period. For example, the Census Bureau reports in *Historical Statistics of the United States, Colonial Times to 1970* that the GNP in 1945 was nearly $212 billion. The GNP is calculated by summing consumer and government spending, business and residential investments, and the net value of U.S. exports (exports minus imports).

At first, GNP estimates were made annually. Eventually, they were calculated on a quarterly basis. The GNP provides

FIGURE 1.8

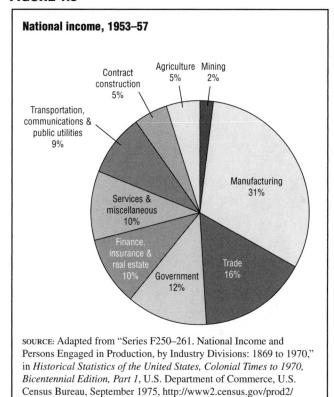

National income, 1953–57

SOURCE: Adapted from "Series F250–261. National Income and Persons Engaged in Production, by Industry Divisions: 1869 to 1970," in *Historical Statistics of the United States, Colonial Times to 1970, Bicentennial Edition, Part 1*, U.S. Department of Commerce, U.S. Census Bureau, September 1975, http://www2.census.gov/prod2/statcomp/documents/CT1970p1-07.pdf (accessed June 10, 2008)

a valuable tool for tracking national productivity over time. By the end of the 1940s an entire set of NIPAs had been developed to report macroeconomic data on the state of the U.S. economy.

A Postwar Spending Spree

Following World War II many U.S. industries demobilized from producing military goods and returned to producing consumer goods. Well-paid workers who had been frustrated by wartime shortages were ready to spend money. Returning soldiers received government incentives to buy houses and start businesses. Postwar euphoria drove a spending spree and a baby boom.

New industries in aviation and electronics arose after World War II. Many existing industries underwent consolidation and growth as corporations merged into giant conglomerates. Figure 1.8 shows the national income produced by the business sector for 1953 to 1957. Manufacturing accounted for 31% of the national income during this period.

The 1950s also experienced a boom in business franchises. In this arrangement an individual could purchase permission from a company in one geographic area to sell the company's products or services in another area. Franchising proved to be an extremely effective means of spreading brand recognition and was widely practiced in the surging fast-food industry. In 1955 Des Plaines, Illinois, became the site of the first McDonald's franchise, after the

businessman Ray Kroc (1902–1984) became a franchisee for the McDonald brothers, who owned a small chain of restaurants in California. By 1959 there were more than one hundred McDonald's franchises around the country. Over the next decade franchising was practiced in a number of other businesses, many of which grew into major corporations.

Dwight D. Eisenhower (1890–1969) was president from 1953 through 1961. His administration is associated with a growing economy that experienced low inflation rates and general prosperity. However, the prosperity of the 1950s was not shared equally in American society. Once again, farmers found themselves in trouble due to overproduction. An oversupply of agricultural goods meant lower prices (and lower profits). Agriculture became increasingly an industry in which large factory farms run by corporations were able to survive, whereas many smaller farmers could not compete.

Minority populations (largely African-American) also suffered financial hardship during this era. Figure 1.9 shows the dramatic difference between the unemployment rates for whites and minorities during the postwar decades. By the mid-1950s unemployment among minorities was twice as high as it was among white workers, a disparity that lingered well into the 1960s. It was in this atmosphere that the civil rights movement gained in strength and urgency. In 1954 segregation was ruled unconstitutional by the Supreme Court. A year later, the African-American seamstress and activist Rosa Parks (1913–2005) was arrested in Alabama for refusing to move from the "white" section of a public bus. This incident spurred a bus boycott and ultimately brought Martin Luther King Jr. (1929–1968) and other leaders of the movement to national prominence.

The Cold War, Korea, and Vietnam

The United States left World War II in sound economic shape. During the war, all other industrialized nations had suffered great losses in their infrastructure, financial stability, and populations. The United States invested heavily in the postwar economies of Western Europe and Japan, hoping to instill an atmosphere conducive to peace and the spread of capitalism. U.S. barriers to foreign trade were relaxed to build new markets for U.S. exports and to allow some war-ravaged nations to make money selling goods to American consumers.

The Soviet Union had been a wartime ally of the United States, but relations became strained after the war. The Soviet Union had adopted communism following a period of revolution and civil war in the late 1910s and early 1920s. During World War II the Soviet Union "liberated" a large part of eastern Europe from Nazi occupation. Through various means the Union of Soviet Socialist Republics (USSR) assumed political control over these nations. The USSR had been largely industrialized before

FIGURE 1.9

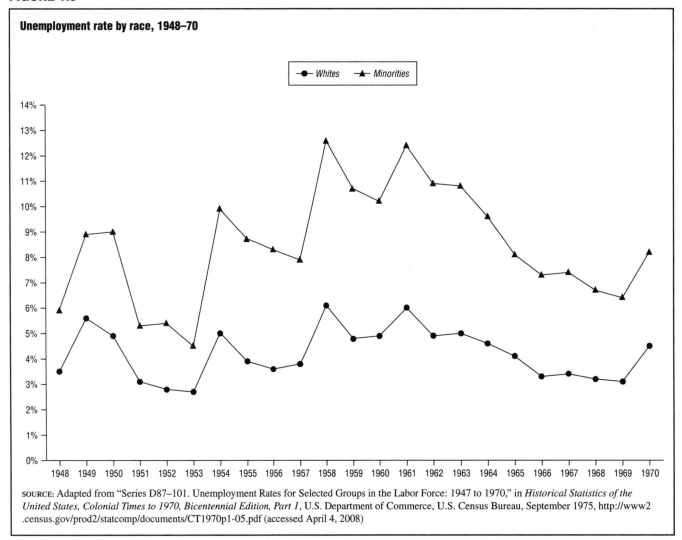

Unemployment rate by race, 1948–70

SOURCE: Adapted from "Series D87–101. Unemployment Rates for Selected Groups in the Labor Force: 1947 to 1970," in *Historical Statistics of the United States, Colonial Times to 1970, Bicentennial Edition, Part 1*, U.S. Department of Commerce, U.S. Census Bureau, September 1975, http://www2 .census.gov/prod2/statcomp/documents/CT1970p1-05.pdf (accessed April 4, 2008)

World War II and quickly regained its industrial capabilities. It soon took a major role in international affairs, placing it in direct conflict with the only other superpower of the time: the United States. A cold war began between the two rich and powerful nations that had completely different political, economic, and social goals for the world.

The cold war was fought mostly by politicians and diplomats. A direct and large-scale military conflict between U.S. and Soviet forces never occurred. Regardless, an expensive arms race began in which both sides produced and stockpiled large amounts of weapons as a show of force to deter a first strike by the enemy. In addition, both sides provided financial and military support to countries around the world in an attempt to influence the political leanings of those populations. Communist China joined the cold war during the 1950s and often partnered with the USSR against U.S. interests.

During the early 1950s U.S. forces became embroiled in two Asian conflicts over communism: the Korean War and

the Vietnam War. The Korean War was relatively short, lasting from 1950 through 1953. The fight in Vietnam turned out to be a long and difficult one in which U.S. forces, assisted by a handful of other countries, were pitted against highly motivated forces equipped and backed by the USSR and China. The United States was engaged in the Vietnam War from 1955 until it withdrew the last of its troops in 1975, leaving South Vietnam to a communist takeover. In *Outline of U.S. History* (November 2005, http://usinfo .state.gov/products/pubs/histryotln/historytln.pdf), Alonzo L. Hamby of Ohio University states that the total cost of the Vietnam War exceeded $150 billion.

In both the Korean and Vietnam wars the United States chose to fight in a limited manner without using its arsenal of nuclear weapons or engaging Chinese or Soviet troops directly for fear of sparking another world war. Full-scale mobilization of U.S. industries was not required for these wars, as it had been during World War II. Instead, a defense industry developed during the cold war to supply the U.S. military on a continuous basis with the arms and goods it needed.

FIGURE 1.10

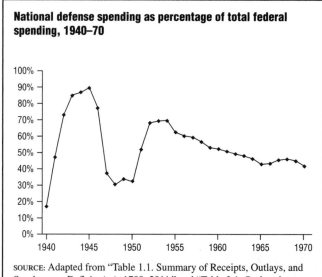

National defense spending as percentage of total federal spending, 1940–70

SOURCE: Adapted from "Table 1.1. Summary of Receipts, Outlays, and Surpluses or Deficits (−): 1789–2011," and "Table 3.1. Outlays by Superfunction and Function: 1940–2011," in *Budget of the United States Government, Fiscal Year 2007*, Office of Management and Budget, 2006, http://www.gpoaccess.gov/usbudget/fy07/pdf/hist.pdf (accessed June 10, 2008)

Figure 1.10 shows the percentage of the national budget that was devoted to national defense between 1940 and 1970. Spending on national defense soared during World War II and then declined dramatically following the war's end. However, military spending quickly climbed again as the cold war heated up, remaining above 40% for nearly two decades.

The Birth of the Modern Fed

The nation's central bank—the Federal Reserve System—was formed in 1913 to furnish currency and supervise financial institutions. Gradually, it took on other roles that affected the amount of money circulating in the United States and the interest rates charged by banks to their customers. The Federal Reserve System consists of twelve regional banks located around the country and is overseen by a seven-member board of governors headquartered in Washington, D.C.

The Fed, as it came to be called, was designed to be as independent as possible from political pressures from the U.S. president and the Congress. This safeguard was included to prevent the Fed from having to bow to demands for short-term economic fixes requested by politicians seeking reelection. The Fed was charged with taking a big-picture, long-term approach to economic policy for the good of the nation as a whole.

Robert L. Hetzel and Ralph F. Leach explain in "After the Accord: Reminiscences on the Birth of the Modern Fed" (*Economic Quarterly*, vol. 87, no. 1, winter 2001), that from its inception until the early 1950s, the Fed was influenced by the policies of the U.S. Department of the Treasury, a federal agency created in 1789. During the late 1940s Fed and Treasury officials disagreed about how best to handle the large debt accumulated by the United States during World War II. This conflict and other contentious issues led to a new agreement, or accord, between the two agencies about the roles of each in the U.S. economy. This accord is considered the birth of the modern Fed, an organization that has grown to exert great power in the U.S. economy.

The chairman of the board of governors at the time of the accord was William McChesney Martin Jr. (1906–1998). Martin was a dynamic leader who maintained his post for nearly two decades. Under his leadership the Fed assumed greater control over the nation's financial policies. This control was exercised primarily by influencing interest rates on loans. Lowering interest rates encouraged borrowing, which put more money into circulation for spending or investing. However, if demand outpaced supply, price inflation became a problem. Then, the Fed would raise interest rates to make borrowing less attractive and dampen demand. Martin reportedly summed this up by saying, "You have to take away the punch bowl when the party is warming up." His policy proved to be fruitful during the prosperous decades of the 1950s and 1960s.

The 1960s: Social Upheaval and Economic Growth

The 1960s were a time of social and economic change for the United States. The decade began with the election of President John F. Kennedy (1917–1963), who promised to ensure economic growth and address growing social problems within the United States. In 1963 Kennedy's efforts were cut short by his assassination. Lyndon B. Johnson (1908–1973) took over as president and dramatically enlarged the federal government and its role in socioeconomic affairs. Johnson's administration initiated large-scale programs for the needy, including the health-care programs Medicare (for the elderly) and Medicaid (for the poor), jobs programs, federal aid to schools, and food stamps for low-income Americans. The so-called war on poverty and the escalating war in Vietnam proved to be extremely expensive. At the same time, the United States was pursuing a costly (but ultimately successful) endeavor to land astronauts on the moon before the end of the decade.

Consumer and government spending drove the nation's GNP during the 1960s. According to the article "1970: The Year of the Hangover" (*Time*, December 28, 1970), it grew to $977 billion by 1970. However, inflation became a problem (as it often does in a fast-growing economy) in the late 1960s. At the macroeconomic level, there was too much money in the hands of consumers, which resulted in consumer demand that was higher than supply. In *Consumer Price Index* (June 13, 2008,ftp://ftp.bls.gov/pub/special .requests/cpi/cpiai.txt), the U.S. Bureau of Labor Statistics (BLS) notes that by 1970 the inflation rate had reached 5.7%.

FIGURE 1.11

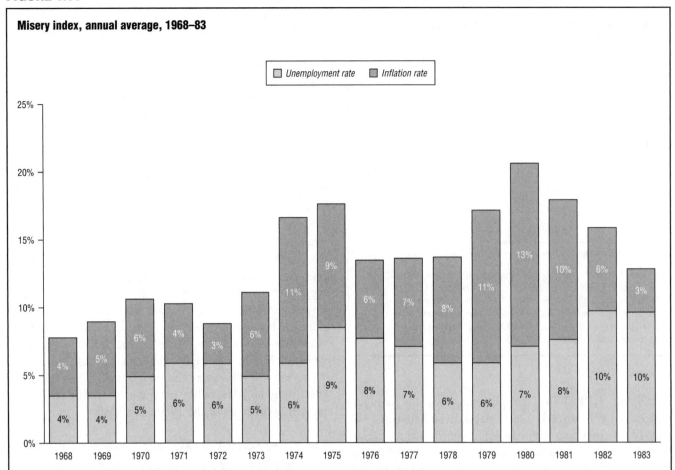

Misery index, annual average, 1968–83

☐ Unemployment rate   ■ Inflation rate

SOURCE: Adapted from "Labor Force Statistics from the Current Population Survey: Unemployment Rate, Annual Average," in *Bureau of Labor Statistics Data*, U.S. Department of Labor, Bureau of Labor Statistics, 2006, http://data.bls.gov/PDQ/servlet/SurveyOutputServlet?data_tool=latest_numbers&series_id=LNU04000000&years_option=all_years&periods_option=specific_periods&periods=Annual+Data (accessed June 10, 2008), and "Consumer Price Index, All Urban Consumers—(CPI-U), U.S. City Average, All Items, 1982–84=100," in *Consumer Price Index*, U.S. Department of Labor, Bureau of Labor Statistics, March 14, 2008, ftp://ftp.bls.gov/pub/special.requests/cpi/cpiai.txt (accessed April 3, 2008)

The nation was preoccupied with the explosive social problems of the time. During the mid- to late 1960s the country was plagued by protests against the Vietnam War and riots in blighted urban areas populated by poor African-Americans. By 1968 there were half a million U.S. troops in Vietnam. Nightly television coverage provided a bleak picture of the war's progress and helped turn public opinion against the war and President Johnson. In 1968 Johnson announced he would not seek reelection. That same year King and Robert F. Kennedy (1925–1968)—John Kennedy's brother and an aspiring presidential candidate—were assassinated.

According to the NBER, in "US Business Cycle Expansions and Contractions" (March 27, 2008, http://www.nber.org/cycles.html/), the United States left the 1960s having experienced the longest continuous stretch of positive GNP growth in history—the first quarter of 1961 through the last quarter of 1969. However, high inflation was about to become a major problem.

The 1970s: Stagflation and Energy Crises

Stagflation is a word coined during the 1970s to describe an economy suffering stagnant growth, high inflation, and high unemployment all at the same time. This combination of economic problems was unprecedented in U.S. history. Previously, high inflation had occurred when the economy was growing quickly, such as during World War II. However, high production had meant high employment levels. By contrast, economic downturns were associated with higher unemployment but lower inflation (and even deflation). These relationships had been considered natural and certain.

The 1970s were unique because both unemployment and inflation were high, by historical standards. The economist Robert Joseph Barro (1944–) invented a new term called the Misery index to describe this condition. The Misery index is computed by summing the unemployment rate and inflation rate. Figure 1.11 shows the annual Misery index calculated for 1968 through 1983. By the mid-1970s each rate exceeded 5%.

FIGURE 1.12

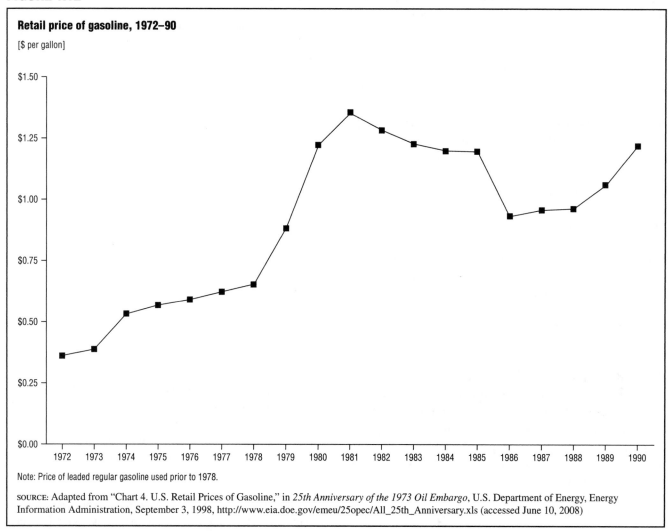

Retail price of gasoline, 1972–90

[$ per gallon]

Note: Price of leaded regular gasoline used prior to 1978.

SOURCE: Adapted from "Chart 4. U.S. Retail Prices of Gasoline," in *25th Anniversary of the 1973 Oil Embargo*, U.S. Department of Energy, Energy Information Administration, September 3, 1998, http://www.eia.doe.gov/emeu/25opec/All_25th_Anniversary.xls (accessed June 10, 2008)

There were three presidents during the 1970s—Richard M. Nixon (1913–1994), Gerald R. Ford (1913–2006), and Jimmy Carter (1924–). Each tried a variety of measures to stem stagflation, but none was considered effective. Nixon implemented wage and price controls and increased government spending. In 1973 he resigned under threat of impeachment for his role in the Watergate scandal. Vice president Ford assumed the presidency. Economic problems continued, and in 1976 the country elected Carter as the new president. Carter had emphasized the high Misery index during his presidential campaign, but his administration was unable to turn the tide. By 1980 the Misery index had climbed to 20%. (See Figure 1.11.)

FOREIGN OIL AND COMPETITION. The United States' economic problems were aggravated by its dependence on foreign oil and competition from foreign industries. In 1973 the Middle Eastern members of the Organization of Petroleum Exporting Countries halted oil exports to the United States in retaliation for U.S. support of Israel. The oil embargo lasted five months. When shipments resumed, the price of oil had dramatically increased. Americans faced high prices, long lines, and shortages at the gas pumps. Figure 1.12 shows that the average retail price of gasoline surged from around $0.35 per gallon in 1972 to $1.35 per gallon in 1981. To save fuel, a 55-mile-per-hour (89 kph) speed limit was imposed on the nation's interstates. The federal government called on Americans to conserve energy and provided an example by not lighting the White House Christmas tree. During the late 1970s a revolution in oil-rich Iran brought a second wave of shortages to U.S. energy supplies.

The "energy crisis" of the 1970s had a ripple effect through the U.S. economy, causing the prices of other goods and services to increase. Lower profits and uncertainty about the future caused businesses to slow down and reduce their workforces. At the same time, U.S. industries in steel, automobiles, and electronics endured stiff foreign competition, particularly from Japan. Small energy-efficient Japanese cars became popular in the United States. By 1980 gasoline cost more than $1.00 per gallon, which was quadruple the price in 1970. (See Figure 1.12.) U.S. car makers struggled to compete, having always relied on consumer demand for large automobiles—which were now considered "gas guzzlers."

DEREGULATION. One of the measures that President Carter used to combat stagflation was deregulation. For decades, certain industries in the United States had been given government immunity from market supply and demand factors. The railroad, trucking, and airline industries were prime examples. Companies in these industries were guaranteed rates and routes and were allowed to operate contrary to antitrust laws. In 1978 the airline industry was deregulated. The result was that airlines began to compete with each other over fares and routes, and new companies entered the industry. Some of the large, well-established companies were unable to compete in the new environment and went out of business. However, demand increased as prices came down and flying became available to many more Americans. By 1980 deregulation had been completed or was under way for the railroad, trucking, energy, financial services, and telecommunications industries.

The 1980s: Recession and Reaganomics

In November 1980 the American people elected Ronald Reagan (1911–2004) as the new president. Inflation was at 13% that year, which was incredibly high for a peacetime economy. (See Figure 1.11.) Unemployment was at 7%, meaning that millions of people were unemployed and faced with rapidly increasing prices in the marketplace. The economic situation was dire, and drastic measures were required to turn the economy around.

SLAYING THE INFLATIONARY DRAGON. In late 1979 President Carter had appointed a new governor of the Federal Reserve, Paul A. Volcker (1927–), who promised to "slay the inflationary dragon." Volcker began by tightening the nation's money supply. This had the effect of making credit more difficult to obtain, which drove up interest rates. The government knew that rising interest rates would probably trigger a production slowdown (a recession) that would push unemployment even higher. It was a trade-off that policymakers during the previous decade had been unwilling to accept.

Volcker forged ahead with his policies, and by the early 1980s interest rates had reached historical highs. Figure 1.13 shows that the prime loan rate—the interest rate that banks charge their best customers—peaked at 21.5% in December 1980. In 1981 the average interest rate for a conventional thirty-year mortgage soared to nearly 18.5%, the highest rate ever recorded by the Federal Home Loan Mortgage Corporation, in "30-Year Conventional Mortgage Rate" (June 3, 2008, http://research.stlouisfed .org/fred2/data/MORTG.txt).

The lack of credit caused a business slowdown—a reduction in GNP growth (or recession). As expected,

FIGURE 1.13

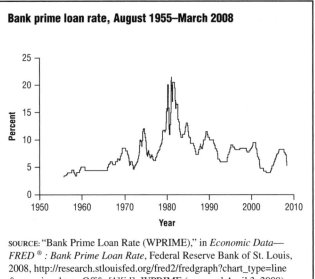

Bank prime loan rate, August 1955–March 2008

SOURCE: "Bank Prime Loan Rate (WPRIME)," in *Economic Data—FRED ® : Bank Prime Loan Rate*, Federal Reserve Bank of St. Louis, 2008, http://research.stlouisfed.org/fred2/fredgraph?chart_type=line &recession_bars=Off&s[1][id]=WPRIME (accessed April 3, 2008)

the recession put more people out of work. Unemployment climbed at first, averaging 10% in 1982 and 1983, but then began to decline. (See Figure 1.11.) By the end of the decade it was down around 5%. According to the BLS, in *Consumer Price Index*, the inflation rate dropped from a high of 13.5% in 1980 to 4.8% by 1989. Even though the spike in unemployment had been painful for Americans, the inflationary dragon was finally dead.

REAGANOMICS. When Reagan took office in 1981, he brought a new approach to curing the nation's financial woes: supply-side economics. Traditionally, the government had focused on the demand side—the role of consumers in stimulating businesses to produce more. Reagan preferred economic policies that directly helped producers. In "Supply Side Economics" (2005, http://www.auburn.edu/~johnspm/ gloss/supply_side), Paul Johnson of Auburn University describes the philosophy this way: "Supply-side policy analysts focus on barriers to higher productivity—identifying ways in which the government can promote faster economic growth over the long haul by removing impediments to the supply of, and efficient use of, the factors of production."

One of the cornerstones of supply-side economics is reducing taxes so that people and businesses have more money to invest in private enterprise. Reagan enacted tax cuts through two pieces of legislation: the Economic Recovery Tax Act of 1981 and the Tax Reform Act of 1986. The result was a much lower number of tax brackets (the various rates at which individuals are taxed based on their income), a broader tax base (wealth within a jurisdiction that is liable to taxation), and reduced tax rates on income and capital gains (the profit made from selling an investment, such as land).

FIGURE 1.14

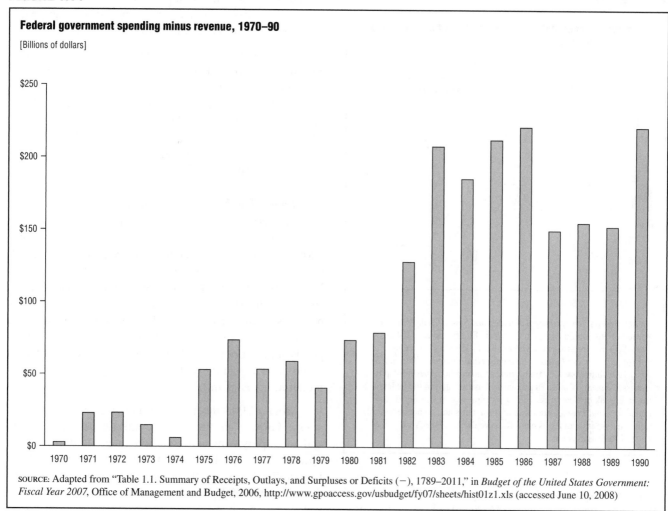

Federal government spending minus revenue, 1970–90

[Billions of dollars]

SOURCE: Adapted from "Table 1.1. Summary of Receipts, Outlays, and Surpluses or Deficits (−), 1789–2011," in *Budget of the United States Government: Fiscal Year 2007*, Office of Management and Budget, 2006, http://www.gpoaccess.gov/usbudget/fy07/sheets/hist01z1.xls (accessed June 10, 2008)

At the same time, Reagan pushed for greater national defense spending as part of his "peace through strength" approach to the Soviet Union and selective cuts in social services spending. However, no cuts were made to the largest and most expensive programs within the social services budget. The combination of all these factors resulted in high federal deficits during the 1980s. In other words, the federal government was spending more than it was making each year. As shown in Figure 1.14, the federal deficits of the mid-1980s were more than twice what they had been during the mid-1970s. According to the article "U.S. Debt Past $1 Trillion" (*New York Times*, October 23, 1981), the national debt (the sum of all accumulated federal deficits since the nation began) reached $1 trillion in 1981.

The 1990s: Sparkling Economic Performance

The 1990s were a time of phenomenal economic growth for the United States, even amid the shadows of war and an ever-increasing federal deficit. In August 1990 the military forces of Iraq under President Saddam Hussein (1937–2006) invaded the small neighboring country of Kuwait. President George H. W. Bush (1924–) had taken office in 1989 and quickly acted to put together a coalition of international forces that successfully forced Iraq out of Kuwait. The Gulf War, as it came to be known, was short lived and would be seen as a triumphant, if incomplete, victory by allied forces. Even though his military strength was weakened, Hussein was not removed from power in Iraq. As a result, he continued to pose foreign relations problems for the United States for many years.

President Bush had been elected in large part because of his promise not to raise taxes. During his presidential campaign he famously said, "Read my lips: No new taxes." However, the promise was not one he could keep, given the economic realities of the time. During the late 1980s there had been a severe financial crisis in the savings and loan industry, which had been recently deregulated. A series of unwise loans and poor business decisions left most of the industry in shambles and necessitated a government bailout. According to Hamby, by 1993 the cost of the bailout had reached nearly $525 billion. At the same time, the government faced rapidly

FIGURE 1.15

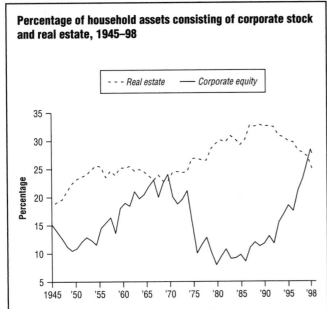

Percentage of household assets consisting of corporate stock and real estate, 1945–98

SOURCE: Joseph Tracy, Henry Schneider, and Sewin Chan, "Chart 1. Portion of Household Assets in Corporate Equity and Real Estate, 1945–98," in "Are Stocks Overtaking Real Estate in Household Portfolios?" *Current Issues in Economics and Finance*, vol. 5, no. 5, April 1999, http://www.ny.frb.org/research/current_issues/ci5-5.pdf (accessed June 10, 2008). Reprinted with permission of the Federal Reserve Bank of New York. The views expressed in *Current Issues in Economics and Finance* are those of the authors and do not necessarily reflect the position of the Federal Reserve Bank of New York or the Federal Reserve System.

rising expenditures on health-care programs for the elderly (Medicare) and the needy (Medicaid). Bush reluctantly agreed to a tax increase, a move that was politically damaging. In 1992 he lost his reelection bid to the Arkansas governor Bill Clinton (1946–), who was reelected in 1996.

Joseph Tracy, Henry Schneider, and Sewin Chan indicate in "Are Stocks Overtaking Real Estate in Household Portfolios?" (*Current Issues in Economics and Finance*, vol. 5, no. 5, April 1999) that, overall, the 1990s were a period of peace and prosperity for the United States. The cold war ended when the Soviet Union disintegrated into individual republics. Technological innovations, particularly in the computer industry, helped push the economy to new heights. Sterling business success led to robust investor confidence in the stock markets. Figure 1.15 shows the portion of household assets invested in real estate and corporate equity (stocks) between 1945 and 1998. Even though real estate was the preferred investment through nearly all of this period, the 1990s witnessed tremendous increases in the holdings of corporate equity by the average American. In the mid-1980s the average household had only 10% of its assets in corporate equity. By 1998 this percentage had reached nearly 30%, roughly equal to the percent held in real estate. The Dow Jones Industrial Average is a stock market index—a measure used by economists to gauge the value (and performance) of the stock of thirty large companies. Between the late 1970s and the late 1990s

the index soared from around one thousand points to eleven thousand points—reflecting the tremendous value gained by these companies over this period.

The combination of low interest rates, low unemployment, and high investment rates and business growth combined to greatly expand the U.S. economy. According to the article "Excerpts from Federal Reserve Chairman's Testimony" (*New York Times*, January 21, 1999), Alan Greenspan (1926–), the chair of the Federal Reserve Board, described this expansion as "America's sparkling economic performance."

The 2000s: The Economy Begins to Falter

The first decade of the twenty-first century has been a tumultuous one for the U.S. economy. During the early 2000s the United States endured the September 11, 2001, terrorist attacks, the outbreak of wars in Afghanistan and Iraq, corporate scandals, devastating hurricanes, and a slump in the stock market. Nevertheless, the economy remained robust, as evidenced by healthy growth in the gross domestic product (the total market value of final goods and services produced within an economy in a given year), relatively low unemployment rates, and moderate rates of inflation.

Around 2005 the economy began showing signs of stress. Growth in the gross domestic product slowed and unemployment and inflation rates started creeping upward. The housing market took a nosedive, and the U.S. dollar lost strength against international currencies. As of July 2008, investors and consumers nervously watched economic indicators amid speculation that a recession could be imminent.

THE GLOBAL WAR ON TERROR. In January 2001 George W. Bush (1946–) was inaugurated as the nation's new president. He entered the executive office with plans to overhaul many federal programs and enacted a tax cut within his first few months of being in office. On September 11, 2001, four commercial airliners were commandeered by hijackers. Two of the planes were flown into the twin towers of the World Trade Center in New York City. A third plane was flown into the Pentagon in Washington, D.C. The fourth plane crashed in a field in Pennsylvania after passengers likely struggled with their hijackers. The attacks killed more than twenty-nine hundred people and stunned the world.

The so-called 9/11 attacks dramatically altered the priorities of the U.S. government. The United States went to war, first in Afghanistan (2001) and then in Iraq (2003). Even though the military campaigns were technically successful, U.S. military forces were unable to bring stability to these troubled nations. As of the summer of 2008, the U.S. military continued its presence in Afghanistan and Iraq. Both nations were trying to rebuild with U.S. assistance. Amy Belasco of the Congressional Research Service estimates in *The Cost of Iraq, Afghanistan, and Other Global War on Terror Operations since 9/11* (June 23,

2008, http://www.fas.org/sgp/crs/natsec/RL33110.pdf) that in June 2008 the Afghanistan and Iraq campaigns had cost the United States over $828 billion.

THE INTERNET BUBBLE BURSTS. During the late 1990s the stock market witnessed tremendous growth, driven in large part by investor enthusiasm for Internet-related businesses. Access to the Internet became widespread in the United States and much of the developed world, creating many new market opportunities for entrepreneurs. Investors enthusiastically poured money into the stock of these new businesses. The National Association of Securities Dealers Automated Quotation System (NASDAQ) is a U.S.-based stock market on which the stock of many technology companies is traded. The NASDAQ composite index is a measure of the performance of many of the stocks on NASDAQ. In 1990 the index was less than five hundred. In early 2000 it peaked above four thousand during the height of the Internet stock craze. Many of the stocks had become overvalued; their high prices could not be sustained based on the actual financial results that the companies were producing. What followed was a sharp market correction, as investors sold off many Internet-based stocks, and the prices plummeted. By late 2002 the NASDAQ composite index was around twelve hundred, from which it slowly began to climb again.

In economics a bubble is a phenomenon in which investors overzealously invest (speculate) in a particular commodity or market sector that becomes overvalued. Excitement about possible gains overrules frank analysis of the underlying financial factors. Unfortunately, the very existence of a bubble is not evident until after the fact, when the bubble has burst and much value has been lost in the investments and the businesses involved.

THE HOUSING MARKET COLLAPSE. During the middle of the decade another bubble burst; this one was the U.S. housing market. Its collapse had serious and far-reaching consequences on the U.S. economy as a whole. As shown in Figure 1.13, the United States experienced historically low interest rates during the early 2000s. This spurred demand throughout the housing industry. Rising demand pushed prices upward. Homes in many areas of the country began to appreciate (rise in value) at an unprecedented rate. Investors eagerly bought houses and sold them a short time later for more money. Many banks and financial institutions became caught up in the frenzy and lowered their normally strict loan standards. They introduced new types of mortgages in which payments were low at first and then quickly rose over a certain period. Eager homebuyers, especially first-time buyers, entered into these agreements without adequately considering the consequences to their personal finances.

In late 2005 and early 2006 the housing bubble burst. Overspeculation had pushed home prices above sustainable levels. Demand suddenly plummeted, and homes depreciated (lost value) in many areas of the country. Some mortgage holders defaulted (quit making payments) on their loans, putting extreme pressure on mortgage lenders. The housing market collapse put an enormous strain on the overall economy. As of July 2008, many analysts believed the full effects from the collapse had not been completely realized and would continue to plague the economy for several years to come.

CHAPTER 2
ECONOMIC INDICATORS AND PUBLIC PERCEPTIONS

Because the U.S. economy is so large and complex, it is difficult to assess its overall health at any given time. Economists use a variety of numerical measures to analyze and track macroeconomic factors, such as employment and production. These economic indicators are widely broadcast in the media and are the subject of much analysis by leaders in government, industry, and the financial markets. The American public tends to gauge the health of the economy based on other factors, including their own personal and community-wide experiences and expectations.

ECONOMIC INDICATORS

Economists gauge the strength of the economy using data on wages, spending, saving, unemployment, and the production and consumption of goods and services. Some of these data are called economic indicators, because they provide key information about the macroeconomic condition of the country. One example is the National Income and Product Accounts compiled by the U.S. Bureau of Economic Affairs (BEA) under the U.S. Department of Commerce. The U.S. Census Bureau, the U.S. Department of Labor, and some private organizations also publish key economic indicators. (See Table 2.1.)

Three of the most important and telling economic indicators are the gross domestic product, the consumer price index, and the unemployment rate.

Gross Domestic Product

The gross domestic product (GDP) measures in dollars the total value of U.S. goods and services newly produced or newly provided during a given time period. It is calculated and published by the BEA and is one of the most important and accurate ways the government tracks the health of the economy. The GDP can be calculated in different ways. One method is the expenditure approach. It sums all the spending that takes place during a specified time period on final goods and services that are newly produced or newly provided. The components of this calculation are:

- Consumption—the amount spent by consumers on final goods and services. This includes food, clothing, household appliances, and so on, and payments for medical care, haircuts, dry cleaning, and other types of services. One major item not included in this category is the purchase of residential housing, which is considered an investment, rather than a consumption expense.

- Investment—this category has three components. One is the amount spent by businesses on assets they will use to provide goods and services (e.g., new machines and equipment, warehouses, software, and company vehicles). Also included are changes in the value of business inventories. This amount can be positive or negative. Residential housing is the third component of the investment category.

- Government expenditures—the amount spent by the government (local, state, and federal) on final goods and services. This category does not include transfer payments to the public (such as Social Security and unemployment compensation) because these expenditures do not represent goods or services purchased.

- Net exports—the difference between the value of U.S. exports and imports. In other words, net exports equal the amount that foreigners paid for American goods minus the amount that Americans spent on foreign goods. If the United States exports more than it imports, this value will be positive. If the country imports more than it exports, this value will be negative.

It should be noted that the GDP counts only the final value paid for goods and services, not the value of intermediate transactions. For example, the value of steel sold by a steel company to an automaker is not counted. The value of the car made from the steel is counted when the car is sold in the marketplace. To be counted in the GDP, a product must be new. The sales of used items are not included.

TABLE 2.1

Key economic indicators for U.S. economy

Economic indicator	Description	Source	Website
Gross domestic product	Value of goods and services produced in a given time period.	U.S. Department of Commerce, Bureau of Economic Affairs http://www.bea.gov/bea	http://www.bea.gov/bea/dn/home/gdp.htm
Personal income and outlays	Personal income, disposable personal income, and personal consumption expenditures.		http://www.bea.gov/bea/dn/home/personalincome.htm
Corporate profits	Corporate profits based on current production.		http://www.bea.gov/bea/dn/home/corporateprof.htm
Fixed assets	Net stocks, depreciation, and investment for private residential and nonresidential fixed assets.		http://www.bea.gov/bea/dn/home/fixedassets.htm
Balance of payments (International transactions)	Quarterly trade in goods, services, income, unilateral transfers, and financial assets.		http://www.bea.gov/bea/di/home/bop.htm
Consumer price index	Monthly changes in the prices paid by urban consumers for a representative basket of goods and services.	U.S. Department of Labor, Bureau of Labor Statistics http://www.bls.gov	http://www.bls.gov/cpi/
Producer price index	Group of indexes that measure the average change over time in the prices received by U.S. producers of goods and services.		
Unemployment rate	Number of unemployed people divided by total labor force. Based on monthly survey.		http://www.bls.gov/cps/home.htm
Monthly retail trade	Survey of companies that sell merchandise and related services to final consumers.	U.S. Department of Commerce, U.S. Census Bureau http://www.census.gov/econ/www/	
Monthly wholesale trade	Survey of companies that are primarily engaged in merchant wholesale trade in the U.S.		
Consumer confidence index	Consumers' assessment of economic conditions based on monthly surveys of a representative sample of 5,000 U.S. households.	The Conference Board http://www.conference-board.org/economics	http://www.conference-board.org/economics/consumerConfidence.cfm
Leading indicators	Index based on vendor performance, stock prices, consumer expectations, manufacturers' new orders, manufacturing hours, interest rate spread, building permits, claims for unemployment insurance, and real money supply.		http://www.conference-board.org/economics/
ISM report on business	Economic activity in many manufacturing and nonmanufacturing industries based on orders, production, employment, supplier deliveries, imports, prices, and inventories.	Institute for Supply Management http://www.ism.ws/ISMReport/	http://www.ism.ws/ISMReport/

SOURCE: Created by Kim Masters Evans for Cengage Learning, Gale, 2008

COMPARISON WITH THE GROSS NATIONAL PRODUCT. Before 1991 the U.S. government used an economic indicator called the gross national product (GNP) to measure U.S. productivity. The GNP was calculated the same way that the GDP is calculated today, except that the GNP included the contribution of U.S. production in foreign countries (e.g., an American-owned factory in Mexico). The GDP includes only production occurring within the boundaries of the United States.

NOMINAL VERSUS REAL GDP. Economists refer to GDP values as being nominal (based on current dollar values) or real (based on inflation-adjusted dollar values). Consider a simple example in which a nation's only production is one thousand identical new cars produced and sold each year. Assume this nation suffers from inflation, meaning that the price charged and paid for each car increases each year. A graph of this nation's GDP would go upward, indicating that production increases each year, while actually it is just the price of the cars that is increasing.

To remedy this problem, economists adjust the actual GDP values (nominal values) to account for inflation. The adjusted values are called real GDP values. They are useful for comparing GDP changes over time. Figure 2.1 shows real GDP values for the U.S. economy from 1929 through 2007. These values were calculated assuming that a dollar had the exact same value over time—the value it had in 2000.

Figure 2.2 shows the annual percentage change in real GDP from 1997 to 2007. Real GDP was up by 2.2% in 2007, down slightly from 2.9% in the previous year.

Consumer Price Index

The consumer price index (CPI) provides a measure of price changes in consumer goods and services over a

FIGURE 2.1

Real gross domestic product, 1929–2007

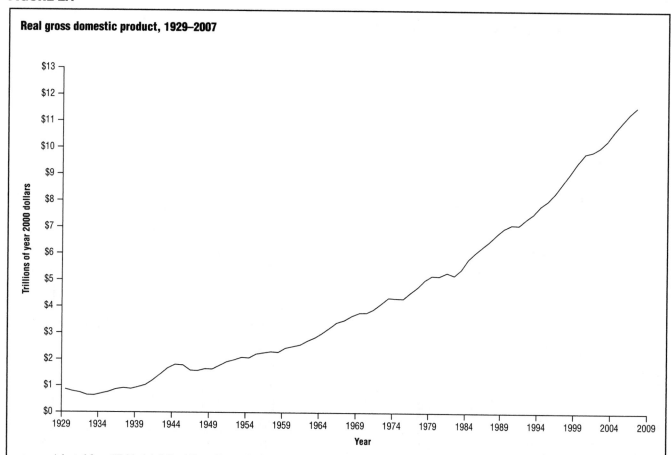

SOURCE: Adapted from "Table 1.1.6. Real Gross Domestic Product, Chained Dollars [Billions of chained (2000) dollars]," in *National Income and Product Accounts Table*, U.S. Department of Commerce, Bureau of Economic Analysis, March 27, 2008 http://www.bea.gov/bea/dn/nipaweb/TableView.asp? SelectedTable=6&FirstYear=3005&Freq=Year (accessed April 4, 2008)

specific period. Each month the U.S. Bureau of Labor Statistics (BLS), a division of the U.S. Department of Labor, calculates the purchase price of a fixed "basket" of thousands of goods and services commonly purchased for consumption by U.S. households. These purchases are divided into eight major categories:

- Food and beverages—at-home and away-from-home consumption

- Housing—includes rent of primary residence or owners' equivalent rent

- Apparel

- Transportation—includes insurance payments

- Medical care

- Recreation—includes pet expenses

- Education and communication—includes computer software

- Other goods and services—haircuts, cigarettes, funeral expenses, and so on

The basket price includes sales and excise taxes paid on goods purchased. Payments for income taxes and investments, such as stocks and bonds, are not included.

An index is a useful tool for comparing changes over time. The index for the basket price for a selected time period is arbitrarily set to one hundred. This is the reference index. All other basket prices are compared to the reference index using this equation: index = (basket price/reference basket price) × 100. Therefore, a graph of CPI data over time does not show the actual prices paid for the baskets but a series of index numbers useful for determining price changes. Figure 2.3 shows the average annual CPI from 1913 through 2007. It uses the time period of 1982 through 1984 as the reference time period for which the CPI value is arbitrarily set to one hundred.

Percent changes in price between two years can be determined based on the difference in index values. For example, according to the BLS, in *Consumer Price Indexes* (March 14, 2008, ftp://ftp.bls.gov/pub/special .requests/cpi/cpiai.txt), the average CPI was 113.6 in 1987. By 2007 it had risen to 207.3—a difference of 93.7 index points. Dividing 93.7 by 113.6 and multiplying by

FIGURE 2.2

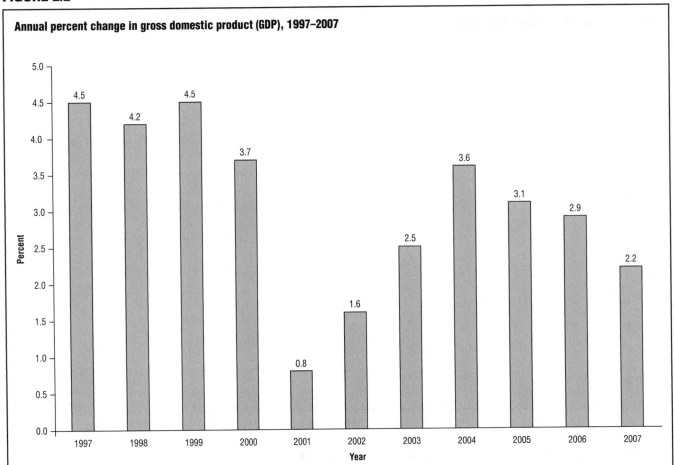

Annual percent change in gross domestic product (GDP), 1997–2007

SOURCE: Adapted from "Table 7. Real Gross Domestic Product: Percent Change from Preceding Year," in *Gross Domestic Product: First Quarter 2008 (Advance)*, U.S. Department of Commerce, Bureau of Economic Analysis, April 30, 2008, http://www.bea.gov/newsreleases/national/gdp/2008/pdf/gd108a .pdf (accessed May 7, 2008)

100 provides a percentage difference of 82.5%. On average, prices increased by 82.5% over this twenty-year period.

The data presented in Figure 2.3 are for urban households. According to the BLS (November 30, 2007, http://www.bls.gov/cpi/cpifaq.htm), the urban CPI (CPI-U) represents the buying habits of approximately 87% of the U.S. population. The BLS also calculates a CPI for urban dwellers employed in clerical or wage occupations, which are a subset of people included in the CPI-U. This subset represents approximately 32% of the U.S. population. Besides the national average, the BLS publishes CPI data for specific regions of the United States and for dozens of metropolitan areas.

CALCULATING AVERAGE ANNUAL INFLATION RATES FROM THE CPI. Price inflation can be defined as the increase in price over time of a fixed basket of goods and services. Thus, the CPI provides economists with a tool for quantifying inflation rates. The percent change in CPI from year to year is the inflation rate for that year. Figure 2.4 shows the annual average inflation rate for the U.S. economy for each year between 1915 and 2007

based on CPI-U data. In *Consumer Price Indexes*, the BLS states that the average CPI-U for 2006 was 201.6, and for 2007 it was 207.3. The inflation rate was ([207.3-201.6]/201.6) × 100 = 2.8%. This means that, on average, the price of consumer goods and services increased by 2.8% between 2006 and 2007. It also means that the purchasing power of a dollar went down over that time. For example, an item that cost $1.00 in 2006 cost nearly $1.03 in 2007.

In general, annual inflation rates of 2% to 3% are considered signs of a healthy growing economy where demand slightly outpaces supply. Larger inflation rates can be worrisome. The U.S. economy has suffered from double-digit inflation rates due to the effects of the world wars and during the 1970s and very early 1980s. Deflation (the lowering of average prices) occurred during the 1920s and 1930s.

CALCULATING ANNUAL INFLATION RATES ON A DECEMBER-TO-DECEMBER BASIS. The average annual inflation rate increase of 2.8% from 2006 to 2007 does not give the complete picture of price behavior during

FIGURE 2.3

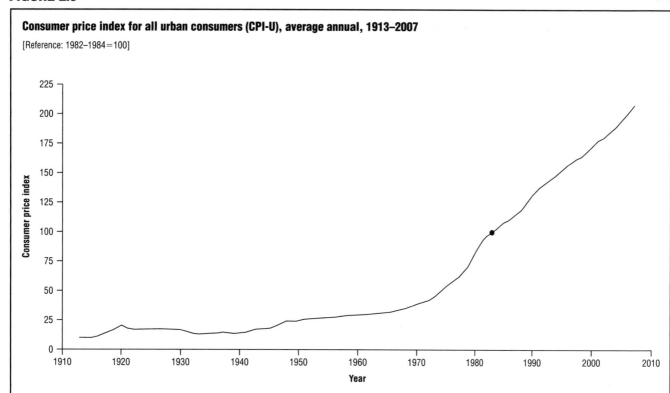

Consumer price index for all urban consumers (CPI-U), average annual, 1913–2007

[Reference: 1982–1984 = 100]

SOURCE: Adapted from "Consumer Price Index, All Urban Consumers—(CPI-U), U.S. City Average, All Items, 1982–84 = 100," in *Consumer Price Index*, U.S. Department of Labor, Bureau of Labor Statistics, March 14, 2008, ftp://ftp.bls.gov/pub/special.requests/cpi/cpiai.txt (accessed April 3, 2008)

2007. Another way to look at annual inflation rates is on a December-to-December basis. The BLS indicates in *Consumer Price Indexes* that in December 2006 the CPI-U was 201.8; by December 2007 it was 210. These values provide an annual inflation rate of ([210-201.8]/ 201.8) × 100 = 4.1%. This increase is higher than the increase calculated on an annual average basis and more accurately represents the price pressures faced by consumers in the marketplace during 2007. From a macro-economic standpoint, the December 2006 to December 2007 inflation rate of 4.1% was higher than "normal" for a "healthy" economy.

Unemployment Rate

The U.S. government calculates the nation's unemployment rate for a given time period by dividing the number of unemployed people by the total labor force (unemployed plus employed people). The employment status of people is determined based on responses by the public to a monthly government survey called the Current Population Survey (CPS). The CPS is administered by the Census Bureau for the BLS. According to the BLS, in "How Is the Unemployment Rate Related to Unemployment Insurance Claims?" (March 4, 2004, http://www.bls.gov/cps/uiclaims.htm), the survey is administered to more than sixty thousand households per month.

The BLS counts people as being unemployed if they meet all the following criteria:

- Do not have a job

- Have actively looked for work in the previous four weeks

- Are currently available for work

The BLS does not consider active-duty military personnel or institutionalized workers (such as prison inmates) to be in the labor force. In addition, some Americans are neither employed nor unemployed under the BLS definitions and thus are not in the labor force. The most obvious examples are patients in long-term care facilities and retirees. Many students and stay-at-home parents also fall into this category.

Figure 2.5 shows the U.S. unemployment rate from 1925 through 2007. For years through 1945, the rate is calculated based on people aged fourteen and older. Because of the passage of child labor laws, the unemployment rate for years following 1945 includes only people aged sixteen and older. The unemployment rate soared during the Great Depression, reaching nearly 25% in 1933. More typically, it has ranged between 3% and 8%. During the early 1980s the unemployment rate was nearly 10%, its highest rate since the 1930s. Since 1995 is has hovered between 4% and 6%, which is generally considered to be a reasonable range for a healthy economy.

FIGURE 2.4

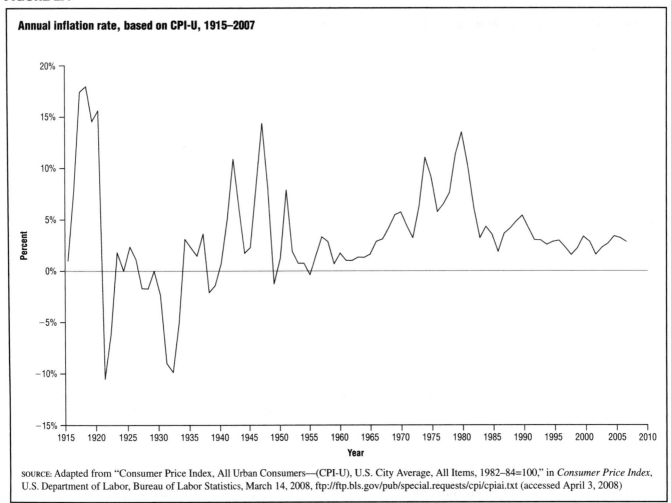

Annual inflation rate, based on CPI-U, 1915–2007

SOURCE: Adapted from "Consumer Price Index, All Urban Consumers—(CPI-U), U.S. City Average, All Items, 1982–84=100," in *Consumer Price Index*, U.S. Department of Labor, Bureau of Labor Statistics, March 14, 2008, ftp://ftp.bls.gov/pub/special.requests/cpi/cpiai.txt (accessed April 3, 2008)

Critics believe that the BLS data are not representative of the nation's actual unemployment rate, because the data do not include people who become discouraged and quit actively looking for work.

THE NUMERICAL STATE OF THE U.S. ECONOMY

Government and industry statistics on the state of the U.S. economy are released with varying frequency. Some economic indicators are published monthly, whereas others are published quarterly. Three government agencies—the BLS, the BEA, and the Census Bureau—publish updated economic indicators regularly.

The BLS: Unemployment, Wages, and Prices

The BLS publishes *U.S. Economy at a Glance*, which includes the latest statistics gathered by the agency on unemployment, wages, prices, and other economic factors. Table 2.2 shows the latest data available at the end of April 2008.

The unemployment rate in April 2008 was 5%. (See Table 2.2.) The rate had dropped slightly from March 2008, when it was 5.1%, but was up from 4.7% in November

2007. Comparison with the historical unemployment chart in Figure 2.5 shows that the rates for November 2007–April 2008 are moderate rates for post-depression America.

The BLS (April 25, 2008, http://www.bls.gov/ces/) also tracks changes in nonfarm payroll employment and average hourly earnings. These data are based on monthly surveys conducted of 150,000 businesses and government agencies as part of the agency's Current Employment Statistics program. Approximately twenty thousand jobs were lost in April 2008. (See Table 2.2.) Even larger losses were reported in the first three months of 2008—seventy-six thousand jobs lost in January, eighty-three thousand jobs lost in February, and eighty-one thousand jobs lost in March. New jobs were added in November and December of 2007. The average hourly wage for production and nonsupervisory workers was $17.88 in April 2008, up slightly from November 2007 when it was $17.64. Note that some data in Table 2.2 are considered preliminary and may change after further analysis by the BLS.

The CPI increased by 0.2% from March 2008 to April 2008. (See Table 2.2.) This value was down slightly

FIGURE 2.5

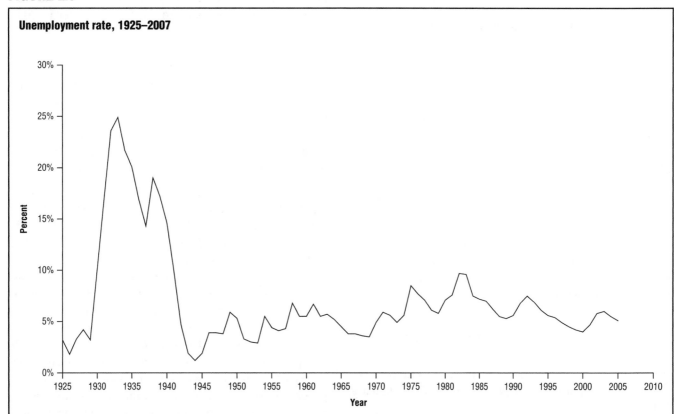

Unemployment rate, 1925–2007

Note: Rate calculated through 1946 for people age 14 years and above. After that, the rate is based on people age 16 years and above.

SOURCE: Adapted from "Series D85–86. Unemployment: 1890 to 1970," in *Historical Statistics of the United States, Colonial Times to 1970, Bicentennial Edition, Part 1*, U.S. Department of Commerce, U.S. Census Bureau, September 1975, http://www2.census.gov/prod2/statcomp/documents/CT1970p1-05 .pdf (accessed April 4, 2008), and "Labor Force Statistics from the Current Population Survey: Unadjusted Unemployment Rate," in *Bureau of Labor Statistics Data*, U.S. Department of Labor, Bureau of Labor Statistics, April 4, 2008, http://data.bls.gov/PDQ/servlet/SurveyOutputServlet?data_tool= latest_numbers&series_id=LNU04000000&years_option=all_years&periods_option=specific_periods&periods=Annual+Data (accessed April 4, 2008)

TABLE 2.2

U.S. Department of Labor economic indicators, November 2007–April 2008

Data series	Nov 2007	Dec 2007	Jan 2008	Feb 2008	Mar 2008	Apr 2008
Unemployment rate[a]	4.7	5	4.9	4.8	5.1	5
Change in payroll employment[b]	60	41	−76	−83	−81 (P)	−20 (P)
Average hourly earnings[c]	17.64	17.70	17.75	17.81	17.87 (P)	17.88 (P)
Consumer price index[d]	0.9	0.4	0.4	0.0	0.3	0.2
Producer price index[e]	2.6	−0.5	1.1 (P)	0.3 (P)	1.1 (P)	0.2 (P)
U.S. import price index[f]	3.2	−0.2	1.5	0.2[i]	2.9[i]	1.8[i]
Employment cost index[g, j]	0.8	0.7				
Productivity[h]	1.8	2.2				

(p) Preliminary
[a]In percent, seasonally adjusted. Annual averages are available for not seasonally adjusted data.
[b]Number of jobs, in thousands, seasonally adjusted.
[c]For production and nonsupervisory workers on private nonfarm payrolls, seasonally adjusted.
[d]All items, U.S. city average, all urban consumers, 1982–84 = 100, 1-month percent change, seasonally adjusted.
[e]Finished goods, 1982 = 100, 1-month percent change, seasonally adjusted.
[f]All imports, 1-month percent change, not seasonally adjusted.
[g]Compensation, all civilian workers, quarterly data, 3-month percent change, seasonally adjusted.
[h]Output per hour, nonfarm business, quarterly data, percent change from previous quarter at annual rate, seasonally adjusted.
[i]Revised.
[j]Includes wages, salaries, and employer costs for employee benefits.

SOURCE: Adapted from *U.S. Economy at a Glance*, U.S. Department of Labor, Bureau of Labor Statistics, May 28, 2008, http://www.bls.gov/eag/eag.us.htm (accessed May 31, 2008)

FIGURE 2.6

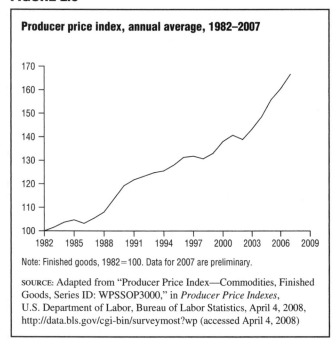

Producer price index, annual average, 1982–2007

Note: Finished goods, 1982=100. Data for 2007 are preliminary.

SOURCE: Adapted from "Producer Price Index—Commodities, Finished Goods, Series ID: WPSSOP3000," in *Producer Price Indexes*, U.S. Department of Labor, Bureau of Labor Statistics, April 4, 2008, http://data.bls.gov/cgi-bin/surveymost?wp (accessed April 4, 2008)

from the previous month, and relatively low compared to the changes reported from November 2007 to January 2008.

There are three other indexes reported by the BLS:

- Producer price index (PPI)—a family of indexes that measure changes over time in the selling prices received by the makers and providers of goods and services. The PPI has risen dramatically over the past two decades from its reference value of one hundred in 1982. (See Figure 2.6.) The PPI increased by 0.2% between March and April 2008. (See Table 2.2.) PPI values can differ from CPI values because of factors such as taxes and distribution costs.

- U.S. import price index (MPI)—indicates monthly changes in the prices of nonmilitary goods and services imported to the United States from the rest of the world. The MPI increased by 1.8% between March and April 2008. (See Table 2.2.) The BLS also tracks an export price index as part of its International Price Program.

- Employment cost index (ECI)—tracks quarterly changes in nonfarm civilian business labor costs based on a national compensation survey. It includes wages, salaries, and employer costs for employee benefits. The ECI increased by 0.7% from the fourth quarter in 2007 to the first quarter in 2008. (See Table 2.2.)

Finally, the BLS includes in *U.S. Economy at a Glance* a measure of national productivity (or efficiency). This number is a quarterly estimate of the change in output per hour of nonfarm businesses. It is calculated by comparing the amount of goods and services produced with the inputs that were used to produce them. Accord-

ing to the BLS, productivity was up 2.2% in the first quarter in 2008, compared to the fourth quarter in 2007. (See Table 2.2.)

The BEA: GDP, Income, Savings, and Profits

The BEA publishes *Overview of the Economy*, which includes the latest agency statistics for the GDP, corporate profits, personal income and savings, and other economic factors. It should be noted that until they are dubbed "final," these statistics are estimates and are frequently revised by the BEA as new data become available.

REAL GDP. Figure 2.7 shows the quarterly changes in real GDP for the second quarter in 2004 through the first quarter in 2008. Real GDP grew by only 0.6% during the last quarter of 2007 and the first quarter of 2008, based on preliminary estimates. These values represent a substantial downturn from previous recent quarters. In the press release "Gross Domestic Product: First Quarter 2008 (Advance)" (April 30, 2008, http://www.bea.gov/newsreleases/national/gdp/2008/pdf/gdp108a.pdf), the BEA reports that the growth slowdown in the first quarter in 2008 real GDP was primarily due to decreases in residential fixed investments and consumer spending on durable (long-lasting) goods and to an increase in U.S. imports. Positive factors included consumer spending on services, business investments in inventory, U.S. exports, and federal government spending. Overall, real GDP grew by 2.2% during 2007.

NOMINAL GDP. The BEA reports that nominal GDP (GDP in current dollars) was $13.8 trillion in 2007. A breakdown by component is detailed in Table 2.3 and shown graphically in Figure 2.8. Personal consumption expenditures (PCE) accounted for 67% of positive GDP during 2007. This is consumer spending on goods and services. Services accounted for more than half of PCE, totaling $5.8 trillion. Medical care was the largest single service component, accounting for nearly $1.7 trillion of the total. Housing costs were the second largest component, at nearly $1.5 trillion. Spending on nondurable goods, such as food, clothing, and so on, amounted to $2.8 trillion, or 19% of positive GDP. Durable goods expenditures totaled nearly $1.1 trillion, or 7% of positive GDP.

Private investments totaled $2.1 trillion in 2007 and accounted for 15% of positive GDP. (See Table 2.3.) More than half of this total was devoted to nonresidential (business) investments in structures, equipment, and software. Residential fixed investments totaled $640.7 billion. The contribution from the change in private inventories was $2.9 billion.

Government spending and investment amounted to nearly $2.7 trillion, or 18% of positive GDP. (See Table 2.3.) State and local governments accounted for more than half of this total. Net exports were a negative contributor to the GDP during 2007, because the value of imports ($2.4 trillion) was greater than the value of exports ($1.6 trillion).

FIGURE 2.7

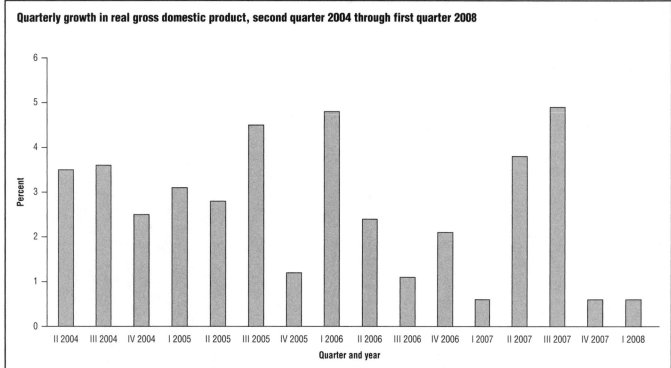

Quarterly growth in real gross domestic product, second quarter 2004 through first quarter 2008

Note: GDP growth is measured at seasonally adjusted annual rates.

SOURCE: Adapted from "Table 1. Real Gross Domestic Product and Related Measures: Percent Change from Preceding Period," in *Gross Domestic Product: First Quarter 2008 (Advance)*, U.S. Department of Commerce, Bureau of Economic Analysis, April 30, 2008, http://www.bea.gov/newsreleases/national/gdp/2008/pdf/gdp108a.pdf (accessed May 7, 2008)

PERSONAL INCOME AND SAVINGS. The BEA also tracks changes in personal income and its disposition. Personal income includes wages and salaries (the largest component), wage and salary supplements (e.g., employer contributions to private pension funds on behalf of employees), rental income, proprietors' income (earned by entrepreneurs, small businesses, and farmers), and interest and dividend income. Most of the data are based on private and government payrolls. In the press release "Personal Income and Outlays" (June 27, 2008, http://www.bea.gov/newsreleases/national/pi/pinewsrelease.htm), the BEA notes that personal income increased by 1.9% in May 2008. This was a major increase compared to changes recorded in the previous four months.

Disposable personal income (DPI) is the amount of income received by people after taxes are subtracted. In other words, the DPI is the income available to people for spending or saving. According to the BEA, the DPI increased by 5.7% in May 2008, compared to 0.4% in April 2008. Personal savings (DPI minus personal outlays) was $555.7 billion in May 2008, up from $39.7 billion in April 2008.

CORPORATE PROFITS. The BEA reports in the press release "Gross Domestic Product: Fourth Quarter 2007 (Final)" (March 27, 2008, http://www.bea.gov/newsreleases/national/gdp/2008/gdp407f.htm) that corporate profits from current production decreased $52.9 billion during the fourth quarter 2007 after decreasing by $20.5 billion the third quarter.

The Census Bureau: Housing Starts and Home Sales

A high rate of homeownership is considered a positive sign of financial health by the U.S. government. As such, the Census Bureau tracks two important indicators in this area: housing starts and home sales. Housing starts is the number of new housing units (or homes) that have been started over a particular period. According to the Census Bureau, approximately 690,000 single-family homes were started in April 2008. (See Figure 2.9.) This value is down from more than 1.8 million homes started in early 2006. In general, monthly housing start numbers increased steadily through early 2006 and then plummeted. Sales of existing and newly built single-family homes plunged at around the same time. (See Figure 2.10.) This signaled a significant downturn in the real estate market.

PUBLIC PERCEPTION OF THE ECONOMY

According to the government's various economic indicators, the overall condition of the U.S. economy is good. In reality, the state of the nation's economy is a reflection of the financial condition of the hundreds of millions of individuals and businesses that contribute to it. Thus, economic conditions at the national level can be

TABLE 2.3

Composition of gross domestic product (GDP), 2007

[Billions of current dollars, seasonally adjusted at annual rates, 2007ʳ]

Gross domestic product: $13,841.30

	Component	Percent of positive GDP
Personal consumption expenditures	**$9,734.20**	**67%**
Durable goods	**$1,078.20**	**7%**
Motor vehicles and parts	$441.2	3%
Furniture and household equipment	$416.1	3%
Other	$221.0	2%
Nondurable goods	**$2,833.2**	**19%**
Food	$1,336.4	9%
Clothing and shoes	$370.5	3%
Gasoline, fuel oil, and other energy goods	$364.2	3%
Other	$762.2	5%
Services	**$5,822.80**	**40%**
Housing	$1,465.9	10%
Household operation	$531.1	4%
Electricity and gas	$226.9	2%
Other household operation	$304.2	2%
Transportation	$358.4	2%
Medical care	$1,689.3	12%
Recreation	$402.2	3%
Other	1,375.8	9%
Gross private domestic investment	**$2,125.40**	**15%**
Nonresidential fixed investment	**$1,481.8**	**10%**
Structures	$472.1	3%
Equipment and software	$1,009.7	7%
Residential fixed investment	**$640.7**	**4%**
Change in private inventories	**$2.9**	**0.0%**
Government consumption expenditures and gross investment	**$2,689.80**	**18%**
Federal	**$976.0**	**6.7%**
State and local	**$1,713.8**	**11.8%**
Net exports of goods and services	**−$708.00**	
Exports	**$1,643.00**	
Goods	$1,152.9	
Services	$490.1	
Imports	**$2,351.00**	
Goods	$1,979.4	
Services	$371.6	

ʳRevised

SOURCE: Adapted from "Table 3. Gross Domestic Product and Related Measures: Level and Change from Preceding Period," in *Gross Domestic Product: Fourth Quarter 2007 (Final); Corporate Profits: Fourth Quarter 2007*, U.S. Department of Commerce, Bureau of Economic Analysis, March 27, 2008, http://www.bea.gov/newsreleases/national/gdp/2008/pdf/gdp407f .pdf (accessed April 4, 2008)

FIGURE 2.8

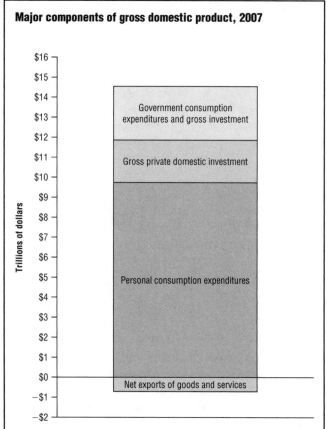

Major components of gross domestic product, 2007

SOURCE: Adapted from "Table 3. Gross Domestic Product and Related Measures: Level and Change from Preceding Period," in *Gross Domestic Product: Fourth Quarter 2007 (Final); Corporate Profits: Fourth Quarter 2007*, U.S. Department of Commerce, Bureau of Economic Analysis, March 27, 2008, http://www.bea.gov/newsreleases/ national/gdp/2008/pdf/gdp407f.pdf (accessed April 4, 2008)

quite different from those experienced by people at the regional and local levels.

Regional and Local Economies

Part of microeconomics study involves the economic health of various geographical regions and communities. A regional economy can be an area as small as a neighborhood or as large as a group of states with climate, geography, industry, or culture in common. The relative strength of a regional economy reflects broader national trends. For example, in the late nineteenth and early twentieth centuries—with the economy of the American South in shambles after the Civil War—northern cities attracted millions of workers to their rapidly growing industrial centers, such as the steel mills of Pittsburgh and the car factories of Detroit. Later, as the population migrated elsewhere, this region became known as the Rust Belt. Similarly, in the late twentieth century, western states experienced substantial growth with the rise of the computer industry, thanks in large part to Microsoft, which is headquartered in Seattle, Washington, and the dot-com companies centered in California's Silicon Valley. Other major economic regions of the United States include the Farm Belt of the Great Plains and the Sun Belt states of the South and Southwest, with warm climates that make them popular tourist destinations and strong agricultural regions.

When a region or community experiences a serious economic downturn—such as that which happened in the

FIGURE 2.9

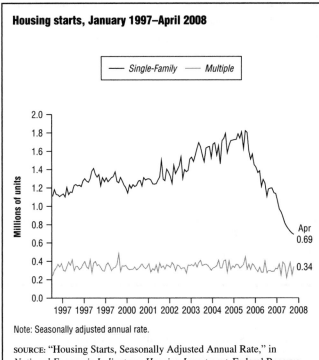

Housing starts, January 1997–April 2008

Note: Seasonally adjusted annual rate.

SOURCE: "Housing Starts, Seasonally Adjusted Annual Rate," in *National Economic Indicators: Housing Investment*, Federal Reserve Bank of New York, May 23, 2008, http://www.ny.frb.org/research/directors_charts/ibcd_04.pdf (accessed May 23, 2008)

FIGURE 2.10

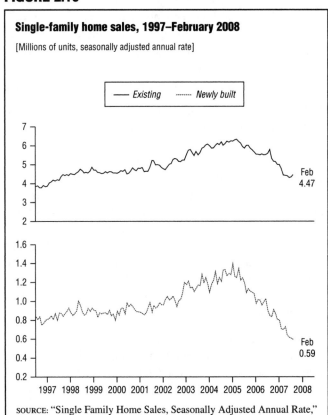

Single-family home sales, 1997–February 2008

[Millions of units, seasonally adjusted annual rate]

SOURCE: "Single Family Home Sales, Seasonally Adjusted Annual Rate," in *National Economic Indicators: Housing Investment*, Federal Reserve Bank of New York, April 4, 2008, http://www.ny.frb.org/research/directors_charts/ibcd_04.pdf (accessed April 5, 2008)

upper Midwest, when the auto and steel manufacturers started losing ground to foreign competitors, and in the Farm Belt, with the rise of agribusiness and the subsequent demise of the small family farm—its citizens often fall into a cycle of unemployment and poverty, leading federal and local governments and private nonprofit organizations to step in to offer assistance.

The Role of the Individual in the Economy

Almost every aspect of American life is influenced by, and further influences, the economy. Whether a person drives or flies during his or her next vacation, how he or she will pay for college and save for retirement, what advertisements he or she sees, what movies he or she watches, and what magazines he or she reads all involve making economic decisions, which then affect the way the economy functions. If a person works or plans to work, that person is a small but important part of the economy. Likewise, every time an individual buys goods or saves money, he or she is participating in economic activity.

Economists maintain that the better off the economy is, the better its participants will be. In a healthy economy people tend to have more job security, earn more money, and are able to increase opportunities for themselves and their family—thus lifting their overall quality of life. However, in an unstable, bad economy—such as in the United States during the Great Depression and during recessions—people are less certain of the future, face increasing pressures at work and may lose their jobs, and have less flexibility in being able to pay for goods and services, which in turn affects trends in employment, interest rates, the cost of living, the money supply, and all other aspects of the economy, on both the macro and micro levels.

Public Opinion Polls

PROBLEMS FACING THE COUNTRY. The Gallup Organization is a U.S.-based firm that conducts frequent public opinion polls to gauge the mood and attitudes of the American people on a variety of subjects. In April 2008 Gallup asked Americans to name "the most important problem facing the country today." Poll participants' first responses were recorded. The results are featured in *Gallup Poll Social Series: Economy & Personal Finance* (http://brain.gallup.com/documents/questionnaire.aspx?STUDY=P0804015). The most common first response was the economy. Nearly 41% of those asked named it as the nation's most important problem. The two next most common responses were the war in Iraq (13%) and fear of war (10%).

RATING THE U.S. ECONOMY. Since 1992 Gallup has asked poll participants to provide their assessment of the overall economic condition of the country by rating it as "excellent," "good," "only fair," or "poor." Table 2.4 shows the results of this survey for April 2008. Only a

TABLE 2.4

Public opinion poll on economic conditions, April 2008

HOW WOULD YOU RATE ECONOMIC CONDITIONS IN THIS COUNTRY TODAY—AS EXCELLENT, GOOD, ONLY FAIR, OR POOR?

Mean: 1.68		Total N: 1021
	%	**N**
Excellent	0.79	8
Good	12.50	128
Only fair	40.03	409
Poor	46.48	475
Don't know	0.20	2
Refused	0.00	0

N = Population.

SOURCE: "Question qn5. How Would You Rate Economic Conditions in This Country Today—As Excellent, Good, Only Fair, or Poor?" in *Gallup Poll Social Series: Economy & Personal Finance*, The Gallup Organization, April 2008, http://brain.gallup.com/documents/questionnaire.aspx?STUDY= P0804015 (accessed May 13, 2008). Copyright © 2008 by The Gallup Organization. Reproduced by permission of The Gallup Organization.

TABLE 2.5

Public opinion poll on personal financial situation, April 2008

HOW WOULD YOU RATE YOUR FINANCIAL SITUATION TODAY—AS EXCELLENT, GOOD, ONLY FAIR, OR POOR?

Mean: 2.35	Total N: 1021	
	%	**N**
Excellent	7.15	73
Good	37.98	388
Only fair	37.42	382
Poor	17.34	177
Don't know	0.06	1
Refused	0.05	1

N=Population.

SOURCE: "Question qn7. How Would You Rate Your Financial Situation Today—As Excellent, Good, Only Fair, or Poor?" in *Gallup Poll Social Series: Economy & Personal Finance*, The Gallup Organization, April 2008, http://brain.gallup.com/documents/questionnaire.aspx?STUDY=P0804015 (accessed May 13, 2008). Copyright © 2008 by The Gallup Organization. Reproduced by permission of The Gallup Organization.

small percentage of respondents (0.79%) rated the economy as "excellent." A higher number (12.5%) described the economy as "good." More than 40% said the economy was "only fair" and over 46% described it as "poor."

In *Consumers' Negative Attitudes Unchanged in Early May* (May 15, 2008, http://www.gallup.com/poll/107290/consumers-negative-Attitudes-Unchanged-Early-May.aspx?), Lydia Saad of the Gallup Organization compares the results of surveys conducted on this same topic in January 2008 through May 2008. Saad lumps together the "excellent" and "good" responses. In January 2008 nearly an equal percentage of respondents described the economy as "excellent/good" (27%) or "poor" (28%). Over the following months, pessimism grew considerably. By May 2008 the percentage rating the economy as "excellent/good" decreased to 16%, whereas the percentage rating the economy as "poor" increased to 43%.

In the same polls the participants were asked to give their opinion on whether economic conditions in the country as a whole are getting better or worse. Saad indicates that in January 2008, 78% of those asked believed the nation's economy is getting worse. By May 2008 this value grew to 86%.

NATIONAL ECONOMIC MOOD. Gallup uses poll response data to calculate a value it calls an Economic Mood measure. People describing the economy as excellent or good and either staying the same or getting better are considered to have a "positive" mood. Those who believed the economy is fair or poor and either staying the same or getting worse are considered to have a "negative" mood. Other viewpoints outside of these two categories are considered "mixed." According to Saad, 78% of those asked in May 2008 had a negative outlook on the economy, compared to only 7% with a positive outlook. Another 13% had a mixed outlook.

Saad notes that economic attitudes varied based on the family income and political persuasion of the poll respondents. Eleven percent of respondents making $7,500 or more per month had a positive outlook, and 73% had a negative outlook. By contrast, 5% of those making less than $2,000 per month had a positive outlook, whereas 83% had a negative outlook. There were large differences based on political party affiliation. Eighty-seven percent of Democrats and 81% of Independents had a negative outlook, compared to 62% of Republicans. Similarly, 15% of Republicans had a positive outlook, whereas 5% of Independents and 3% of Democrats did so.

PERSONAL FINANCIAL SITUATION. As part of *Gallup Poll Social Series: Economy and Personal Finance*, pollsters asked Americans to rate their financial situation as excellent, good, only fair, or poor. Only a small percentage (7.2%) of respondents gave an answer of excellent. (See Table 2.5.) More than a third (38%) rated their financial situation as good. Nearly as many (37.4%) felt it was only fair. Another 17.3% said their financial situation was poor. When asked if their financial situation was "getting better" or "getting worse," nearly half (49%) of poll participants said their financial situation was getting worse. Close to one-third (32%) said their financial situation was getting better. Another 17% said their financial situation was staying the same.

Poll participants were asked to name "the most important financial problem" facing their families. First responses were recorded by Gallup. The ten problems cited most often were:

- Energy costs/oil/gas prices—14%
- None—13%
- Lack of money/cash flow—11%

- Costs of owning/renting a home—10%
- Health-care costs—10%
- High cost of living/inflation—10%
- Not enough money to pay debts—9%
- College expenses—7%
- Unemployment/loss of jobs—6%
- Retirement savings—5%

Gallup pollsters also asked people to indicate their level of worry about being able to "maintain the standard of living" they currently enjoyed. A quarter of respondents said they were very worried about that issue. Nearly 30% were moderately worried, and almost 24% were not too worried. Another 20% of respondents indicated they were not worried at all.

Dennis Jacobe of the Gallup Organization examines the standard of living poll results in detail in *In U.S., Record Worry about Maintaining Standard of Living* (April 25, 2008, http://www.gallup.com/poll/106831/US-Record-Worry-About-Maintaining-Standard-Living.aspx). According to Jacobe, the 55% of respondents indicating they were very worried or moderately worried about maintaining their standard of living was the highest percentage recorded by Gallup since the question was first asked in 2001. In that year 43% of respondents said they were very worried or moderately worried about maintaining their standard of living. The percentage varied over the following six years between 35% and 49%.

Jacobe notes that in April 2008 the greatest amount of worry on this issue was expressed by lower-income Americans. Nearly three-quarters (72%) of respondents earning less than $30,000 per year were very or moderately worried about being able to maintain their standard of living. By comparison, 58% of respondents making $30,000 to $74,999 per year and 41% of respondents earning $75,000 or more per year expressed a similar degree of worry.

SPECIFIC NATIONAL ECONOMIC CHALLENGES. In April 2008 Gallup conducted a poll asking Americans to rate specific national economic challenges on their seriousness. Respondents could use the following ratings:

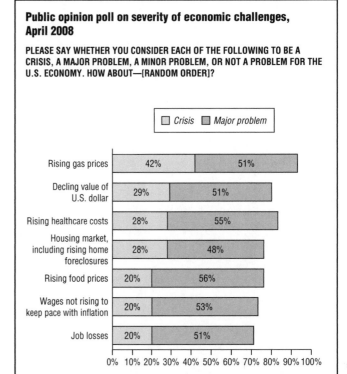

FIGURE 2.11

Public opinion poll on severity of economic challenges, April 2008

PLEASE SAY WHETHER YOU CONSIDER EACH OF THE FOLLOWING TO BE A CRISIS, A MAJOR PROBLEM, A MINOR PROBLEM, OR NOT A PROBLEM FOR THE U.S. ECONOMY. HOW ABOUT—[RANDOM ORDER]?

Crisis / Major problem

	Crisis	Major problem
Rising gas prices	42%	51%
Decling value of U.S. dollar	29%	51%
Rising healthcare costs	28%	55%
Housing market, including rising home foreclosures	28%	48%
Rising food prices	20%	56%
Wages not rising to keep pace with inflation	20%	53%
Job losses	20%	51%

0% 10% 20% 30% 40% 50% 60% 70% 80% 90% 100%

SOURCE: Dennis Jacobe, "Please Say Whether You Consider Each of the Following To Be a Crisis, a Major Problem, a Minor Problem, or Not a Problem for the U.S. Economy. How about—[RANDOM ORDER]?" in *Economic Issues Reaching "Crisis" Level for Many Americans*, The Gallup Organization, May 1, 2008, http://www.gallup.com/poll/106939/Economic-Issues-Reaching-Crisis-Level-Many-Americans.aspx?version=print (accessed June 1, 2008). Copyright © 2008 by The Gallup Organization. Reproduced by permission of The Gallup Organization.

crisis, major problem, minor problem, or not a problem. Forty-two percent of respondents rated rising gas prices as a crisis. (See Figure 2.11.) More than a quarter of poll participants considered the declining value of the U.S. dollar, rising health costs, and the housing market (including rising home foreclosures) to be a crisis. Twenty percent of respondents thought rising food prices, wages not rising to keep pace with inflation, and job losses were crises. Roughly half of respondents rated each of these economic challenges as a major problem in the country.

CHAPTER 3
THE AMERICAN CONSUMER

The use of money is all the advantage there is in having money.

—Benjamin Franklin, *Poor Richard's Almanack* (1737)

Americans love to spend money, and their aggressive spending helps fuel both the U.S. and global economies, as imported goods are widely available and popular in the U.S. market. In fact, consumer spending is the single largest contributing factor to the nation's growth in gross domestic production. High consumer spending rates produce a ripple effect that spreads across many other macroeconomic sectors, including employment, wages, corporate profits, and interest rates.

THE RISE OF THE CONSUMER CULTURE
World War II

World War II (1939–1945) is generally credited with lifting the United States out of the Great Depression—the period of economic disaster that lasted from 1929 through the early 1940s. The urgent need for weapons, tanks, planes, and other war goods led the government to invest heavily in getting the nation's factories running again, especially after the United States joined the fighting in late 1941. At the war's end, many factories were converted into facilities to manufacture civilian products such as appliances and automobiles, for which demand was especially high after the war.

RATIONING AND THE WAR PRODUCTION BOARD. During the war citizens were encouraged to exercise restraint in spending to conserve materials for the war effort. Some items were temporarily banned from public use; for example, platinum was declared a "strategic metal" to be used only in the manufacture of military goods, so its use in jewelry making was halted. The government also established rationing (tight controls over how much of an item a person can use or consume in a certain amount of time). All citizens were issued coupon books for rationed items every six months; once they used up their

coupons for the month, they had to wait until the next month to buy more rationed goods. Coffee, sugar, meat, butter, and canned vegetables were rationed, as were gasoline, rubber, silk (which was used to make parachutes), fuel oil, and other goods put to military purposes. Victory gardens became common as the government encouraged Americans to grow their own vegetables rather than buy them.

In 1942 the War Production Board (WPB) was created to oversee production programs for war-related commodities. The agency's first move was to halt all American automobile production and order car factories to produce only planes, tanks, machine guns, diesel engines, and military trucks. Producers of other consumer goods were also ordered to join the war effort; for example, a domestic housewares company called International Silver converted its manufacturing facilities to the production of military goods such as surgical instruments, machine gun clips, and gasoline bombs. To conserve materials needed to clothe soldiers and make other fabric items for the war effort, the WPB regulated every aspect of U.S. clothing design. Silk stockings were banned, so women drew seams on the backs of their legs to simulate them. The WPB mandated that dresses and skirts be made shorter and that men's suits—marketed as "victory suits"—had narrower lapels and pants with no cuffs, to conserve fabric. Women's two-piece bathing suits became popular because they used less fabric than one-piece suits.

The Postwar Boom

When the war came to an end in 1945, Americans were divided about becoming consumers again. Whereas some had felt deprived for so long that they could not wait to start spending, others were reluctant. To help create jobs for the tens of thousands of soldiers returning to the workforce from the war and build on the country's newfound economic prosperity, the government, along with businesses and marketing firms, began a campaign to stir up consumer activity. Spending was promoted as a civic duty and an expression of patriotism rather than as a personal indulgence. A postwar baby boom also changed Americans' perspective on spending.

Growing families purchased bigger houses, many of which were built in the suburbs. The suburban population shift was accompanied by a growth in shopping centers, supermarkets, and car ownership. According to Alonzo L. Hamby of Ohio University, in *Outline of U.S. History* (November 2005, http://usinfo.state.gov/products/pubs/histryotln/historytln.pdf), the annual production of automobiles quadrupled between 1946 and 1955. Television and air conditioning became widely available following World War II. Air conditioning spurred migration from the Northeast and Midwest to the Southeast and Southwest. By the end of the 1950s three-fourths of all American families owned at least one television set. Television advertising reached a large audience and promoted more consumer spending.

THE COLD WAR: BEATING COMMUNISM BY SHOPPING. By the late 1940s the cold war—a decades-long period of political tension between the United States and the former Soviet Union that began just after World War II and ended in the early 1990s—was well under way. To contrast the U.S. open market system with Soviet socialism—under which private ownership was generally disallowed—U.S. politicians argued that widespread ownership of more possessions would create greater social equality, thereby proving the superiority of the market system. Therefore, consumer spending acted as a function of the drive to defeat communism.

HOMEOWNERSHIP. Foremost on the list of items that many American citizens wanted was new housing, and the ideal housing, according to the standards of the time, was a mass-produced single-family home in the suburbs. Lizabeth Cohen explains in "The Landscape of Mass Consumption" (February 2003, http://www.nthposition.com/landscapeofmass.php) that residential housing construction after the war occurred at rates never before seen in the United States, with the federal government helping veterans buy homes with guaranteed loans and connecting the new suburbs to cities with an immense system of federally built highways. Between 1947 and 1953 the number of people living in the suburbs increased by 43%, and by 1960, 62% of Americans owned their own homes.

AUTOMOBILES. Homeownership generated the need for many items, but few had more far-reaching effects than automobiles. With such a large proportion of Americans living in the suburbs, the ability to commute to work and shopping centers became essential, so a family car went from being a luxury to being a necessity in the 1950s. This was the birth of the American car culture.

Car ownership led to more travel, which spawned more business opportunities. Fast-food restaurants allowed people to eat in their cars. Motels (motor hotels) provided inexpensive places to stay (and park cars) overnight. Convenience stores sprang up along the new highways, encouraging drivers to stop and shop while they were on the road. Even the camping and outdoor industry saw a rush to its products, as Americans purchased campers and other outdoor equipment and took to the road for family vacations. In *What We Work for Now: Changing Household Consumption Patterns in the Twentieth Century* (December 2001, http://www.rprogress.org/newpubs/2001/whatwework.pdf), Jerome Segal, Cynthia Pansing, and Brian Parkinson state that by 1950, 60% of U.S. households had a car and that transportation-related expenses accounted for one out of every seven dollars spent by the typical U.S. household.

TELEVISION. Along with the widespread ownership of automobiles, the introduction of television into daily U.S. life represented one of the most important social, economic, and technological changes of the twentieth century. Television was promoted as a social equalizer that would, again, prove the superiority of U.S. capitalism over Soviet communism. With such unprecedented access to information, U.S. citizens were predicted to achieve equality across all classes and social groups. Lyn Spigel explains in "Television" (*Encyclopedia of American Cultural and Intellectual History*, 2001) that in 1948 about 2% of U.S. households had a television. By 1960 approximately 90% of U.S. households were equipped with at least one television.

CONTEMPORARY CONSUMER SPENDING

The U.S. Bureau of Labor Statistics (BLS) tracks consumer spending and publishes the results in two different formats. Personal Consumer Expenditure (PCE) data are used on a quarterly basis to calculate the nation's gross domestic product (GDP; the total market value of final goods and services produced within an economy in a given year). The PCE is based on aggregate data (data summed to represent the entire population). The BLS also publishes an annual Consumer Expenditure Survey that estimates the consumer spending of an average U.S. household during a given year.

One economic indicator extremely relevant to consumer spending is the inflation rate based on the Consumer Price Index (CPI). The BLS indicates in *Consumer Price Index* (March 14, 2008, ftp://ftp.bls.gov/pub/special.requests/cpi/cpiai.txt) that the average annual inflation rate based on the CPI for all urban consumers (CPI-U) was 2.8% in 2007. However, the annual rate calculated from December 2006 to December 2007 was much higher at 4.1%. This means that consumer prices rose at an uncomfortably high rate during 2007. Table 3.1 shows the annual percent change in the CPI-U for all items and specific categories of items for 2007 on a

TABLE 3.1

Annual percent change in the urban Consumer Price Index (CPI-U) for selected expenditure categories, December 2006–December 2007

Expenditure category	Percentage change 12 months ended in December	
	2006	2007
All items	**2.5**	**4.1**
Food and beverages	2.2	4.8
Housing	3.3	3.0
Apparel	.9	−.3
Transportation	1.6	8.3
Medical care	3.6	5.2
Recreation	1.0	.8
Education and communication	2.3	3.0
Other goods and services	3.0	3.3
Special indexes:	2.9	17.4
Energy		
Energy commodities	6.1	29.4
Energy services	−.6	3.4
All items less energy	2.5	2.8
Food	2.1	4.9
All items less food and energy	2.6	2.4

SOURCE: Adapted from Malik Crawford, ed., "Table Q1. Annual Percent Changes in the CPI for All Urban Consumers, 2001–2008," in *CPI Detailed Report: Data for March 2008*, U.S. Department of Labor, Bureau of Labor Statistics, April 2008, http://www.bls.gov/cpi/cpid0803.pdf (accessed May 6, 2008)

TABLE 3.2

Personal consumption expenditures (PCE), 2007

[Billions of current dollars, seasonally adjusted at annual rates, 2007[r]]

	Component	Percent of PCE
Personal consumption expenditures	**$9,734.20**	
Durable goods	**$1,078.20**	**11%**
Motor vehicles and parts	$441.2	5%
Furniture and household equipment	$416.1	4%
Other	$221.0	2%
Nondurable goods	**$2,833.2**	**29%**
Food	$1,336.4	14%
Clothing and shoes	$370.5	4%
Gasoline, fuel oil, and other energy goods	$364.2	4%
Other	$762.2	8%
Services	**$5,822.80**	**60%**
Housing	$1,465.9	15%
Household operation	$531.1	5%
Electricity and gas	$226.9	2%
Other household operation	$304.2	3%
Transportation	$358.4	4%
Medical care	$1,689.3	17%
Recreation	$402.2	4%
Other	1,375.8	14%

[r] = Revised.

SOURCE: Adapted from "Table 3. Gross Domestic Product and Related Measures: Level and Change from Preceding Period," in *Gross Domestic Product: Fourth Quarter 2007 (Final); Corporate Profits: Fourth Quarter 2007*, U.S. Department of Commerce, Bureau of Economic Analysis, March 27, 2008, http://www.bea.gov/newsreleases/national/gdp/2008/pdf/gdp407f.pdf (accessed April 4, 2008)

December 2006 to December 2007 basis. These numbers represent annual inflation rates. The overall inflation rate of 4.1% in 2007 for all items was exceeded by the rates for food and beverages (4.8% increase), medical care (5.2% increase), transportation (8.3% increase), and energy (17.4% increase).

Personal Consumer Expenditures

In 2007 the nation's personal consumption expenditures (PCE) totaled $9.7 trillion. (See Table 3.2.) Major PCE categories include durable goods (items expected to last at least one year, such as cars and refrigerators), nondurable goods (items expected to last less than one year, such as food and gasoline), and services. Note that housing is listed under services. This category includes rent paid by renters and the estimated equivalent of rent for owner-occupied houses (in other words, the amount of money the owner occupants would have paid if they had been renting the space from someone else).

Services accounted for the largest portion (60%) of the PCE in 2007, totaling more than $5.8 trillion. (See Table 3.2.) Medical care ($1.7 trillion) and housing ($1.5 trillion) were the two largest components of service spending. Americans spent more than $2.8 trillion on nondurable goods in 2007. Nearly half of this amount ($1.3 trillion) was devoted to food. Another $1.1 trillion was spent on durable goods, such as motor vehicles and furniture. Note that PCE data are based on industry information. In other words, the BLS estimates con-

sumer spending by calculating the final value of goods and services sold by businesses.

Consumer Expenditure Survey

According to the BLS, in the Consumer Expenditure Survey (October 26, 2007, http://www.bls.gov/cex/2006/standard/multiyr.pdf), the average U.S. household spent $48,398 during 2006. Nearly two-thirds of this amount was devoted to three expenses: housing ($16,366, or 33%), transportation ($8,508, or 17%), and food ($6,111, or 13%). (See Figure 3.1.) However, the Consumer Expenditure (CE) housing component does not include mortgage principal payments, because they are considered repayment of a loan, rather than a consumer expense. Thus, CE data underreport the true cost of housing for Americans with mortgages.

CE data are compiled based on consumer-supplied information. Purchase diaries are sent to sample households around the country. Participants record their everyday purchases and expenses in the diaries. Periodic interviews are conducted to collect diary information and quiz participants about their finances and spending habits. CE data are collected from households (called "consumer units") that are representative of the civilian noninstitutional population of the United States (i.e., people not in

FIGURE 3.1

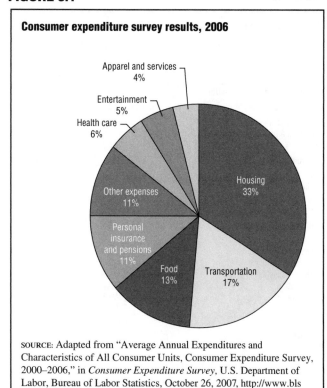

Consumer expenditure survey results, 2006

- Apparel and services 4%
- Entertainment 5%
- Health care 6%
- Other expenses 11%
- Personal insurance and pensions 11%
- Food 13%
- Transportation 17%
- Housing 33%

SOURCE: Adapted from "Average Annual Expenditures and Characteristics of All Consumer Units, Consumer Expenditure Survey, 2000–2006," in *Consumer Expenditure Survey*, U.S. Department of Labor, Bureau of Labor Statistics, October 26, 2007, http://www.bls.gov/cex/2006/standard/multiyr.pdf (accessed May 5, 2008)

the military and not in institutions, such as prisons or long-term-care facilities).

According to the BLS, the average consumer unit in 2006 included 2.5 people and had pretax annual income of $60,533. Most of the consumer units owned their homes (67%), and a large majority (88%) owned or leased at least one motor vehicle.

The Consumer Expenditure Survey results provide detailed data on American spending habits. For example, participants break down food purchases as to meal location (at home or away from home). The 2006 survey indicates that the average household spent $2,694 eating out, representing 44% of total food expenses. Each household averaged $117 per year for reading materials and $888 per year for educational expenses. Another $497 per year was spent on alcohol and $327 per year on tobacco products. The average U.S. household reported donating $1,869 in cash to charitable causes.

HISTORICAL TRENDS IN CONSUMER SPENDING

Expenditures for some components making up the PCE have changed dramatically over time. Figure 3.2 shows spending on medical care, housing, durable goods, nondurable goods, and "other" services as a percentage of the total

FIGURE 3.2

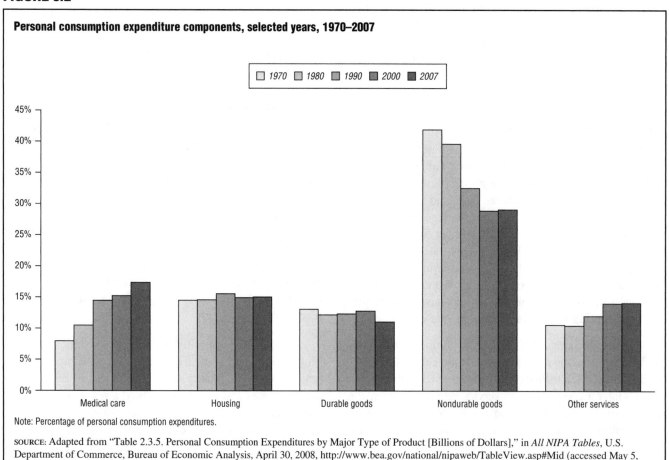

Personal consumption expenditure components, selected years, 1970–2007

Legend: 1970, 1980, 1990, 2000, 2007

Categories (y-axis 0% to 45%): Medical care, Housing, Durable goods, Nondurable goods, Other services

Note: Percentage of personal consumption expenditures.

SOURCE: Adapted from "Table 2.3.5. Personal Consumption Expenditures by Major Type of Product [Billions of Dollars]," in *All NIPA Tables*, U.S. Department of Commerce, Bureau of Economic Analysis, April 30, 2008, http://www.bea.gov/national/nipaweb/TableView.asp#Mid (accessed May 5, 2008)

FIGURE 3.3

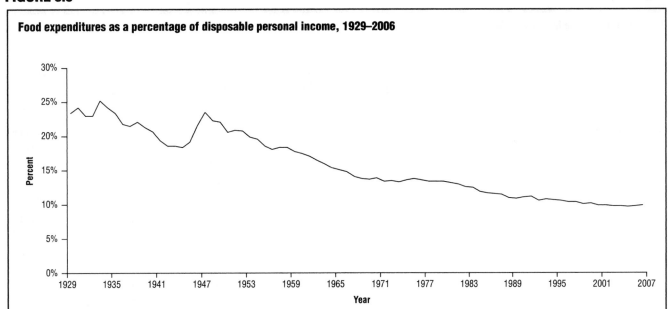

Food expenditures as a percentage of disposable personal income, 1929–2006

SOURCE: Adapted from "Food Expenditures by Families and Individuals as a Share of Disposable Personal Income," in *Food Market Indicators: CPI for Food, and Food Expenditures Data*, U.S. Department of Agriculture, Economic Research Service, 2007, http://www.ers.usda.gov/data/foodmarketindicators/cpiandexpenditures/table7.xls (accessed April 5, 2008)

PCE for 1970, 1980, 1990, 2000, and 2005. These categories have historically been the five largest components of the PCE.

The data show that the percentage of the PCE dedicated to housing and durable goods remained steady between 1970 and 2007. Housing hovered between 14% and 16%, and durable goods stayed between 11% and 13%. (See Figure 3.2.) A slight downward trend is evident in the percent spent on durable goods over time. A much more dramatic decrease is seen in the percentage of the PCE devoted to nondurable goods—from 42% in 1970 to around 29% in 2000 and 2007. A percentage decrease in one component making up the PCE means a percentage increase in one or more of the other components.

The percentage of the PCE devoted to "other" services increased slightly, from around 10% in 1970 and 1980 to around 14% in 2000 and 2007. (See Figure 3.2.) Medical care increased from only 8% of the PCE in 1970 to 17% in 2007. In other words, the percentage of the PCE devoted to medical care more than doubled between 1970 and 2007.

Food and Energy Price Volatility

Over the short term, food and energy prices can vary tremendously. Food prices are dependent on a variety of factors, including weather conditions (which affect growing costs), transportation and processing costs, and subsidies paid to farmers by the government that influence supply and demand ratios. Energy prices, particularly for oil, are affected by political and economic factors in the Middle East. Energy prices in the United States can also be affected by weather, as evidenced by the rise in gasoline prices following Hurricanes Katrina and Rita in 2005. Because of the volatile nature of food and energy prices, these costs are not included in the economic indicator called the core inflation.

FOOD PRICES. One component of the PCE that has historically become more affordable over time is food. Figure 3.3 shows data from the U.S. Department of Agriculture (USDA) on food prices as a percentage of personal disposable income between 1929 and 2006. Personal disposable income is also known as after-tax income or take-home pay. During the early 1930s the average U.S. household spent nearly a quarter of its disposable income on food. By the 1960s the percentage had fallen to around 15% and continued to decrease. In 2006 U.S. consumers spent just under 10% of their disposable income on food. Enormous gains in agricultural productivity and crop yields were responsible for keeping food prices relatively low.

This downward trend began to change in 2007 with dramatic increases in some food prices. The Economic Research Service (ERS) uses a food price index to track U.S. food prices. The price index for all food increased by 4% in 2007. (See Figure 3.3.) This increase exceeded the increase in the overall average U.S. inflation rate for the year of 2.8% based on the CPI-U.

According to the ERS, in "Food CPI, Prices, and Expenditures: Analysis and Forecasts of the CPI for Food" (June 20, 2008, http://www.ers.usda.gov/Briefing/CPIFoodAndExpenditures/consumerpriceindex.htm), the 4% increase in 2007 was the largest annual increase

TABLE 3.3

Changes in food price indexes, 2004–08

Item	Relative importance[a]	Final 2004	Final 2005	Final 2006	Final 2007	April 25, 2008 Forecast 2008[b]
Consumer price indexes	Percent			Percent change		
All food	100.0	3.4	2.4	2.4	4.0	**4.0 to 5.0**
Food away from home	44.6	3.0	3.1	3.1	3.6	**3.5 to 4.5**
Food at home	55.4	3.8	1.9	1.7	4.2	4.0 to 5.0
Meats, poultry, and fish	12.2	7.4	2.4	0.8	3.8	2.0 to 3.0
Meats	7.9	8.4	2.3	0.7	3.3	1.5 to 2.5
Beef and veal	3.8	11.6	2.6	0.8	4.4	2.0 to 3.0
Pork	2.4	5.6	2.0	−0.2	2.0	1.5 to 2.5
Other meats	1.7	4.5	2.4	1.8	2.3	0.0 to 1.0
Poultry	2.3	7.5	2.0	−1.8	5.2	**2.5 to 3.5**
Fish and seafood	2.0	2.3	3.0	4.7	4.6	3.0 to 4.0
Eggs	0.9	6.2	−13.7	4.9	29.2	**3.0 to 4.0**
Dairy products	6.4	7.3	1.2	−0.6	7.4	3.0 to 4.0
Fats and oils	1.5	6.6	−0.1	0.2	2.9	**8.0 to 9.0**
Fruits and vegetables	8.4	3.0	3.7	4.8	3.8	3.0 to 4.0
Fresh fruits and vegetables	6.0	3.5	3.9	5.3	3.9	3.0 to 4.0
Fresh fruits	3.4	2.8	3.7	6.0	4.5	3.5 to 4.5
Fresh vegetables	3.2	4.3	4.0	4.6	3.2	2.5 to 3.5
Processed fruits and vegetables	1.8	1.3	3.3	2.9	3.6	**3.5 to 4.5**
Sugar and sweets	2.0	0.7	1.2	3.8	3.1	**3.0 to 4.0**
Cereals and bakery products	7.4	1.6	1.5	1.8	4.4	**7.5 to 8.5**
Nonalcoholic beverages	6.7	0.4	2.9	2.0	4.1	3.5 to 4.5
Other foods	9.9	0.5	1.6	1.4	1.8	2.5 to 3.5

[a]Bureau of Labor Statistics (BLS) estimated expenditure shares, December 2007.
[b]Forecasts updated by the 25th of each month.

SOURCE: "Changes in Food Price Indexes, 2004 through 2008," in Briefing Rooms: Food CPI, Prices, and Expenditures: CPI for Food Forecasts, U.S. Department of Agriculture, Economic Research Service, April 25, 2008, http://www.ers.usda.gov/Briefing/CPIFoodAndExpenditures/Data/April2008CPI.xls (accessed May 6, 2008)

recorded in the food price index since 1990. The agency blames higher food prices on five factors:

• Higher commodity and energy costs for retailers

• Growing global demand for food

• An increase in U.S. food exports due to strong global demand and the relative weakness of the U.S. dollar

• Weather-related food production problems in some parts of the world

• Increasing use of some food commodities, such as corn, for bioenergy purposes

The ERS projects particularly large price increases in 2008 for fats and oils (up 8% to 9%) and cereals and bakery products (up 7.5% to 8.5%). (See Table 3.3.) The latter products are expected to be more expensive due to increasing prices for wheat and corn and rising energy costs associated with the production of cereals and baked goods.

ENERGY EXPENDITURES AND PRICES. Nondurable energy goods accounted for only a small amount (4%) of the PCE during 2007. (See Table 3.2.) This category does not include electricity and gas for household operation, which fall under services. Nondurable energy goods include products such as gasoline, other motor fuels, and lubricants. In 2007 U.S. consumers spent $364.2 billion on nondurable energy goods; gasoline accounted for the vast majority of this total.

December-to-December inflation rates based on the CPI-U for energy goods and services are shown from 2002 through 2007 in Table 3.4. In 2007 the inflation rate for gasoline was 29.6%, and for fuel oil it was 32.5%. Inflation rates for electricity and natural gas for home heating and/or cooling were much lower at 5.2% and −0.4%, respectively.

GASOLINE PRICES. According to the U.S. Department of Energy, the average retail price for a gallon of regular-grade gasoline was $3.61 per gallon as of May 5, 2008. This value was up from $3.05 per gallon on May 5, 2007. Gasoline prices have risen dramatically since the mid-1990s, when the average retail price for a gallon of regular-grade gasoline was between $1 and $1.50 per gallon. (See Figure 3.4.)

Figure 3.5 illustrates that the retail price for a gallon of gasoline in the United States in March 2008 had four contributing components:

• Crude oil price—72%

• Federal and state taxes—12%

TABLE 3.4

Annual percent change in the urban Consumer Price Index (CPI-U) for energy expenditure categories, December to December, 2002–07

Expenditure category	2002	2003	2004	2005	2006	2007
Energy	**10.7**	**6.9**	**16.6**	**17.1**	**2.9**	**17.4**
Energy commodities	23.7	6.9	26.7	16.7	6.1	29.4
Motor fuel	24.6	6.8	26.1	16.2	6.4	29.5
Gasoline	24.8	6.8	26.1	16.1	6.4	29.6
Fuel oil	14.7	7.8	39.5	27.2	2.3	32.5
Energy services (electricity and natural gas)	0.4	6.9	6.8	17.6	−0.6	3.4
Electricity	−1.9	2.6	2.1	10.7	7.5	5.2
Natural gas	6.7	17.4	16.4	30.2	−14.2	−0.4

Note: Figures are percent changes for 12 months ended December.

SOURCE: Adapted from Malik Crawford, ed., "Table Q1. Annual Percent Changes in the CPI for All Urban Consumers, 2001–2008," in *CPI Detailed Report : Data for March 2008*, U.S. Department of Labor, Bureau of Labor Statistics, April 2008, http://www.bls.gov/cpi/cpid0803.pdf (accessed May 6, 2008)

FIGURE 3.4

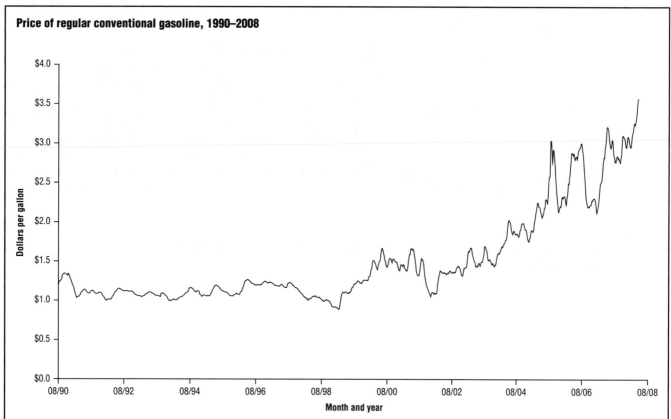

Price of regular conventional gasoline, 1990–2008

SOURCE: Adapted from "Grade: Regular," in *Retail Gasoline Historical Prices*, U.S. Department of Energy, Energy Information Administration, May 5, 2008, http://www.eia.doe.gov/oil_gas/petroleum/data_publications/wrgp/mogas_history.html (accessed May 6, 2008)

- Distribution and marketing costs—8%

- Refining costs—8%

Thus, the cost of crude oil accounts for nearly three-fourths of the retail price of gasoline. Crude oil is sold by the barrel, with each barrel containing forty-two U.S. gallons. In 1997 the average worldwide price for crude oil was around $20 per barrel. (See Figure 3.6.) After a brief decrease over the following year the price of crude oil began to rise in 1999. In April 2008 the price of crude oil rose to an all-time high of $111 per barrel.

All Items Less Food and Energy

Table 3.5 shows annual inflation rates (changes in the CPI-U) on a December-to-December basis for items other than food and energy from 2002 through 2007. The inflation rate for this category in 2007 was 2.4%, well below the overall rate of 4.1%, according to Malik Crawford of

FIGURE 3.5

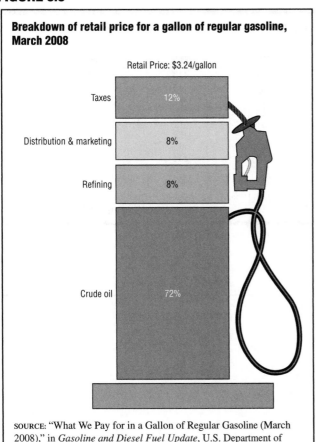

Breakdown of retail price for a gallon of regular gasoline,
March 2008

Retail Price: $3.24/gallon

Taxes — 12%

Distribution & marketing — 8%

Refining — 8%

Crude oil — 72%

SOURCE: "What We Pay for in a Gallon of Regular Gasoline (March 2008)," in *Gasoline and Diesel Fuel Update*, U.S. Department of Energy, Energy Information Administration, May 5, 2008, http://tonto.eia.doe.gov/oog/info/gdu/gasdiesel.asp (accessed May 5, 2008)

the BLS, in *CPI Detailed Report: Data for March 2008* (April 2008, http://www.bls.gov/cpi/cpid0803.pdf). This indicates that inflation was largely driven by rising food and energy costs that year.

Between 2002 and 2007 inflation rates were generally moderate for some items. (See Table 3.5.) Shelter prices increased by 2.2% to 4.2% annually. The prices of alcoholic beverages increased by 1.3% to 3.8% annually. Apparel prices actually decreased in most years; the exception being in 2006, when they increased by 0.9%. Other items with largely negative price trends included televisions, personal computers and peripheral equipment (such as printers), and new vehicles. Mixed positive and negative rates were reported for used cars and trucks (−11.8% to 4.8%), airline fares (−2.4% to 10.6%), and tobacco and smoking products (−0.4% to 9.5%). Items with relatively large inflation rates included college tuition (6.1% to 9.8%) and medical care (3.6% to 5.2%).

THE COST OF MEDICAL CARE

In 2007 medical care expenditures approached $1.7 trillion and accounted for 12% of positive GDP. (See Table 2.3 in Chapter 2.) This made medical care a more expensive component than housing, food, or durable goods. David M. Walker of the U.S. Government Accountability Office notes in *Long-Term Fiscal Outlook: Action Is Needed to Avoid the Possibility of a Serious Economic Disruption in the Future* (January 29, 2008, http://www.gao.gov/new.items/d08411t.pdf) that

FIGURE 3.6

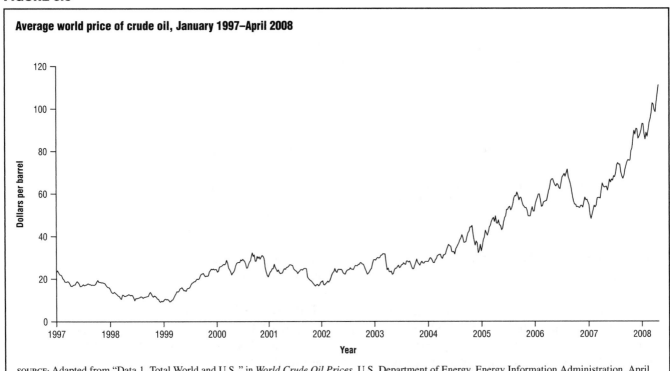

Average world price of crude oil, January 1997–April 2008

SOURCE: Adapted from "Data 1. Total World and U.S.," in *World Crude Oil Prices*, U.S. Department of Energy, Energy Information Administration, April 30, 2008, http://tonto.eia.doe.gov/dnav/pet/xls/PET_PRI_WCO_K_W.xls#'Data 1'!A1 (accessed May 6, 2008)

TABLE 3.5

Annual percent change in the urban Consumer Price Index (CPI-U) for expenditure categories other than food and energy, December to December, 2002–07

Expenditure category	2002	2003	2004	2005	2006	2007
All items less food and energy	1.9	1.1	2.2	2.2	2.6	2.4
Shelter	3.1	2.2	2.7	2.6	4.2	3.1
Rent of primary residence	3.1	2.7	2.9	3.1	4.3	4.0
Owners' equivalent rent of primary residence	3.3	2.0	2.3	2.5	4.3	2.8
Hotels and motels	0.0	3.1	5.0	3.3	3.9	4.5
Apparel	−1.8	−2.1	−0.2	−1.1	0.9	−0.3
Medical care	5.0	3.7	4.2	4.3	3.6	5.2
Medical care commodities	3.1	2.1	2.2	3.7	1.8	2.7
Prescription drugs	4.5	2.5	3.5	4.4	1.9	3.3
Medical care services	5.6	4.2	4.9	4.5	4.1	5.9
Televisions	−10.6	−14.3	−12.3	−14.4	−22.6	−18.3
Personal computers and peripheral equipment	−22.1	−17.8	−14.2	−15.8	−12.0	−13.2
New vehicles	−2.0	−1.8	0.6	−0.4	−0.9	−0.3
Used cars and trucks	−5.5	−11.8	4.8	1.4	−2.2	0.5
Airline fares	−2.4	−0.1	−1.5	6.4	−1.0	10.6
College tuition	7.0	9.8	8.6	6.6	7.0	6.1
Tobacco and smoking products	9.5	−0.4	3.1	5.8	2.8	7.5
Alcoholic beverages	2.2	2.1	2.8	1.3	2.4	3.8

Note: Figures are percent changes for 12 months ended December.

SOURCE: Adapted from Malik Crawford, ed., "Table Q1. Annual Percent Changes in the CPI for All Urban Consumers, 2001–2008," in *CPI Detailed Report: Data for March 2008*, U.S. Department of Labor, Bureau of Labor Statistics, April 2008, http://www.bls.gov/cpi/cpid0803.pdf (accessed May 6, 2008)

FIGURE 3.7

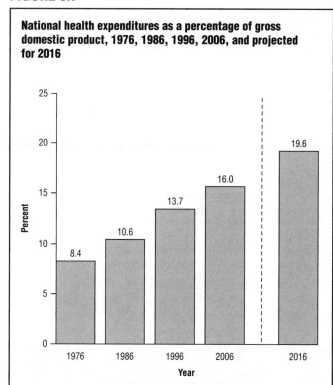

National health expenditures as a percentage of gross domestic product, 1976, 1986, 1996, 2006, and projected for 2016

Notes: The figure for 2016 is projected. The most current data available on health care spending are for 2006.

SOURCE: David M. Walker, "Figure 6. Health Care Spending as a Percent of GDP," in *Long-Term Fiscal Outlook: Action Is Needed to Avoid the Possibility of a Serious Economic Disruption in the Future*, U.S. Government Accountability Office, January 29, 2008, http://www.gao .gov/new.items/d08411t.pdf (accessed April 8, 2008)

the percentage of GDP comprised by medical care spending was 8.4% in 1976, 10.6% in 1986, 13.7% in 1996, and 16% in 2006, and projected it to be 19.6% in 2016. (See Figure 3.7.) On a national basis, health-care expenditures are expected to comprise an ever-increasing percentage of GDP through 2016.

Figure 3.8 compares the CPI-U between all items and medical care only on an annual average basis between 1998 and 2007 using the time period of 1982–84 as the reference period (CPI = 100). Medical inflation has outpaced overall inflation in each of these years. In other words, medical care prices are increasing at a faster pace than overall prices in the economy. Medical inflation is blamed, in part, on technological advances in medicine that have increased expenses associated with the diagnosis and treatment of patients.

Recipients and Costs

The Agency for Healthcare Research and Quality (AHRQ) is a division of the U.S. Department of Health and Human Services. The AHRQ conducts large-scale surveys of medical care recipients and providers as part of its Medical Expenditure Panel Survey (MEPS; http://www.meps.ahrq .gov/), which provides detailed data and reports on medical utilization and expenditures. As of July 2008, comprehensive MEPS data were available for calendar year 2005.

According to the AHRQ, 84.7% of the U.S. civilian noninstitutional population had some kind of medical expense during 2005. (See Table 3.6.) The rate was much higher among the elderly (people aged sixty-five and

FIGURE 3.8

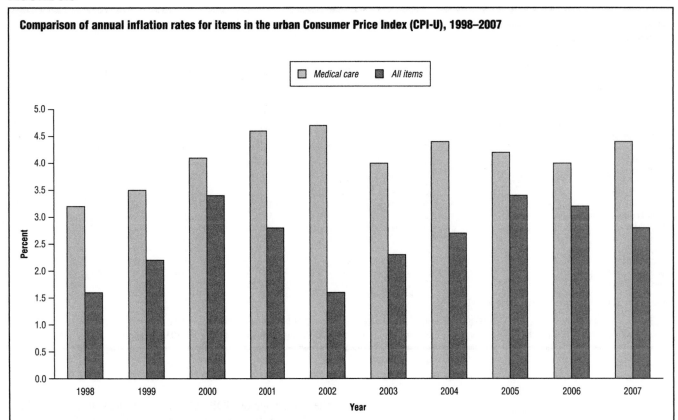

Comparison of annual inflation rates for items in the urban Consumer Price Index (CPI-U), 1998–2007

Note: Percent based on U.S. city average, not seasonally adjusted, 1982–84=100.

SOURCE: Adapted from "Consumer Price Index, All Urban Consumers, 12-Month Percent Change, Series ID: CUUR0000SAM, Medical Care," and "Medical Care and Consumer Price Index, All Urban Consumers, 12 Months Percent Change, Series ID: CUUR0000SA0, All Items," in *Consumer Price Index*, U.S. Department of Labor, Bureau of Labor Statistics, April 7, 2008, http://www.bls.gov/cpi/home.htm#tables (accessed April 7, 2008)

TABLE 3.6

Health care expenses and sources of payment, by age of patient, 2005

Population characteristic	Population (in thousands)	Percent with expenses	Per person with an expense Median	Per person with an expense Mean	Total expense (in millions)	Out of pocket	Private insurance[a]	Medicare	Medicaid	Other[b]
Total	296,185	84.7	1,166	4,082	1,023,763	18.8	41.6	21.1	11.2	7.2
Age in years										
Under 65	258,708	82.9	912	3,239	695,048	19.6	53	5.9	14.2	7.3
Under 5	19,793	88.9	444	1,638	28,822	10.2	45.3	7.3	29.6	7.6
5–17	53,770	83.4	467	1,598	71,692	20.5	52.6	0.2	21.9	4.8
18–44	111,067	77.1	824	2,880	246,619	19.6	52.4	3.6	17.2	7.1
45–64	74,078	89.7	2,025	5,233	347,915	20.2	54.1	8.5	9.2	8
65 and over	37,477	96.7	4,085	9,074	328,715	17.1	17.6	53.4	5	6.8

[a]Private insurance includes Tricare (Armed-Forces-related coverage).
[b]Other includes other public programs such as Department of Veterans Affairs (except Tricare); other federal sources (Indian Health Service, military treatment facilities, and other care provided by the federal government); other state and local sources (community and neighborhood clinics, state and local health departments, and state programs other than Medicaid); and other public (Medicaid payments reported for persons who were not enrolled in the Medicaid program at any time during the year). Other also includes worker's compensation; other unclassified sources (e.g., automobile, homeowner's, liability, and other miscellaneous or unknown sources); and other private insurance (any type of private insurance payments reported for persons without private health insurance coverage during the year, as defined in the medical expenditure plan survey).

SOURCE: Adapted from "Table 1. Total Health Services-Median and Mean Expenses per Person with Expense and Distribution of Expenses by Source of Payment: United States, 2005," in *Medical Expenditure Panel Survey*, U.S. Department of Health and Human Services, Agency for Healthcare Research and Quality, 2008, http://meps.ahrq.gov/cgi-bin/texis/webinator/search/?pr=MEPSFULLSITE&query=Table%201&submit=Submit&cmd=Simple (accessed May 6, 2008)

older); 96.7% of them reported having a medical expense during the year.

Overall, expenses for medical services (excluding insurance premiums) exceeded $1 trillion. (See Table 3.6.) The average (mean) expense during the year for each treated person was $4,082. According to the AHRQ, the average was lower ($3,239 per treated person) for people aged sixty-four and younger and much higher ($9,074 per treated person) for people aged sixty-five and older.

Who Pays the Bill?

During 2005 private health insurance paid the largest portion (41.6%) of medical service expenditures. (See Table 3.6.) Another 18.8% was paid out of pocket, that is, directly by consumers. Medicare and Medicaid are government-operated health-care programs. Medicare covers the elderly and includes some younger people with certain disabilities and illnesses. Medicaid provides insurance coverage for needy people. During 2005 Medicare and Medicaid paid 21.1% and 11.2%, respectively, of the nation's health-care expenditures. An additional 7.2% was paid by other sources, such as workers' compensation programs or automobile insurance companies.

THE COST OF LIVING

The nontechnical term *cost of living* refers to the cost of basic necessities to U.S. households, such as food, clothing, and shelter. Even though many factors affect the prices of these commodities, one economic factor has played a major role in recent decades: inflation. Because of inflation, the cost of living increases each year as the prices of necessities become more expensive. The CPI is the economic indicator commonly used to gauge changes in inflation and the cost of living.

A cost of living adjustment (COLA) is an adjustment made to wages or benefits to compensate consumers for the effects of inflation. The government applies annual COLAs to increase the amounts paid out to recipients of certain benefits, such as Social Security and food stamps. This is designed to help people keep up with the rising cost of living due to inflation.

The COLA for Social Security recipients is calculated on the CPI for urban wage earners and clerical workers (CPI-W) from the third quarter of one year to the third quarter of the next year. For example, in "2008 Social Security Changes" (October 2007, http://www.social security.gov/cola/colafacts2008.htm), the U.S. Social Security Administration notes that in December 2007 the government calculated a 2.3% increase in the CPI-W between the third quarter in 2006 and the third quarter in 2007. As a result, monthly Social Security benefits payable during 2008 were increased by 2.3%.

PUBLIC OPINION ON CONSUMER ISSUES

The Gallup Organization conducts many polls questioning Americans about their consumer habits and concerns. In April 2008 pollsters asked Americans to rate their level of concern about their ability to pay certain costs based on their "current financial situation." Nearly half (44%) of respondents were moderately or very worried about having enough money to pay their "normal monthly bills." (See Table 3.6.) A quarter of those asked said they were "not too worried." Another 29% of respondents expressed no worry about this issue.

Poll participants were also asked about specific costs for housing and medical care. Thirty-six percent of respondents were very or moderately worried about being able to pay their rent, mortgage, or other housing costs. (See Figure 3.9.) Less than a quarter (24%) were "not too worried" about these costs. A larger percentage (35%) were not worried at all about these costs.

Gallup found that medical costs posed a greater concern for Americans. Forty-four percent of poll participants were very or moderately worried about being able to pay medical costs for "normal health care." (See Figure 3.9.) Twenty-four percent said they were "not too worried," and 28% were not worried at all about these expenses. Respondents were slightly more concerned about medical costs they could incur in the event of a serious illness or accident. More than half (56%) of those asked were very or moderately worried about being able to afford such costs. Twenty percent were "not too worried," and 21% expressed no worry about this issue.

CONSUMER SPENDING, JOB CREATION, AND INTEREST RATES

Consumer spending is essential to economic growth in the United States and is greatly affected by two things: employment and interest rates, which are interdependent factors in the economy. Historically, when interest rates have been lower, people have spent more money, which has in turn stimulated the job market. When people have steady and dependable work, they are more likely to spend money, which also adds jobs to the economy.

Consumer buying choices can also stimulate—and even shift—job growth among industries. The higher the demand is for certain products and services, the more growth those industries will experience. The goods and services that are purchased by the consumer are called final goods; those that are used in the production of final goods are called intermediate goods. Demand for both final and intermediate goods leads to expansion in their respective industries, which in turn adds jobs to the economy.

Interest Rates and Spending

Interest rates are determined by the Federal Reserve Board, which is the central bank of the United States. The

FIGURE 3.9

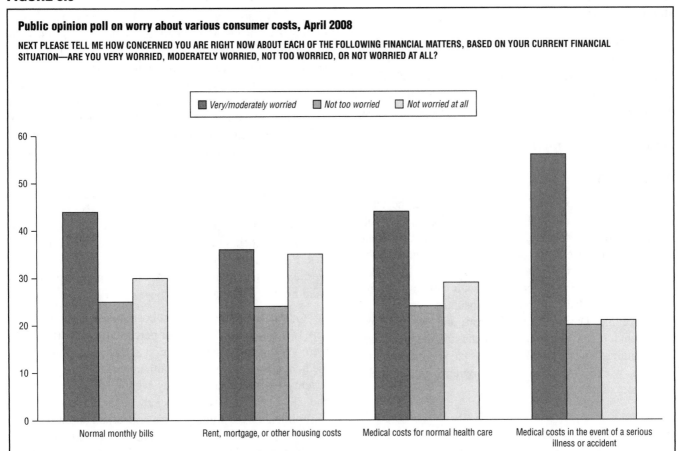

Public opinion poll on worry about various consumer costs, April 2008

NEXT PLEASE TELL ME HOW CONCERNED YOU ARE RIGHT NOW ABOUT EACH OF THE FOLLOWING FINANCIAL MATTERS, BASED ON YOUR CURRENT FINANCIAL SITUATION—ARE YOU VERY WORRIED, MODERATELY WORRIED, NOT TOO WORRIED, OR NOT WORRIED AT ALL?

SOURCE: Adapted from "Question qn19. Next Please Tell Me How Concerned You Are Right Now about Each of the Following Financial Matters, Based on Your Current Financial Situation—Are You Very Worried, Moderately Worried, Not Too Worried, or Not Worried at All?" in *Gallup Poll Social Series: Economy & Personal Finance*, The Gallup Organization, April 2008, http://brain.gallup.com/documents/questionnaire.aspx?STUDY=P0804015 (accessed May 13, 2008). Copyright © 2008 by The Gallup Organization. Reproduced by permission of The Gallup Organization.

Federal Reserve sets the federal funds rate (the interest rate banks charge for overnight loans to each other), which then influences the prime rate (the rate that banks charge their best customers; the prime rate is usually set at about three percentage points above the federal funds rate). From there, creditors set competitive rates for lending money to consumers. When interest rates are high, consumer spending, particularly for high-priced items such as cars and houses, tends to slow down because the cost of borrowing money is higher. Lower interest rates stimulate the economy because consumers can afford to borrow more at lower rates.

For example, the historically low interest rates of the early 2000s led to a high number of mortgage refinancings, which gave homeowners more money to spend monthly as their mortgage payments were lowered. Because of lower interest rates, many homeowners also had access to a source of disposable income unrelated to their wages: their homes. In 2003 U.S. homeowners took advantage of rising property values and low interest rates by withdrawing $200 billion in equity from their homes. (Equity is the proportion of a house's mortgage value that a homeowner has paid off

and actually owns; when people get a home equity loan, they have access to that part of their home's value in the form of credit, which they must then pay back.) In this sense, low interest rates are not always good for individual finances or the economy, because they lead to more debt in the form of home equity loans, car loans, and credit cards.

CONSUMERISM

Some critics say that American consumer habits are a sign of chronic overspending. In *The Overspent American: Why We Want What We Don't Need* (1998), Juliet B. Schor examines the tendency of Americans to overspend. Noting that "competitive acquisition" has been a hallmark of American life since the founding of the country, Schor explains that people used to compare themselves and their belongings to those who lived near them in circumstances similar to their own. More recently, however, as exposure to different economic classes has become commonplace—especially via television, movies, magazines, and the Internet, but also with coworkers and acquaintances—Americans began to compare themselves to people outside of their own economic group, usually looking to the upper classes for direction on what and how much to buy. This seemingly unrealistic comparison eventually became the norm, causing average Americans to expect their material status to equal that of those outside of what Schor calls their "reference groups"—the group of people each of us chooses to identify with most closely. The material possessions of one's reference group quickly come to be considered necessities rather than indulgences; Schor writes of the trend of overspending to keep up with others:

> Oddly, it doesn't seem as if we're spending wastefully, or even lavishly. Rather, many of us feel we're just making it, barely able to stay even. But what's remarkable is that this feeling is not restricted to families of limited income. It's a generalized feeling, one that exists at all levels. Twenty-seven percent of all households making more than $100,000 a year say they cannot afford to buy everything they really need. Nearly twenty percent say they "spend nearly all their income on the basic necessities of life." In the $50,000–100,000 range, 39 percent and one-third feel this way, respectively. Overall, half the population in the richest country in the world say they cannot afford everything they really need. And it's not just the poorest half.

Elizabeth Warren and Amelia Warren Tyagi find in *The Two-Income Trap: Why Middle-Class Mothers and Fathers Are Going Broke* (2003) that many Americans overspend for practical reasons, citing education as an example. Even though public schools were once considered more or less reliably similar in different communities, the perception in the 1990s and 2000s has been that families who plan to send their children to public schools must buy houses in more affluent neighborhoods, whether or not they can afford them because those areas have better school districts. Many parents consider this to be a fair trade-off, but it often strains a family's finances. Additionally, Warren and Tyagi note that, unlike earlier generations that typically had one parent working full time and the other at home and available to take on a job to supplement the family's income if necessary, families in the late twentieth and early twenty-first centuries already tended to have both parents working full time and putting about 75% of their pay toward household essentials.

CHAPTER 4
PERSONAL DEBT

Beautiful credit! The foundation of modern society.

—Mark Twain and Charles Dudley Warner, *The Gilded Age* (1873)

He who goes a borrowing, goes a sorrowing.

—Benjamin Franklin, *Poor Richard's Almanack* (1757)

Personal debt has both good and bad effects on the U.S. economy. Americans borrow money to buy houses, cars, and other consumer goods. They also take out loans to pay for vacations, investments, and educational expenses. All of this spending helps businesses and boosts the nation's gross domestic product (the total market value of final goods and services produced within an economy in a given year). As long as debt is handled prudently, it can be a positive economic force. However, some Americans take on too much debt and get into financial difficulties. Debt becomes a problem on a macroeconomic scale when people must devote large amounts of their disposable income (after-tax income or take-home pay) to repaying loans instead of spending or investing their money.

In response to consumer demand, a credit industry has developed in the United States that encompasses a wide variety of businesses. Consumers and regulators complain that some creditors engage in practices that victimize debtors, particularly those who are poor and uneducated. In addition, identity theft has become a major problem in the industry. This is a crime in which personal and financial data are stolen so that criminals can use the good credit histories of others for illegal purposes.

HISTORICAL DEVELOPMENTS

For centuries religious teachings about making and taking loans affected societal attitudes about the appropriateness of personal debt. The promise to repay a loan was considered a sacred pledge; thus, violating such an agreement was morally reprehensible. The Bible and the Koran (the sacred text of Islam) include scriptures that were interpreted as prohibiting the charging of excessive interest (or even any interest) on loans made to certain groups of people. Granting or assuming debt were actions that aroused disapproval in many circumstances. In William Shakespeare's (1564–1616) play *Hamlet*, which was first performed around 1600, one of the characters advises: "Neither a borrower, nor a lender be."

English common law allowed for imprisonment of debtors who could not repay their debts. This practice carried over to the fledgling United States. In fact, Robert Morris (1734–1806), one of the signers of the Declaration of Independence, was later imprisoned in Philadelphia for failing to repay personal debt. The use of debtor's prisons in the United States was gradually phased out during the 1800s because of changing societal attitudes and the enactment of bankruptcy laws.

David A. Skeel Jr. explains in *Debt's Dominion: A History of Bankruptcy Law in America* (2001) that federal bankruptcy laws were passed in the United States in 1800, 1841, and 1867. However, each law was in force for only a few years before being repealed. Legislators had a difficult time drafting bills considered fair to both creditors and debtors. In 1898 a more workable law was passed that became the foundation for modern bankruptcy law.

As the twentieth century progressed, social taboos about personal debt diminished in the face of growing consumer demand for immediate access to goods. In 1919 the General Motors Acceptance Corporation (the financial arm of the automobile company General Motors) formed to allow Americans to borrow money to acquire new automobiles. The venture proved to be wildly successful and inspired other companies to enter the credit business. During the 1920s middle-class Americans seized on the opportunity to use credit to buy newly available durable (long-lasting) goods, such as appliances. Installment loans became a popular financing method. In the 1950s the first all-purpose credit cards were introduced. Over the next few decades their use became commonplace, representing a major shift in American buying habits and attitudes about the acceptability of debt.

CATEGORIES OF DEBT

Economists divide personal debt into two broad categories: investment debt and consumer debt. Money borrowed to buy houses and real estate is considered investment debt. Because most property appreciates (increases in value) over time, the debt assumed to finance its purchase will likely be a wise investment. Likewise, money borrowed to start a business or pay for a college education can bring financial benefits. All of this assumes that the investment was a wise one and that the short-term costs of the debt can be borne. By contrast, consumer debt is assumed purely for consumption purposes. The money is spent to gain immediate access to goods and services that will not appreciate in value (and may well lose value) over time to help offset the costs of the debt.

Credit falls into two other categories: nonrevolving credit and revolving credit. Nonrevolving loans require regular payments of amounts that will ensure that the original debt (the principal) plus interest will be paid off in a particular amount of time. They are also known as closed-end loans and are commonly used to finance the purchase of real estate, cars, and boats or to pay for educational expenses. Nonrevolving loans feature predictable payment amounts and schedules that are laid out in amortization tables. The term *amortize* is derived from the Latin term *mort*, which means "to kill or deaden." An amortization schedule details how a loan will be gradually eliminated (killed off) over a set period. Revolving debt is a different kind of arrangement in which the debtor is allowed to borrow against a predetermined total amount of credit and is billed for the outstanding principal plus interest. The loans typically require regularly scheduled minimum payments, but not a set time period for repaying the entire amount due. Credit card loans are the primary example of revolving debt.

Loans can also be secured or unsecured. A secured loan is one in which the borrower puts up an asset called collateral to lessen the financial risk of the loaner. If the borrower defaults (fails to pay back the loan), the loaner can seize the collateral and sell it to recoup some or all the money that was loaned. Mortgages on homes and property and loans on cars, boats, motor homes, and other goods of high value are typically secured loans. In all these cases the collateral can be legally repossessed by the loaners. Unsecured loans are not backed by collateral. They are granted solely on the good financial reputation of the borrower. Credit card debts and debts owed to medical practitioners and hospitals are the major types of unsecured debts.

FIGURE 4.1

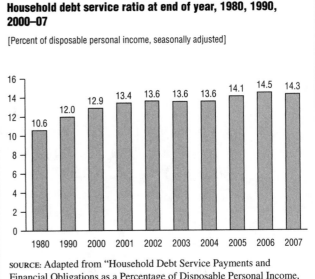

Household debt service ratio at end of year, 1980, 1990, 2000–07

[Percent of disposable personal income, seasonally adjusted]

SOURCE: Adapted from "Household Debt Service Payments and Financial Obligations as a Percentage of Disposable Personal Income, Seasonally Adjusted," in *Household Debt Service and Financial Obligations Ratios*, The Federal Reserve, March 11, 2008, http://www .federalreserve.gov/releases/housedebt/default.htm (accessed April 7, 2008)

HOUSEHOLD DEBT SERVICE

The Federal Reserve Board, the national bank of the United States, compiles an economic indicator called the household debt service ratio (DSR). The DSR is the ratio of household debt payments to disposable personal income. It indicates the estimated fraction of disposable income that is devoted to payments on outstanding mortgage and consumer debt.

The DSR has gradually increased since the 1980s. During the last quarter of 1980 the DSR was 10.6%. (See Figure 4.1.) A decade later it had climbed to 12%. By the end of 2000 the DSR was 12.9%, and it continued to rise to 14.5% in 2006. It decreased slightly to 14.3% by the fourth quarter of 2007. This means that by the end of 2007, Americans as a whole were spending 14.3% of their disposable income on their debt.

INTEREST RATES

One of the chief factors affecting the amount of debt that people assume is the amount of interest charged on loans. Banks and other financial institutions charge interest to make money on loaning money. The interest rate charged must be low enough to tempt potential borrowers, but high enough to make a profit for lenders. In general, commercial lenders base their interest rates on the rates charged by the Federal Reserve. Lower interest rates encourage consumers to borrow money.

The Federal Reserve makes short-term loans to banks at an interest rate called the discount rate. If the Federal Reserve raises or lowers the discount rate, then banks

TABLE 4.1

Interest payments for particular loans

Interest rate	Years of loan	Amount borrowed	Total interest paid	Total principal + interest paid
5%	30	$100,000	$93,256	$193,256
10%	30	$100,000	$215,926	$315,926
15%	30	$100,000	$355,200	$455,200
5%	15	$100,000	$42,343	$142,343
10%	15	$100,000	$93,429	$193,429
15%	15	$100,000	$151,926	$251,926
12%	4	$20,000	$5,280	$25,280
12%	5	$20,000	$6,693	$26,693

SOURCE: Created by Kim Masters Evans for Cengage Learning, Gale, 2008

TABLE 4.2

Residential mortgage debt outstanding, 1990–2007

[Dollars in millions except where noted]

	Residential mortgage debt outstanding
1990	$2,909,563
1991	$3,073,707
1992	$3,226,434
1993	$3,382,901
1994	$3,561,122
1995	$3,734,685
1996	$3,970,772
1997	$4,217,362
1998	$4,607,678
1999	$5,074,182
2000	$5,531,095
2001	$6,124,447
2002	$6,922,584
2003	$7,792,665
2004	$8,888,396
2005	$10,061,950
2006	$11,184,546
2007	$11,966,836

Note: Data for mortgage debt outstanding from the Federal Reserve Boards Flow of Funds Accounts of the United States, Annual Flows and Outstandings, March 6, 2008.

SOURCE: Adapted from "Total Mortgages Held or Securitized by Fannie Mae and Freddie Mac as a Percentage of Residential Mortgage Debt Outstanding, 1990–2007," in *Enterprise Share of Residential Mortgage Debt Outstanding, 1990–2007*, U.S. Department of Housing and Urban Development, Office of Federal Housing Enterprise Oversight, March 6, 2008, http://www.ofheo.gov/media/marketdata/ESRMDOutstanding19902007.xls (accessed May 12, 2008)

adjust the federal funds rate, which is the rate they charge each other for loans. This affects the prime rate, the interest rate banks charge their best customers (typically large corporations), which in turn affects the rates on other loans. Figure 1.13 in Chapter 1 shows the bank prime loan rate between 1955 and 2008. The rate has varied widely over time from less than 5% in 1955 to more than 20% in the early to mid-1980s. Since 1990 the prime rate has consistently remained below 10% and temporarily dipped below 5% in the early 2000s.

When a loan is granted, the creditor sets terms that specify whether the interest rate to be paid will be fixed or variable. A fixed interest rate remains constant throughout the life of the loan. A variable rate changes and is typically tied to a publicly published interest rate, such as the prime rate. For example, a loan can be made with the stipulation that the interest rate charged each month will be one percentage point higher than the prime rate. As the prime rate changes, so will the interest rate on the loan and the borrower's monthly payments.

Table 4.1 shows the tremendous difference between loans with differing interest rates and repayment periods. A $100,000 mortgage with a thirty-year fixed interest rate of 5% will result in $193,256 being paid over the lifetime of the loan. The same loan at 10% interest will cost $315,926. Loans for new cars typically have a repayment period of four to five years. A 12% fixed interest car loan for $20,000 paid over four years results in a total payment of $25,280. The same loan spread over five years will end up costing $26,693. However, the trade-off to the borrower for a shorter loan period will be higher monthly payments. Borrowers must consider the financial consequences of monthly payments and interest rates to get a loan they can afford in the short and long term.

MORTGAGES

For most Americans a mortgage is the largest personal debt they will ever incur. Mortgage debt is a form of investment debt, because real estate usually increases in value. Thus, assuming mortgage debt is generally considered a sensible economic move, as long as the payments are well matched to the borrower's income and ability to pay.

Mortgage loans have been in use in Europe for centuries, developing along with private ownership of land. In modern times a mortgage represents a lien, or binding charge, against a piece of property for the payment of a debt. In other words, the loan is granted on the condition that the property can be claimed by the loaner (creditor) in the event the borrower defaults. If the loan is satisfactorily paid, full ownership of the property is granted to the borrower. In 2007 the outstanding residential mortgage debt totaled $11.9 trillion. (See Table 4.2.)

There are two types of mortgages in common use: conventional mortgages and government-underwritten mortgages. Conventional mortgages are loans made by nongovernmental businesses, such as banks and finance companies. Government-underwritten mortgages are insured by a federal, state, or local government agency.

The Federal Government's Role in Mortgages

Because high rates of homeownership are considered good for the U.S. economy, the government has taken an active role in the mortgage markets. Mortgage terms have changed dramatically since the early 1930s. At that time home buyers could borrow only up to half of a property's market value. A typical repayment plan included three to five years of regular payments and then one large balloon payment of the remaining balance. According to the Federal Housing Administration (FHA; September 6, 2006, http://www.hud.gov/offices/hsg/fhahistory.cfm), these terms discouraged many potential homeowners. As a result, the homeownership rate stood at around 40%. Most people preferred to rent.

During the 1930s the federal government introduced a variety of initiatives to boost a housing industry devastated by the Great Depression and increase homeownership. These efforts were focused on encouraging the supply side of the mortgage industry. They benefited consumers by enhancing the availability and flexibility of home mortgages. For example, amortization schedules covering fifteen years or more became common, eliminating balloon payments and making it much easier for consumers to afford houses. Following World War II the Veteran's Administration offered mortgages on favorable terms to returning veterans. Postwar economic prosperity and relatively low interest rates led to a housing boom. In the press release "Census Bureau Reports on Residential Vacancies and Homeownership" (April 28, 2008, http://www.census.gov/hhes/www/housing/hvs/qtr108/q108press .pdf), the U.S. Census Bureau states that the nation's homeownership rate was 64% by the mid-1980s. It was 67.8% in the first quarter of 2008.

There are several agencies and organizations that operate under government control or mandate to increase homeownership among Americans.

FEDERAL HOUSING ADMINISTRATION. The FHA was created in 1934 and later placed under the oversight of the U.S. Department of Housing and Urban Development. The FHA provides mortgage insurance on loans made by FHA-approved lenders to buyers of single- and multifamily homes. FHA-insured loans require less cash down payment from the home buyer than most conventional loans. The insurance provides assurances to lenders that the government will cover losses resulting from homeowners defaulting on their loan. In "About the Federal Housing Administration" (March 12, 2007, http://portal.hud.gov/portal/page?_pageid=33,717454 &_dad=portal&_schema= PORTAL), the FHA states that it has insured over thirty-four million home mortgages since 1934.

FEDERAL NATIONAL MORTGAGE ASSOCIATION. The Federal National Mortgage Association (Fannie Mae) was created in 1938. Fannie Mae began buying FHA-insured mortgages from banks and other lenders, bundling the mortgages together and selling the mortgage packages as investments on the stock market. In essence, Fannie Mae created a secondary market for home mortgages. Lenders benefited because they received immediate money that could be loaned to new customers. Home buyers benefited from the increased availability of mortgage loans. The

mortgage packages were attractive to investors because the mortgages were backed by FHA insurance. In 1968 Fannie Mae was converted to a private organization and expanded its portfolio beyond FHA-insured mortgages. However, as of 2008 it remained under congressional charter to enhance the availability and affordability of home mortgages for low- to middle-income Americans.

FEDERAL HOME LOAN MORTGAGE CORPORATION. The Federal Home Loan Mortgage Corporation (Freddie Mac) was created by the government in 1970 as a competitor for Fannie Mae, to prevent Fannie Mae's monopolization of the mortgage market. Like Fannie Mae, Freddie Mac sells home mortgages on the secondary market and is a private organization operating under a government charter.

TROUBLE FOR FANNIE MAE AND FREDDIE MAC. The 2005–06 housing market crash put tremendous financial pressure on Fannie Mae and Freddie Mac. Like many other mortgage providers, the two companies suffered large losses due to defaulted loans. Investors became increasingly nervous that Fannie Mae and Freddie Mac would be unable to raise sufficient money to cover these losses.

Katie Benner reports in "The $5 Trillion Mess" (CNNMoney.com, July 11, 2008) that shares in Fannie Mae and Freddie Mac had dropped in value by 65% and 75%, respectively, since the beginning of 2008. Benner notes that the two companies held and/or guaranteed approximately $5 trillion in mortgage loans. Some economists and federal regulators had become deeply worried about the financial soundness of the two companies, whereas others expressed confidence in their ability to survive the housing market slump. To calm investor fears, the federal government announced a plan to pump billions of dollars into Fannie Mae and Freddie Mac if the need arises. As of mid-July 2008, it remained to be seen whether this promise of a government bailout would help save the financially troubled companies.

Mortgage Interest Rates: Fixed and Adjustable

A fixed-rate mortgage charges a set interest rate over the entire lifetime of the loan, typically thirty years. Figure 4.2 shows the average annual interest rate charged on a thirty-year fixed mortgage from 1972 through 2007. Comparison to Figure 1.13 in Chapter 1 shows that fixed mortgage rates mirror the ups and downs of the prime rate. One feature of a fixed-rate mortgage is that the monthly payment remains the same throughout the lifetime of the loan.

Creative financing terms introduced by creditors since the late 1990s have led to many alternatives to the conventional thirty-year fixed-rate mortgage. One alternative is a shorter loan period, for example, fifteen years, instead of thirty years. Another popular option has been

FIGURE 4.2

Interest rate on conventional 30-year fixed mortgage, 1972–2007

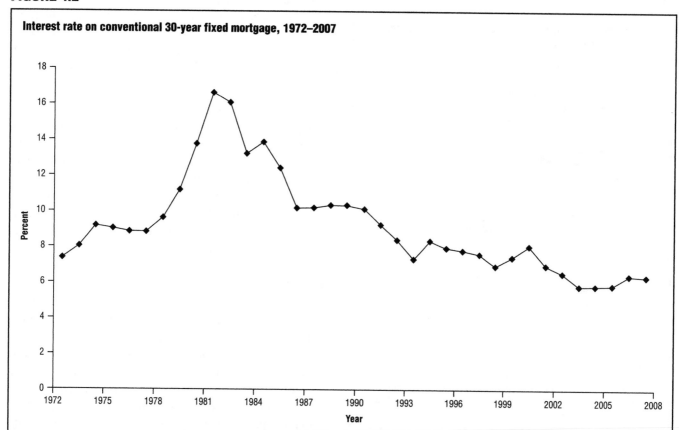

SOURCE: Adapted from "Contract Rate on 30-Year, Fixed-Rate Conventional Home Mortgage Commitments," in *Federal Reserve Statistical Release H.15: Selected Interest Rates*, The Federal Reserve, May 5, 2008, http://www.federalreserve.gov/releases/H15/data/Annual/H15_MORTG_NA.txt (accessed May 7, 2008)

the adjustable-rate mortgage (ARM). ARMs feature variable interest rates (and consequently variable monthly payments) over the life of the loan. An ARM rate is typically tied to a published benchmark rate called an index rate. Figure 4.3 displays selected index rates over the period 1996 to 2006. Low index rates during the early 2000s enticed many home buyers to take on ARMs instead of fixed-rate mortgages. Lenders often offer discount (or teaser) rates even lower than the index rate during the early months or years of the ARM repayment period. This translates into extra low monthly payments for an initial period, followed by much higher payments later.

Some creditors offer mortgages that allow homeowners to make interest-only payments for a short initial portion of the loan period. This is followed by a longer period of much higher monthly payments. A similar product is the payment-option mortgage, which allows homeowners to make small minimum payments for an initial short period. Short-term payment schedules requiring one large balloon payment are also offered in some mortgage products.

Mortgage arrangements with changeable monthly payments and balloon payments can pose a financial problem

FIGURE 4.3

Selected index rates for adjustable rate mortgages, 1996–2006

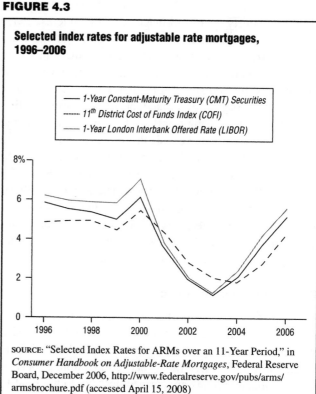

SOURCE: "Selected Index Rates for ARMs over an 11-Year Period," in *Consumer Handbook on Adjustable-Rate Mortgages*, Federal Reserve Board, December 2006, http://www.federalreserve.gov/pubs/arms/armsbrochure.pdf (accessed April 15, 2008)

FIGURE 4.4

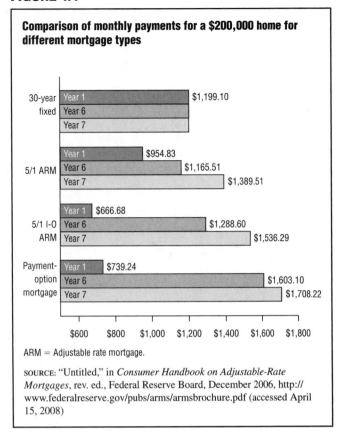

Comparison of monthly payments for a $200,000 home for different mortgage types

ARM = Adjustable rate mortgage.

SOURCE: "Untitled," in *Consumer Handbook on Adjustable-Rate Mortgages*, rev. ed., Federal Reserve Board, December 2006, http://www.federalreserve.gov/pubs/arms/armsbrochure.pdf (accessed April 15, 2008)

for homeowners who overestimate their ability to meet the costs of the mortgage. Figure 4.4 illustrates how monthly payments can vary significantly between different types of mortgages on a $200,000 home. The buyer assuming a fixed-rate thirty-year mortgage at 6% interest pays $1,199.10 per month for the entire lifetime of the loan. The 5/1 ARM is a common ARM arrangement in which the initial interest rate remains fixed for five years and then begins to fluctuate with the index rate. In this example, the buyer pays a discounted rate of 4% during the first year of the ARM. This translates to a monthly mortgage payment of $954.83. In year six the monthly payment is tied to a 6% ARM rate, and the monthly payment jumps to $1,165.51. In year seven the ARM rate increases to 7%; consequently, the monthly payment increases to $1,389.51. Two other mortgage types depicted in Figure 4.4—a 5/1 ARM with initial interest only payments and a payment-option mortgage—both feature large increases in monthly payments after the initial low-rate period.

Prime and Subprime Loans

Lenders divide mortgage loans into two broad categories—prime and subprime—based on the credit-worthiness of mortgage applicants. Prime loans feature better (lower) interest rates than comparable subprime loans. Subprime loans are for people who do not qualify for prime mortgages for various reasons—poor or short

credit history, lack of assets, low income or inability to prove income, and so on. Subprime loan holders are more likely than prime loan holders to default on their loans. As a result, lenders charge higher interest rates on subprime loans because of the greater risk associated with them.

During the early 2000s the United States experienced a subprime mortgage loan boom. In "Who Is to Blame for the Subprime Crisis?" (2007, http://www.investopedia.com/articles/07/subprime-blame.asp), Eric Petroff indicates that only $35 billion in subprime mortgage loans were initiated in 1994. By 2002 the number had risen to $213 billion. Over the next three years the subprime market skyrocketed. In 2005 subprime lenders originated $665 billion of the risky mortgage loans.

Refinancing Mortgages

Most home mortgages cover long periods—up to thirty years. However, interest rates can change dramatically in the short term, rising and falling in response to macroeconomic factors. Home buyers who assume mortgages during times of high interest rates can ask creditors to refinance (adjust the mortgage terms) when interest rates go down. Basically, refinancing entails drawing up a new mortgage contract on a property. Because mortgage contracts are complicated legal documents, creditors usually charge fees to refinance mortgages. Thus, homeowners must weigh the long-term benefits of a reduced interest rate against the expense of refinancing fees.

During the 1990s and early 2000s interest rates trended downward, making mortgage refinancing popular. This was particularly true for consumers who had purchased homes during the 1980s, when interest rates were extremely high by historical standards.

Refinancing frequently results in lower monthly payments for the homeowner because of the lower interest rate and because refinancing is commonly performed after at least several years of payments have been made on the original loan. This frees up the borrowers' money for consumer spending, investing, or saving. However, refinances conducted with a long payment period will keep the homeowner in mortgage debt for a longer period than originally anticipated. Some homeowners opt for a shorter loan payback period when they refinance. For example, consider a homeowner who has been paying for five years on a fixed-rate thirty-year mortgage. There are twenty-five years left in the repayment period. Refinancing at a much lower interest rate with a new fifteen-year payback period may not decrease the monthly payment, but it will reduce by ten years the amount of time the homeowner will be in mortgage debt.

Home Equity Loans

Real estate tends to appreciate in value. Thus, a property can increase in value above the amount originally paid for it (i.e., the amount that was borrowed to pay for it). For example, imagine a homeowner who bought a house in 1990 for $100,000 under a thirty-year fixed-rate mortgage. After making mortgage payments for several years, the homeowner discovers that the principal due on the loan has dropped to $90,000, but the property has increased in value to $140,000. The difference between the amount of principal owed (the outstanding loan balance) and the value of the property is $50,000 and is called home equity. Home equity is an asset that can be borrowed against. Basically, homeowners can liquefy (turn into cash) the equity they have built up in their homes.

Since the late 1980s a combination of rising home values and decreasing interest rates has prompted many homeowners to refinance their mortgages and take out home equity loans. Margaret M. McConnell, Richard W. Peach, and Alex Al-Haschimi of the Federal Reserve Bank of New York examine the macroeconomic effects of this phenomenon in "After the Refinancing Boom: Will Consumers Scale Back Their Spending?" (*Current Issues in Economics and Finance*, vol. 9, no. 12, December 2003). The researchers note that homeowners liquefied $450 billion of home equity in 2003. In 2001 and early 2002 homeowners used 35% of liquefied home equity funds for home improvements. (See Table 4.3.) Another 26% was used to repay other debts, and 16% went to consumer spending. Smaller shares were devoted to financial investments (11%), real estate or business investments (10%), and tax payments (2%).

TABLE 4.3

Uses of funds liquefied in 2001 and 2002 refinancings

	Share of loans[a] (percent)	Share of dollars (percent)
Repayment of other debts	51	26
Home improvements	43	35
Consumer expenditures[b]	25	16
Stock market or other financial investment	13	11
Real estate or business investment	7	10
Taxes	2	2

[a]The percentages sum to more than 100 because multiple uses could be cited for a single loan.
[b]Includes vehicle purchases; vacation, education, or medical expenses; living expenses; and other consumer purchases.

SOURCE: Margaret M. McConnell, Richard W. Peach, and Alex Al-Haschimi, "Table 2. Uses of Funds Liquefied in 2001 and 2002 Refinancings," in "After the Refinancing Boom: Will Consumers Scale Back Their Spending?" *Current Issues in Economics and Finance*, vol. 9, no. 12, December 2003, http://www.newyorkfed.org/research/current_issues/ci9-12.pdf (accessed June 10, 2008). Data from Glenn Canner, Karen Dynan, and Wayne Passmore, "Mortgage Refinancing in 2001 and Early 2002," *Federal Reserve Bulletin*, vol. 88, no.12, December 2002.

Economists are encouraged by the use of home equity money for home improvements. This type of spending is considered an investment, because it adds value to the home. Many homeowners chose to use home equity funds to repay other debt. Because mortgage loans typically have lower interest rates than other loans, this exchange is beneficial. In addition, the interest paid on mortgage loans is tax deductible for most Americans, whereas interest paid on other types of loans is not deductible. Thus, conversion of "bad" types of debt (such as credit cards) to mortgage debt has favorable consequences. More than half (51%) of the loans obtained from 2001 and 2002 refinancings were taken by homeowners to repay other debts. (See Table 4.3.) However, some economists worry that homeowners who use home equity loans to pay off bad kinds of debt may succumb to temptation and run up bad debt again. This could put them in a dire financial situation. They will no longer have their home equity to fall back on if their new debts become more than they can afford, and they might have to default on their loans. Home equity loans, like all mortgage loans, are secured by property. Thus, default on a home equity loan can result in loss of the home by the owner.

The Housing Market Booms and Bursts

The historically low interest rates of the early 2000s spurred demand in the real estate market. This pushed up prices on new homes and appreciated (increased the value) of existing homes. Many lenders relaxed loan standards and extended subprime mortgages to applicants eager to become homeowners. Subprime ARMs were particularly popular, because they featured low initial monthly payments. Lenders and borrowers of these loans expected interest rates to stay low and homes to keep appreciating in value. That would allow the homeowners to refinance and tap into home equity to offset the financial burden of the coming higher monthly payments. This scenario did not materialize. Instead, interest rates began to rise, and demand dropped dramatically in the housing market. (See Figure 4.5.)

The White House notes in *Economic Report of the President* (February 2008, http://www.gpoaccess.gov/eop/2008/2008_erp.pdf) that between 2004 and 2006 the default rate among homeowners with subprime ARMs was around 6%. By late 2007 the rate had skyrocketed to more than 15%. The default rate for prime mortgage loans also increased during this period, from around 1% to nearly 4%.

RECORD FORECLOSURE RATE. Foreclosure is a legal process in which a lender takes possession of the collateral (i.e., the home) of a borrower who has defaulted on a mortgage loan. In "Foreclosure Rate Hits Record High" (*Los Angeles Times*, March 7, 2008), Maura Reynolds reports that the national average foreclosure rate at the end of 2007 was the highest in recorded history. Just over

FIGURE 4.5

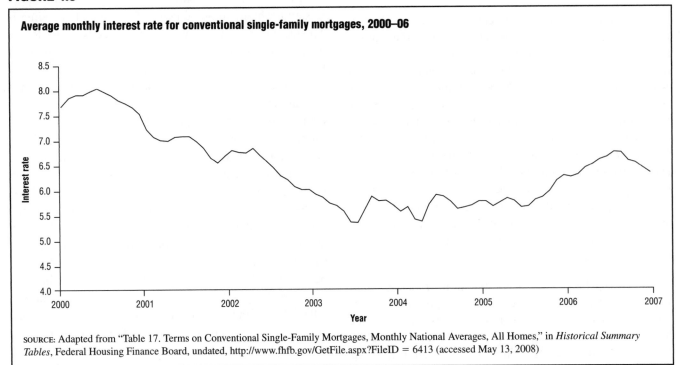

Average monthly interest rate for conventional single-family mortgages, 2000–06

SOURCE: Adapted from "Table 17. Terms on Conventional Single-Family Mortgages, Monthly National Averages, All Homes," in *Historical Summary Tables*, Federal Housing Finance Board, undated, http://www.fhfb.gov/GetFile.aspx?FileID = 6413 (accessed May 13, 2008)

2% of mortgages were in foreclosure at that time. The foreclosure rate was highest in states that had experienced the greatest housing boom (and hence the greatest housing bust): California, Nevada, Florida, and Arizona.

CONSUMER CREDIT

The Federal Reserve defines the term *consumer credit* as credit extended to individuals that does not include loans secured by real estate. In other words, mortgages are excluded from consumer credit. The Federal Reserve states in *Federal Reserve Statistical Release G.19: Consumer Credit, March 2008* (May 7, 2008, http://www.federalreserve.gov/releases/ G19/Current/g19.pdf) that consumer credit topped $2.5 trillion during the first quarter of 2008. (See Figure 4.6.) The amount had risen since 2003, when nearly $2.1 trillion in credit was outstanding. The breakdown for the first quarter of 2008 was $1.6 trillion in nonrevolving loans and $956 million in revolving loans. Nonrevolving debt includes loans for vehicles, boats, vacations, and student loans. Revolving debt is almost entirely comprised of credit card debt.

Figure 4.7 shows the breakdown of outstanding consumer debt by creditor as of March 2008. Nearly one-third (31%) of the total was owed to commercial banks. Pools of securitized assets (bundled debts sold as securities on the stock markets) accounted for 27% of the total. Finance companies held another 23% of the debt and credit unions held 9%. The remaining creditors each accounted for 4% or less of the total.

FIGURE 4.6

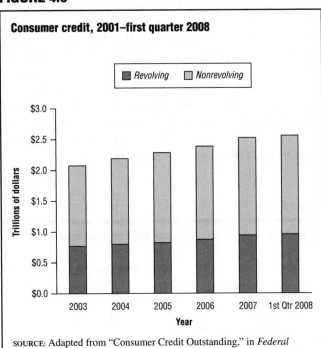

Consumer credit, 2001–first quarter 2008

SOURCE: Adapted from "Consumer Credit Outstanding," in *Federal Reserve Statistical Release G.19: Consumer Credit, March 2008*, The Federal Reserve, May 7, 2008, http://www.federalreserve.gov/releases/ G19/Current/g19.pdf (accessed May 8, 2008)

Interest Rates on Consumer Loans

Consumer loans are not secured by real estate. Because they have a higher risk of default, consumer loans generally have a higher interest rate than mortgage loans. Table 4.4 lists the average interest rates charged on various kinds of consumer loans from 2003 through 2007 and for the first quarter of 2008. It should be noted that borrowers with good credit histories would have likely received lower interest rates than these averages and that borrowers with poor credit histories would have been charged higher rates.

FIGURE 4.7

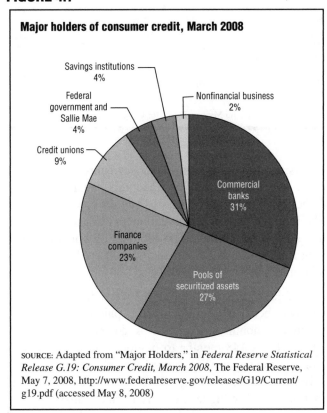

Major holders of consumer credit, March 2008

Savings institutions
4%

Federal government and Sallie Mae
4%

Nonfinancial business
2%

Credit unions
9%

Commercial banks
31%

Finance companies
23%

Pools of securitized assets
27%

SOURCE: Adapted from "Major Holders," in *Federal Reserve Statistical Release G.19: Consumer Credit, March 2008*, The Federal Reserve, May 7, 2008, http://www.federalreserve.gov/releases/G19/Current/g19.pdf (accessed May 8, 2008)

New Car Loans

Loans for the purchase of new cars (and other types of vehicles) are secured by the vehicle being purchased. In other words, the creditor can repossess the vehicle if the loan is in default. As a result of this collateral, the interest rates on new vehicle loans tend to be lower than on other types of consumer loans.

As of the first quarter of 2008, the average interest rate on a four-year loan from a commercial bank for the purchase of a new car was 7.27%. (See Table 4.4.) The interest rate charged by auto finance companies for a new car loan was lower, at 4.85%. According to the Federal Reserve, the latter rate is based on the rates charged by the finance companies of the "big three" automakers: General Motors Corp., Ford Motor Co., and Daimler-Chrysler AG.

The typical loan period reported by the auto finance companies was 62.6 months (just over five years). (See Table 4.4.) This is much longer than the three-year loan period that was common for new car loans in the mid-1970s. Longer loan periods reflect longer car lifetimes. The average loan-to-value ratio reported by the auto finance companies for the first quarter of 2006 was 94%. This means that the average new car buyer borrowed 94% of the value of the new car being purchased. The remaining 6% was a down payment paid by the buyer in cash or via trade-in of another vehicle. The

TABLE 4.4

Terms of credit at commercial banks and finance companies, 2003–first quarter 2008

[Percent except as noted, not seasonally adjusted]

Institution, terms, and type of loan	2003	2004	2005	2006	2007	2008 Q1*
Commercial banks						
Interest rates						
48-mo. new car	6.93	6.60	7.08	7.72	7.77	7.27
24-mo. personal	11.95	11.89	12.05	12.41	12.39	11.40
Credit card plan						
All accounts	12.30	12.72	12.51	13.21	13.38	12.48
Accounts assessed interest	12.73	13.22	14.55	14.73	14.67	13.71
New car loans at auto finance companies						
Interest rates	3.81	4.92	6.02	4.99	4.87	4.85
Maturity (months)	61.3	60.7	60.0	63.0	62.0	62.6
Loan-to-value ratio	95	89	88	94	95	94
Amount financed (dollars)	26,295	24,888	24,133	26,620	28,287	27,586

*Preliminary.

Notes: Interest rates are annual percentage rates (APR) as specified by the Federal Reserve's Regulation Z. Interest rates for new-car loans and personal loans at commercial banks are simple unweighted averages of each bank's most common rate charged during the first calendar week of the middle month of each quarter. For credit card accounts, the rate for *all accounts* is the stated APR averaged across all credit card accounts at all reporting banks. The rate for *accounts assessed interest* is the annualized ratio of total finance charges at all reporting banks to the total average daily balances against which the finance charges were assessed (excludes accounts for which no finance charges were assessed). Finance company data are from the subsidiaries of the three major U.S. automobile manufacturers and are volume-weighted averages covering all loans of each type purchased during the month.

SOURCE: Adapted from "Terms of Credit at Commercial Banks and Finance Companies," in *Federal Reserve Statistical Release G.19: Consumer Credit, March 2008*, The Federal Reserve, May 7, 2008, http://www.federalreserve.gov/releases/G19/Current/g19.pdf (accessed May 8, 2008)

average amount financed during the first quarter of 2008 for a new car purchase was $28,174.

Personal Loans

Personal loans are generally unsecured loans based on the creditworthiness of the borrower. A lack of collateral makes personal loans more risky from the loaners' viewpoint; thus, interest rates are higher for personal loans than for car loans. (See Table 4.4.) In the first quarter of 2008 the average interest rate charged by commercial banks for a twenty-four-month personal loan was 11.4%. The rate varied from 11.89% to 12.41% between 2003 and 2007.

Credit Cards

Credit cards have the highest average interest rates of all types of consumer loans. Most credit card loans are unsecured and are granted based on the creditworthiness of the borrower. The higher risk factor for the creditor and the huge demand for credit cards contribute to the high interest rates that are charged.

The average interest rate charged by commercial banks on credit card loans was 13.71% during the first quarter of 2008. (See Table 4.4.) The rate varied from 12.73% to 14.73% between 2003 and 2007. However, Lucy Lazarony of Bankrate.com explains in "Store Credit Cards: Flashy Perks, High Rates" (2008, http://moneycentral.msn.com/content/Banking/creditcardsmarts/P55860.asp) that rates charged on credit cards issued by department and specialty stores can be much higher. Lazarony notes that even though these stores sometimes offer discounts and "rewards" for items charged on their cards, their interest rates can be more than 20%.

REVOLVING CREDIT AND MINIMUM PAYMENTS. Credit card debt is an example of revolving debt, a type of debt that is not amortized. There is no preset schedule of payments that will eliminate the debt within a particular time frame. The creditor grants the borrower a total amount of credit at a particular interest rate. Even though the interest rate may be fixed for a short introductory period, in general, credit card interest rates are variable.

Each month the borrower is billed for the outstanding balance on the credit card, which includes principal plus interest. The borrower can pay off the entire balance or a lesser amount down to the minimum payment required by the credit card issuer. Payment of any amount less than the minimum required will result in additional finance charges on the remaining balance. This is an example of compound interest (interest charged on an amount that already includes built-up interest charges).

When credit cards were first introduced, it was common for creditors to require 5% or more of the balance as a minimum monthly payment. Minimum payment requirements were gradually reduced to 2% by most credit card

TABLE 4.5

Effects of different minimum monthly payments on credit card debt

Interest rate	Amount borrowed	Minimum monthly payment required	Months to pay off loan	Total interest paid	Total principal+ interest paid
13%	$1,000	2%	148	$815	$1,815
18%	$1,000	2%	232	$1,931	$2,931
21%	$1,000	2%	397	$4,198	$5,198
13%	$1,000	4%	77	$322	$1,322
18%	$1,000	4%	87	$516	$1,516
21%	$1,000	4%	95	$665	$1,665

SOURCE: Created by Kim Masters Evans for Cengage Learning, Gale, 2008

issuers. Low required minimum payments, high interest rates, and the effect of compounding interest make it difficult for many consumers to pay off credit card debt. The Bankruptcy Abuse Prevention and Consumer Protection Act of 2005 requires creditors to tell borrowers how long it will take to pay off their credit card debt if only minimum payments are made.

Table 4.5 illustrates the tremendous difference to the borrower between credit card debts paid off by differing minimum monthly payments. A $1,000 loan at 13% interest takes 148 months to pay off with 2% minimum monthly payments. The same loan takes only seventy-seven months to discharge if 4% of the balance is paid each month. The higher monthly payment also results in far less interest being paid over the life of the debt ($322 compared to $815). Even greater savings are achieved when a minimum monthly sum of 4% is paid on credit card loans that charge 18% or 21% interest.

Student Loans

Student loans are loans obtained to pay for educational expenses, primarily at the college level. Even though they are technically consumer loans, student loans are not for consumption purposes. They fund the advancement of skill and knowledge in individuals, likely increasing the potential for higher future income. Thus, student loans are considered a type of "human investment."

Because the federal government encourages secondary education, it plays a major role in ensuring that student loans are available. There are three major types of student loans:

- Low-interest loans provided by the government through the financial aid departments of participating schools; these loans are available to needy students through the Perkins Loan Program

- Loans provided directly to students by the government through the William D. Ford Federal Direct Loan Program

- Loans guaranteed by the federal government but provided to students by private lenders

TABLE 4.6

Public opinion poll responses regarding credit card payments, April 2008

THINKING ABOUT ALL CREDIT CARDS INCLUDING DEPARTMENT STORES, RETAIL CHAIN STORES, AS WELL AS GENERAL BANK CREDIT CARDS SUCH AS VISA AND MASTERCARD, HOW MANY CREDIT CARDS DO YOU HAVE? [IF ONE OR MORE CREDIT CARD, ASK:] HOW DO YOU GENERALLY PAY YOUR CREDIT CARD(S) EACH MONTH—DO YOU ALWAYS PAY THE FULL AMOUNT, DO YOU USUALLY PAY THE FULL AMOUNT, BUT NOT ALWAYS, OR DO YOU ALWAYS PAY AS MUCH AS YOU CAN, BUT USUALLY LEAVE A BALANCE, DO YOU USUALLY PAY THE MINIMUM AMOUNT DUE, BUT NOT MUCH MORE, OR DO YOU SOMETIMES PAY LESS THAN THE MINIMUM AMOUNT DUE?

Mean: N/A		Total N: 785
	%	N
Do you always pay the full amount	42.87	336
Do you usually pay the full amount, but not always	16.58	130
Do you always pay as much as you can, but usually leave a balance	25.41	199
Do you usually pay the minimum amount due, but not much more	11.95	94
Do you sometimes pay less than the minimum amount due	0.75	6
Other (vol.)	0.89	7
Don't know	0.76	6
Refused	0.79	6

N = Population.

SOURCE: "Question qn21. Thinking about All Credit Cards including Department Stores, Retail Chain Stores, as well as General Bank Credit Cards Such As Visa and MasterCard, How Many Credit Cards Do You Have?) [IF ONE OR MORE CREDIT CARD, ASK:] How Do You Generally Pay Your Credit Card(s) Each Month—Do You Always Pay the Full Amount, Do You Usually Pay the Full Amount, but Not Always, or Do You Always Pay As Much As You Can, but Usually Leave A Balance, Do You Usually Pay the Minimum Amount Due, but Not Much More, or Do You Sometimes Pay Less Than the Minimum Amount Due?" in *Gallup Poll Social Series: Economy & Personal Finance*, The Gallup Organization, April 2008, http://brain.gallup.com/documents/questionnaire.aspx?STUDY= P0804015 (accessed May 13, 2008). Copyright © 2008 by The Gallup Organization. Reproduced by permission of The Gallup Organization.

TABLE 4.7

Public opinion poll responses regarding ability to make minimum payments on credit cards, April 2008

NEXT, PLEASE TELL ME HOW CONCERNED YOU ARE RIGHT NOW ABOUT EACH OF THE FOLLOWING FINANCIAL MATTERS, BASED ON YOUR CURRENT FINANCIAL SITUATION—ARE YOU VERY WORRIED, MODERATELY WORRIED, NOT TOO WORRIED, OR NOT WORRIED AT ALL? IF A PARTICULAR ITEM DOES NOT APPLY TO YOU, PLEASE SAY SO. FIRST, HOW WORRIED ARE YOU ABOUT—NOT BEING ABLE TO MAKE THE MINIMUM PAYMENTS ON YOUR CREDIT CARDS?

Mean: 1.92		Total N: 1021
	%	N
Very worried	11.22	115
Moderately worried	12.30	126
Not too worried	18.71	191
Not worried at all	41.57	424
Doesn't apply (vol)	15.73	161
Don't know	0.07	1
Refused	0.40	4

N = Population.

SOURCE: "Question qn19e. Next, Please Tell Me How Concerned You Are Right Now about Each of the Following Financial Matters, Based on Your Current Financial Situation—Are You Very Worried, Moderately Worried, Not Too Worried, or Not Worried at All? If a Particular Item Does Not Apply to You, Please Say So. First, How Worried Are You about—Not Being Able To Make the Minimum Payments on Your Credit Cards?" in *Gallup Poll Social Series: Economy & Personal Finance*, The Gallup Organization, April 2008, http://brain.gallup.com/documents/questionnaire.aspx?STUDY= P0804015 (accessed May 13, 2008). Copyright © 2008 by The Gallup Organization. Reproduced by permission of The Gallup Organization.

According to the U.S. Department of Education, in *Performance and Accountability Report Fiscal Year 2007: Highlights* (February 1, 2008, http://www.ed.gov/about/reports/annual/2007report/report-highlights.pdf), the loan portfolio of the William D. Ford Federal Direct Loan Program totaled $99 billion as of September 30, 2007. The total outstanding balance of federally guaranteed student loans held by lenders at that time was $363 billion.

CONSUMER OPINIONS ABOUT DEBT

In March 2005 the Gallup Organization, in conjunction with the credit marketing company Experian, began compiling a Personal Credit Index (PCI; http://www.personalcreditindex.com)—an index gauging consumer perceptions and intentions regarding personal credit. The first index value was arbitrarily set to one hundred. Periodic polls have been conducted to calculate a PCI for comparison to the original value. In December 2007 pollsters found that the PCI had declined to a value of seventy-six, indicating a more negative viewpoint about personal credit.

In *Gallup Poll Social Series: Economy & Personal Finance* (April 2008, http://brain.gallup.com/documents/questionnaire.aspx?STUDY=P0804015), Gallup notes that nearly 22% of respondents had no credit cards at all. Another 17% had one credit card. Seventeen percent reported having two credit cards, and nearly 14% had three credit cards. These are credit cards issued by banks, department stores, or retail chains. When asked about their payment habits, nearly 43% of people said they pay off their credit card bills each month. (See Table 4.6.) The remainder usually carry over a balance from month to month. Twelve percent of those asked usually pay only the minimum amount due each month. A small percentage (0.75%) reported they sometimes pay less than the minimum amount required. Nearly a quarter of respondents reported they were "very worried" (11.2%) or "moderately worried" (12.3%) about not being able to make the required minimum payments on their cards. (See Table 4.7.)

PERSONAL BANKRUPTCIES

The word *bankrupt* is derived from the Italian phrase *banca rotta*, which means "bench broken," referring to the benches or tables used by merchants in outdoor markets in sixteenth-century Italy. Bankruptcy is a state of financial ruin. Under U.S. law people with more debts than they can reasonably hope to repay can file for personal bankruptcy. This results in a legally binding agreement between debtors and the federal government worked out in a federal bankruptcy court. The agreement calls for the debtors to pay as much as they can with

FIGURE 4.8

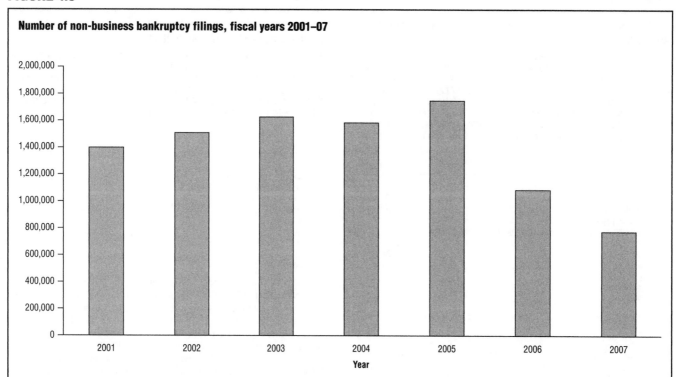

Number of non-business bankruptcy filings, fiscal years 2001–07

SOURCE: Adapted from "Table F-2. U.S. Bankruptcy Courts: Business and Nonbusiness Bankruptcy Cases Commenced, by Chapter of the Bankruptcy Code, during the Twelve-Month Period Ended Sept. 30, 2007," in *Bankruptcy Statistics*, The U.S. Courts, September 2007, http://www.uscourts.gov/bnkrpctystats/sept2007/f2table.xls (accessed May 12, 2008)

whatever assets they have, and after a predetermined amount of time—usually a number of years—the debtors begin again with new credit. Depending on state law, certain belongings may be kept through the bankruptcy.

The American Bankruptcy Institute explains in "General Concepts" (2008, http://consumer.abiworld.org/?q=node/21 #5) that an official declaration of bankruptcy benefits individuals in the short term, because it puts a stop to all collection efforts by creditors. An "automatic stay" goes into effect that prevents creditors from calling, writing, or suing debtors covered by a bankruptcy plan.

Figure 4.8 shows the number of personal bankruptcy cases filed per fiscal year between 2001 and 2007. A fiscal year ends September 30. In fiscal year 2007 over 775,000 individuals filed for bankruptcy, down from nearly 1.1 million cases in fiscal year 2006. After climbing through the early 2000s, the number of personal bankruptcy filings decreased dramatically in 2006 and 2007.

There are three types (or chapters) of personal bankruptcy under which individuals may file:

- Chapter 7—a liquidation plan is developed in which the debtor turns over certain assets that are sold and used to pay creditors.

- Chapter 13—a payment plan is developed under which debtors receiving regular income repay their creditors. Liquidation of assets is not required in most cases.

- Chapter 11—while similar to Chapter 13, Chapter 11 is reserved for individuals with "substantial" debts and assets.

According to the U.S. Courts (September 2007, http://www.uscourts.gov/bnkrpctystats/sept2007/f2table.xls), in fiscal year 2007, 467,248 (60.3%) of personal bankruptcy cases were filed under Chapter 7. Another 307,521 (39.7%) of filings were under Chapter 13, and the remaining 571 (0.1%) were under Chapter 11.

Evolving Bankruptcy Law

The first federal bankruptcy laws were written in the early 1800s but were considered emergency measures to remain in effect for only short periods of time. The first comprehensive federal legislation was the National Bankruptcy Act of 1898, which was extensively amended during the 1930s and later replaced by the Bankruptcy Reform Act of 1978. This law was substantially amended by the Bankruptcy Reform Act of 1994. Major reforms in the law were enacted when the Bankruptcy Abuse Prevention and Consumer Protection Act of 2005 went into effect.

Because of different state laws regulating which assets and belongings a person could keep after a Chapter 7 filing, regulators and creditors believed that some people were using bankruptcy as a way to keep possessions without having to pay for them. The new federal law instituted measures intended to eliminate abuses and loopholes and increased the amount of paperwork and fees required for most filers.

Opponents of the new bill argued that it was designed to make more money for credit card companies and lenders and that it would be detrimental to ordinary people who chose bankruptcy as a last resort.

Bankruptcy Filers

In *The Two-Income Trap: Why Middle-Class Mothers and Fathers Are Going Broke* (2003), Elizabeth Warren and Amelia Warren Tyagi note that women and families with children at home are two of the fastest-growing groups filing for personal bankruptcy. For example, between 1981 and 1999 the number of women who filed for bankruptcy went from about sixty-nine thousand to about five hundred thousand—a 625% increase.

Warren addresses the phenomenon of bankruptcy among middle-class American families in "Financial Collapse and Class Status: Who Goes Bankrupt?" (*Osgoode Hall Law Review*, vol. 41, no. 1, spring 2003). Writing of the importance of documenting who files for bankruptcy, she states, "Knowing who files for bankruptcy can signal information about successes and failures throughout the population, informing research, for example, on the economic progress of different social and racial sub-groups, the heightened vulnerability of the elderly, or the economic risks facing divorced women or mothers of small children." Warren finds that an overwhelming majority of the people she interviewed who had filed for bankruptcy had at least some college education, worked in occupations that are typically rated high in status surveys, and were homeowners—the three factors that Warren used to identify membership in the American middle class. This finding contradicts the idea that people who declare bankruptcy tend to be poorly educated and economically disadvantaged from the outset. Additionally, the most common reasons people give for declaring bankruptcy are sudden financial setbacks, such as job loss, illness or injury, medical debt, or divorce, rather than long-term problems involving chronic overspending (although these cases do exist).

PREYING ON DEBTORS

Consumer demand for credit has led to enormous growth in businesses engaged in making loans, counseling debtors, and arranging debt management plans. Even though these are legitimate enterprises, some businesses have aroused consumer ire and even run afoul of the law with practices considered abusive toward debtors.

Predatory Lending?

Most large creditors, such as banks and finance companies, only make consumer loans to applicants who meet stringent requirements for creditworthiness, excluding people with low incomes and poor credit histories. This has led to the growth of subprime lenders—businesses that make consumer loans to customers considered undesirable by traditional lenders. Because they are assuming higher risk, subprime lenders charge their customers higher interest rates and fees to loan money to them. Some consumers and legislators have accused these businesses of charging excessive fees and interest rates on consumer loans—a practice called predatory lending. Predatory lenders allegedly victimize poor people by imposing loan terms designed to maximize creditor profits and make it difficult for debtors to pay off their debt.

Usury is a word that centuries ago meant "interest" or "the charging of interest." In modern terminology it has come to mean the charging of excessive interest. Even though there are state usury laws against the charging of excessive interest, this issue has not been addressed at the federal level. In fact, most banks are allowed to ignore state usury laws. Other lenders can avoid usury laws through a variety of means, such as charging large loan fees and forcing borrowers to take out expensive insurance policies.

Two particular types of consumer loans are often called predatory: payday loans and refund anticipation loans (RALs). Borrowers obtain payday loans from establishments that agree to accept and hold personal checks until the borrower receives a paycheck. RALs are also short-term loans that must be paid back within two weeks. Creditors offer RALs to people expecting refunds when their income taxes are filed. The Consumer Federation of America claims in "Refund Anticipation Loans: Updated Facts and Figures" (January 17, 2006, http://www.consumerfed.org/pdfs/RAL_2006_Early_info.pdf) that RALs are targeted at uneducated minority populations that "are vulnerable to quick cash loan offers."

Credit Counseling and Debt Management Services

The explosive growth in consumer debt has resulted in many organizations offering credit counseling and debt management services to debtors in financial difficulties. Consumer activists maintain that many of these organizations charge debtors large fees in return for little to no aid. In September 2003 the Permanent Subcommittee on Investigations began investigating alleged abuses in the credit counseling industry and published its findings in *Profiteering in a Non-profit Industry: Abusive Practices in Credit Counseling* (April 13, 2005, http://frwebgate.access.gpo.gov/cgi-bin/getdoc.cgi?dbname=109_cong_reports&docid=f:sr055.109.pdf).

The committee explains that credit counseling as an industry began in the 1960s with the help of large creditors, such as banks, concerned about rising bankruptcy rates. The early credit counseling agencies (CCAs) were locally based nonprofit organizations with trained counselors who met in person with debtors and provided advice on budgeting and paying off debt. CCAs could also arrange debt management plans for debtors in which creditors agreed to charge lower monthly minimum payments, lower interest rates, and waive outstanding late fees. The CCAs collected the new monthly payments from the debtor and paid the creditors. Creditors supported the CCAs with contributions and participated in debt management plans in hopes that the debtors would avoid filing for bankruptcy. Some CCAs also charged small fees to the debtor for administrative costs. These reputable CCAs were members of the National Foundation for Credit Counseling, an organization known for its focus on standards and ethics.

The committee finds that several of the new CCAs that have entered the industry since the 1990s operate in a much different way. Most are Internet-based, communicate with consumers solely by phone, and focus exclusively on enrolling debtors in debt management plans for large fees. Although officially nonprofit organizations, many of these new CCAs have ties to for-profit businesses. The committee concludes that these CCAs engage in deceptive practices and provide no actual counseling services to debtors.

The committee's investigation coincided with a federal crackdown on CCAs. The Internal Revenue Service began revoking the tax-exempt status of CCAs found to be funneling money to for-profit businesses. The Federal Trade Commission (FTC) filed charges against some of the CCAs accused of wrongdoing. Stephen Manning reports in "AmeriDebt Founder Settles with FTC over Alleged Hidden Fees" (Associated Press, January 11, 2006) that in January 2006 Andris Pukke, the founder of AmeriDebt, agreed to pay the FTC a $35-million fine to avoid a trial. AmeriDebt had allegedly collected more than $172 million in fees from an estimated three hundred thousand customers who never received any credit counseling. In "Debt Management Telemarketers Settle FTC Charges" (June 15, 2006, http://www.consumeraffairs.com/news04/2006/06/ftc_debt_management.html), ConsumerAffairs.com notes that in June 2006 the CCA Credit Foundation of America agreed to pay over $926,000 in fines to the FTC for making false claims about its debt management program and operating as part of a for-profit company.

IDENTITY THEFT

Modern technology and compilation of personal and financial information in computer databases has made obtaining loans faster and easier than in the past. No longer are face-to-face meetings required between creditors and borrowers. Loans can be secured through the mail, over the phone, and via the Internet. However, this convenience has a price. It allows unscrupulous people to pretend to be someone else by stealing the identity of people with good credit histories and using it for criminal purposes.

The number of identity theft complaints reported to the FTC has skyrocketed from around 86,000 in 2001 to more than 250,000 complaints in 2007. (See Figure 4.9.) According to the FTC, in *Consumer Fraud and Identity Theft Complaint Data, January–December 2007* (February 2008, http://www.consumer.gov/sentinel/pubs/top10 fraud2007.pdf), the most common outcome of identity theft cases in 2007 was credit card fraud. Nearly one-fourth (23%) of the complaints filed were associated with credit card fraud. More than half of these cases occurred when consumers were opening new accounts with credit card issuers.

The FTC notes that the ten metropolitan areas (in descending order of number of complaints per one hundred thousand population) associated with the most reported cases of identity theft in 2007 were:

1. Albany-Lebanon, Oregon
2. Greeley, Colorado
3. Napa, California
4. Punta Gorda, Florida
5. Allegan, Michigan
6. Roseburg, Oregon
7. Dunn, North Carolina
8. Willimantic, Connecticut
9. Concord, New Hampshire
10. Gainesville, Georgia

FIGURE 4.9

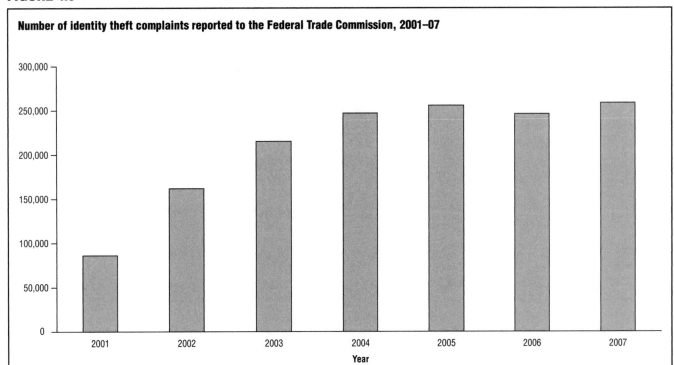

Number of identity theft complaints reported to the Federal Trade Commission, 2001–07

SOURCE: Adapted from "Sentinel Complaints by Calendar Year," in *National and State Trends in Fraud and Identity Theft: January–December 2003, Three-Year Trend for Sentinel Complaints*, U.S. Federal Trade Commission, January 22, 2004, http://www.consumer.gov/sentinel/states03/3year_trends .pdf; "Sentinel Complaints by Calendar Year," in *Consumer Fraud and Identity Theft Complaint Data: January–December 2005*, U.S. Federal Trade Commission, January 25, 2006, http://www.consumer.gov/sentinel/pubs/Top10Fraud2005.pdf; "Sentinel Complaints by Calendar Year," in *Consumer Fraud and Identity Theft Complaint Data: January–December 2006*, U.S. Federal Trade Commission, February 7, 2007, http://www.consumer.gov/ sentinel/pubs/Top10Fraud2006.pdf; and "Sentinel Complaints by Calendar Year," in *Consumer Fraud and Identity Theft Complaint Data: January–December 2007*, U.S. Federal Trade Commission, February 13, 2008, http://www.consumer.gov/sentinel/pubs/Top10Fraud2007.pdf (accessed April 7, 2008)

CHAPTER 5
THE AMERICAN WORKER

When we are all in the business working together, we all ought to have some share in the profits—by way of a good wage, or salary, or added compensation.

—Henry Ford, *My Life and Work* (1922)

The American workforce plays a major role in the U.S. economy. Workers produce goods and provide services, the consumption of which drives the nation's gross domestic product (the total market value of final goods and services produced within an economy in a given year) growth. However, there is an age-old struggle between employers and employees over compensation. Businesses must compensate workers with pay and benefits that are high enough to attract and keep motivated employees, but not so high as to damage the profitability and growth of the business itself. On a macroeconomic scale, gainful employment of large numbers of workers is important to the overall health of the U.S. economy.

THE EMPLOYMENT SITUATION

The Bureau of Labor Statistics (BLS; April 25, 2008, http://www.bls.gov/ces/) conducts a monthly survey of approximately 150,000 nonfarm businesses and government agencies with around 390,000 worksites around the country. Detailed information on employment, work hours, and payroll are obtained as part of the Current Employment Statistics program. These data are published monthly by the BLS in the news release "The Employment Situation." Also included are data collected by the U.S. Census Bureau from approximately sixty thousand households as part of the Current Population Survey.

The BLS defines the civilian labor force as including all civilian noninstitutionalized people aged sixteen years and older who have a job or are actively looking for a job. People are considered to be employed during a given week if they meet any of the following criteria:

- They performed any work that week for pay or profit
- They worked without pay for at least fifteen hours that week in a family operated enterprise
- They had a job but could not work that week due to illness, vacation, personal obligations, leave of absence, bad weather, or labor disputes

People considered not to be in the labor force are those who do not have a job and are not looking for a job. This category includes many students, retirees, stay-at-home moms and dads, the mentally and physically challenged, and people in prison and other institutions, as well as those who are not employed but have become discouraged from looking for work. The unemployed are counted as those who do not have a job but have actively looked for a job during the previous four weeks and are available for work. Also included are people who did not work during a given week due to temporary layoffs.

Table 5.1 lists the major findings from the Current Population Survey and the Current Employment Statistics program for the first quarter of 2008. The civilian labor force averaged nearly 153.7 million people at that time. Another seventy-nine million people were considered to not be in the labor force. Nearly 7.6 million people were counted as unemployed, giving an overall unemployment rate of 4.9%. The unemployment rates were much higher than this for minorities and teenagers. Of the 137.9 million people employed in nonfarm occupations, 116.1 million (84%) held service-providing jobs. The remaining 21.8 million (16%) employees worked at goods-producing jobs, primarily in manufacturing. The average earnings for private-sector production or nonsupervisory workers during the quarter were $17.81 per hour, or $600.80 per week.

Employment and Unemployment as of April 2008

The BLS reports that in April 2008, 146 million people were employed in the United States. (See Table 5.1.)

TABLE 5.1

Labor market activity, first quarter 2008

[Numbers in thousands]

Category	I 2008
Household data	
Civilian labor force	153,661
Employment	146,070
Unemployment	7,591
Not in labor force	79,146
All workers	4.9
Adult men	4.4
Adult women	4.3
Teenagers	16.8
White	4.4
Black or African American	8.8
Hispanic or Latino ethnicity	6.5
Establishment data	
Nonfarm employment	p137,920
Goods-producing[a]	p 21,817
Construction	p 7,381
Manufacturing	p13,690
Service-providing[a]	p116,103
Retail trade[b]	p15,437
Professional and business service	p18,068
Education and health services	p18,663
Leisure and hospitality	p13,660
Government	p22,358
Total private	p33.7
Manufacturing	p41.1
Overtime	p4.0
Indexes of aggregate weekly hours (2002 = 100)[c]	
Total private	p107.4
Earnings[c]	
Average hourly earnings, total private	p$17.81
Average weekly earnings, total private	p600.80

[a]Includes other industries, not shown separately.
[b]Quarterly averages and the over-the-month change are calculated using unrounded data.
[c]Data relate to private production and nonsupervisory workers.
p = preliminary.

SOURCE: Adapted from "Table A. Major Indicators of Labor Market Activity, Seasonally Adjusted," in *The Employment Situation: April 2008*, U.S. Department of Labor, Bureau of Labor Statistics, May 2, 2008, http://www.bls.gov/news.release/archives/empsit_05022008.pdf (accessed June 13, 2008)

FIGURE 5.1

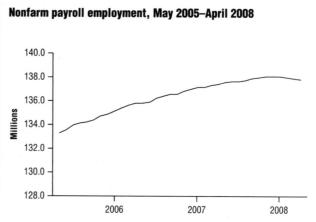

Nonfarm payroll employment, May 2005–April 2008

SOURCE: "Chart 2. Nonfarm Payroll Employment, Seasonally Adjusted, May 2005–April 2008," in *The Employment Situation: April 2008*, U.S. Department of Labor, Bureau of Labor Statistics, May 2, 2008, http://www.bls.gov/news.release/archives/empsit_05022008.pdf (accessed June 13, 2008)

FIGURE 5.2

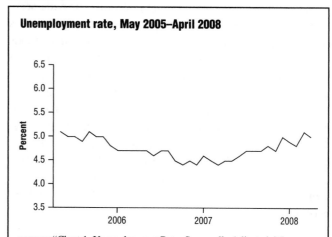

Unemployment rate, May 2005–April 2008

SOURCE: "Chart 1. Unemployment Rate, Seasonally Adjusted, May 2005–April 2008," in *The Employment Situation: April 2008*, U.S. Department of Labor, Bureau of Labor Statistics, May 2, 2008, http://www.bls.gov/news.release/archives/empsit_05022008.pdf (accessed June 13, 2008)

Nonfarm payroll employment totaled 137.9 million people (based on preliminary estimates). This value has steadily increased from May 2005, when it stood at around 133 million people. (See Figure 5.1.) Figure 5.2 indicates that the unemployment rate declined from just above 5% in mid-2005 to around 4.5% in early 2007. Since that time the rate has steadily climbed, reaching 5% in April 2008.

The unemployment rate varied widely according to certain demographic factors in April 2008. (See Figure 5.3.) Teenagers were unemployed at a rate of 15.4%. Racial and ethnic differences were significant; African-American workers had an unemployment rate of 8.6%, and those of Hispanic or Latino ethnicity had a rate of 6.9%. These values were higher than the 4.4% unemployment rate reported for white workers. There was little difference by sex among adults; for adult men the rate was 4.6% and for adult women it was 4.3%.

Table 5.2 provides a breakdown on duration of unemployment as of April 2008. Nearly 2.5 million people had been unemployed for less than five weeks at that time. This represents 32.7% of all the unemployed. Another 2.5 million (32.8%) people had been unemployed for five to fourteen weeks, and nearly 1.3 million (16.7%) had been unemployed for fifteen to twenty-six weeks. Lastly, more than 1.3 million (17.8%) people had been unemployed for at least twenty-seven weeks.

A poll conducted by the Gallup Organization in April 2008 found that only 20% of those asked felt it was a "good time to find a quality job." (See Figure 5.4.) This

FIGURE 5.3

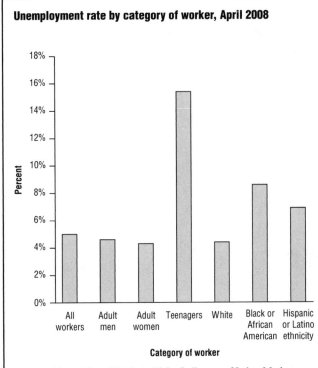

Unemployment rate by category of worker, April 2008

SOURCE: Adapted from "Table A. Major Indicators of Labor Market Activity, Seasonally Adjusted," in *The Employment Situation: April 2008*, U.S. Department of Labor, Bureau of Labor Statistics, May 2, 2008, http://www.bls.gov/news.release/archives/empsit_05022008.pdf (accessed June 13, 2008)

TABLE 5.2

Unemployed persons by duration of unemployment, April 2008

[Numbers in thousands, seasonally adjusted]

Duration	Apr. 2008
Number of unemployed	
Less than 5 weeks	2,484
5 to 14 weeks	2,495
15 weeks and over	2,626
15 to 26 weeks	1,272
27 weeks and over	1,353
Average (mean) duration, in weeks	16.9
Median duration, in weeks	9.3
Percent distribution	
Total unemployed	100.0
Less than 5 weeks	32.7
5 to 14 weeks	32.8
15 weeks and over	34.5
15 to 26 weeks	16.7
27 weeks and over	17.8

Note: Updated population controls are introduced annually with the release of January data.

SOURCE: Adapted from "Table A-9. Unemployed Persons by Duration of Unemployment," in *The Employment Situation: April 2008*, U.S. Department of Labor, Bureau of Labor Statistics, May 2, 2008, http://www.bls.gov/news.release/archives/empsit_05022008.pdf (accessed June 13, 2008)

compares to 75% who believed that it was a "bad time to find a quality job." Optimism about job prospects gen-erally grew from late 2003 through January 2007 and then plummeted over the following sixteen months.

INDUSTRIES AND JOBS

The federal government broadly characterizes jobs as being in the goods-providing or services-providing categories. Goods-providing industries include businesses engaged in manufacturing, construction, mining, and natural resources. The service industry includes businesses whose main function is to provide a professional or trade service, rather than a product. Service-providing industries are extremely diverse and include businesses involved in retail and wholesale trade, professional and business services, education and health services, leisure and hospitality, government, and many other services.

Since the mid-twentieth century the service-providing industries have grown to dominate the U.S. economy. (See Figure 5.5.) In 1960 goods-producing industries employed around nineteen million people. This value rose and fell over time, and was at twenty-two million in 2007. By comparison, the number of people employed in service-providing industries skyrocketed from around thirty-five million in 1960 to more than 116 million in 2007.

Industry Supersectors

The government categorizes jobs by using the North American Industry Classification System (NAICS). Adopted in 1997, the NAICS was devised by the U.S. Economic Classification Policy Committee in conjunction with Statistics Canada and the Instituto Nacional de Estadística, Geografia e Informática of Mexico and is the standard classification system for businesses throughout North America. There are eleven major so-called super-sectors tracked by the BLS that encompass all private and public jobs within the United States and businesses owned by U.S.-based companies operating in other countries.

The eleven supersectors are:

- Construction
- Education and health services
- Financial activities
- Government
- Information
- Leisure and hospitality
- Manufacturing
- Natural resources and mining
- Other services
- Professional and business services
- Trade, transportation, and utilities

FIGURE 5.4

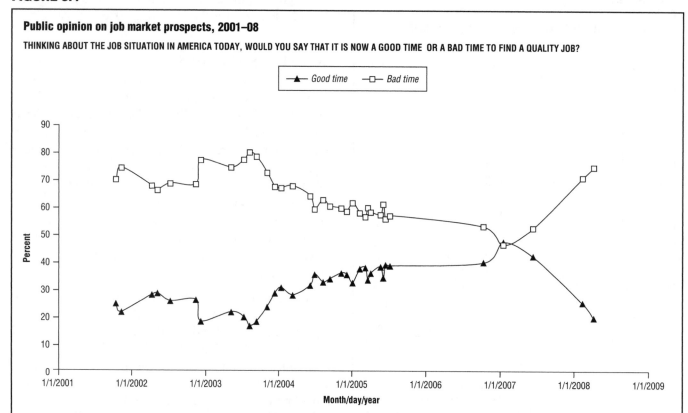

Public opinion on job market prospects, 2001–08

THINKING ABOUT THE JOB SITUATION IN AMERICA TODAY, WOULD YOU SAY THAT IT IS NOW A GOOD TIME OR A BAD TIME TO FIND A QUALITY JOB?

SOURCE: Adapted from "Thinking about the Job Situation in America Today, Would You Say That It Is Now a Good Time or a Bad Time to Find a Quality Job?" in *Gallup Brain: Create a Trend*, May 2008, http://brain.gallup.com/documents/trendQuestion.aspx?QUESTION=164428&Advanced=0& SearchConType=1&SearchTypeAll=thinking%20job%20situation%20american%20today%20say%20good%20time%20bad%20time%20find%20quality% 20job (accessed May 13, 2008). Copyright © 2008 by The Gallup Organization. Reproduced by permission of The Gallup Organization.

Virtually every job can be placed into one of these categories. It should be noted that industry tracking focuses on the core mission of the business rather than on the particular tasks performed by employees. For example, jobs in public schools and government-owned hospitals are considered part of the government sector rather than education and health services.

General industry information in the following sections was obtained from the BLS sources *Career Guide to Industries, 2008–09 Edition* (http://www.bls.gov/oco/cg/home .htm) and *Industry at a Glance* (http://stats.bls.gov/iag/ iaghome.htm), which profiles U.S. businesses.

CONSTRUCTION. The construction supersector includes all businesses that contribute to the development of land, roads, utilities, buildings and houses, and structures such as bridges and dams. Included are firms that build new projects and those that provide maintenance, repairs, and alterations to existing structures. For the most part, such enterprises are managed from a central location with work performed elsewhere. Construction employment often fluctuates throughout the year, especially in areas of the country that experience severe winter weather.

Robyn J. Richards of the BLS indicates in "Payroll Employment in 2007: Job Growth Slows" (*Monthly Labor Review*, vol. 131, no. 3, March 2008) that construction employment increased by 5.9% from 2004 to 2005 and by 2% from 2005 to 2006. (See Table 5.3.) The number of construction jobs fell by 3% in 2007. The largest losses were in residential building (down 9.2%) and residential specialty trade contractors (down 6.3%). These losses reflect the overall downturn in the housing industry.

This supersector employed nearly 7.3 million people in April 2008, down by 5% from the previous year. (See Table 5.4.) The construction unemployment rate in April 2008 was 11.1%, which was higher than the overall nonfarm unemployment rate of 5%. (See Table 5.5.) The BLS (December 18, 2007, http://www.bls.gov/oco/cg/cgs003.htm) predicts that construction employment will increase by 10.2% between 2006 and 2016. This is slightly lower than the 11% growth rate projected for industry overall.

EDUCATION AND HEALTH SERVICES. The education and health services supersector includes all instructional and training facilities, including private schools and universities, that are not funded by the government. Nongovernmental organizations that provide child day care, medical care, and social assistance are also included. Businesses of this type that are government owned (e.g., public schools and hospitals) are considered part of the government sector.

FIGURE 5.5

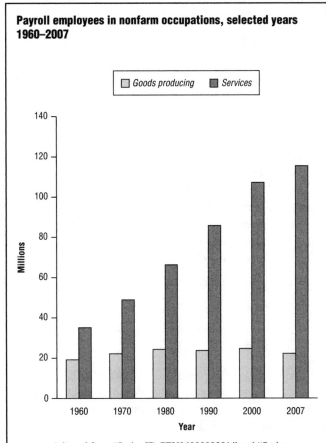

Payroll employees in nonfarm occupations, selected years 1960–2007

Millions

☐ Goods producing ■ Services

SOURCE: Adapted from "Series ID CEU0600000001," and "Series ID CEU0700000001," in *Employment, Hours, and Earnings from the Current Employment Statistics Survey (National)*, U.S. Department of Labor, Bureau of Labor Statistics, May 2008, http://www.bls.gov/webapps/legacy/cesbtab1.htm (accessed May 13, 2008)

Educational services employment increased by 2.2% from 2004 to 2005 and by 1.7% from 2005 to 2006. (See Table 5.3.) The number of educational jobs increased by 2.6% from 2006 to 2007. This sector employed more than three million people in April 2008, up by 3.4% from the previous year. (See Table 5.4.)

According to Richards, employment in health care and social services grew steadily between 2004 and 2007 by 2.6% to 3% per year. (See Table 5.3.) The greatest gains during 2007 were in home health care services (up 5.1%) and social assistance (up 4.3%). As of April 2008, more than 15.7 million people were employed in this sector, up 2.9% from the year before. (See Table 5.4.)

The unemployment rate for the education and health services supersector in April 2008 was 2.8%, lower than the overall nonfarm unemployment rate of 5%. (See Table 5.5.) The BLS (December 18, 2007, http://www.bls.gov/oco/cg/cg1008.htm) projects employment in this supersector from 2006 to 2016 as follows:

- Educational services—10.7% increase

- Health care services—21.7% increase

- Child day care services—33.7% increase

- Social assistance (excluding child day care)—54.8% increase

As noted earlier, the BLS predicts an 11% growth rate for industry overall.

FINANCIAL ACTIVITIES. The financial activities supersector includes the banking, insurance, and real estate industries, including businesses that, according to *Industry at a Glance*, facilitate "transactions involving the creation, liquidation, or change in ownership of financial assets."

TABLE 5.3

Payroll employment change from December to December 2004–07

	2004 to 2005		2005 to 2006		2006 to 2007	
	Level (thousands)	Percent	Level (thousands)	Percent	Level (thousands)	Percent
Construction	420	5.9	152	2	−232	−3.0
Educational services	60.5	2.2	47.4	1.7	74.3	2.6
Financial activities	166	2.1	106	1.3	−104	−1.2
Government	173	0.8	196	0.9	250	1.1
Health care & social services	368.4	2.6	420.4	2.9	453.1	3
Information	−26	−.8	−21	−.7	−15	−.5
Leisure & hospitality	275	2.2	381	3	347	2.6
Manufacturing	−82	−.6	−172	−1.2	−261	−1.9
Natural resources & mining	50	8.3	54	8.3	33	4.7
Other services	8	0.1	62	1.1	41	0.8
Professional & business services	677	4.1	547	3.2	307	1.7
Retail trade	231.5	1.5	55.9	0.4	75	0.5
Transportation & warehousing	102.3	2.4	125.3	2.8	14.9	0.3
Utilities	−4.8	−.9	−1.8	−.3	8	1.5
Wholesale trade	112.6	2	148	2.5	103.7	1.7

SOURCE: Adapted from Robyn J. Richards, "Table 1. Employees on Nonfarm Payrolls, by Industry, Seasonally Adjusted, 2004–07," in "Payroll Employment in 2007: Job Growth Slows," *Monthly Labor Review*, vol. 131, no. 3, March 2008, http://www.bls.gov/opub/mlr/2008/03/art2full.pdf (accessed April 29, 2008)

TABLE 5.4

Employees on nonfarm payrolls by job sector, April 2008

[Seasonally adjusted]

Job sector	Thousands of employees, April 2008	Change from April 2007	April 2007
Government	22,385	1.0%	22,161
Professional & business services	18,068	0.9%	17,903
Health & social services	15,734	2.9%	15,284.9
Retail trade	15,383	−0.7%	15,487
Leisure & hospitality	13,695	2.4%	13,375
Manufacturing	13,596	−2.3%	13,922
Financial activities	8,230	−1.0%	8,315
Construction	7,275	−5.0%	7,660
Wholesale trade	6,044	0.7%	5,999.8
Other services	5,527	0.7%	5,486
Transportation & warehousing	4,540	0.2%	4,532.8
Educational services	3,026	3.4%	2,926.3
Information	3,011	−0.8%	3,034
Natural resources & mining	747	4.0%	718
Utilities	557	1.1%	551.3
Total	**137,818**	**0.3%**	**137,356**

SOURCE: Adapted from "Table B-1. Employees on Nonfarm Payrolls by Industry Sector and Selected Industry Detail," in *The Employment Situation: April 2008*, U.S. Department of Labor, Bureau of Labor Statistics, May 2, 2008, http://www.bls.gov/news.release/archives/empsit_05022008.pdf (accessed May 13, 2008)

TABLE 5.5

Unemployment rates for various job sectors, April 2008

Industry and class of worker	Unemployment rates Apr. 2008
Total, 16 years and over*	4.8
Nonagricultural private wage and salary workers	5.0
Mining	3.6
Construction	11.1
Manufacturing	4.8
Durable goods	4.8
Nondurable goods	5.0
Wholesale and retail trade	4.5
Transportation and utilities	4.0
Information	4.4
Financial activities	3.4
Professional and business services	5.3
Education and health services	2.8
Leisure and hospitality	6.9
Other services	4.0
Agriculture and related private wage and salary workers	8.6
Government workers	1.7
Self employed and unpaid family workers	3.2

*Persons with no previous work experience are included in the unemployed total.
Note: Updated population controls are introduced annually with the release of January data.

SOURCE: Adapted from "Table A-11. Unemployed Persons by Industry and Class of Worker, Not Seasonally Adjusted," in *The Employment Situation: April 2008*, U.S. Department of Labor, Bureau of Labor Statistics, May 2, 2008, http://www.bls.gov/news.release/archives/empsit_05022008.pdf (accessed May 13, 2008)

The real estate sector includes businesses that manage properties for others, appraise real estate, and facilitate property buying, selling, and leasing.

Richards explains that financial activities employment increased by 2.1% from 2004 to 2005 and by 1.3% from 2005 to 2006. (See Table 5.3.) The number of jobs in this supersector fell by 1.2% from 2006 to 2007. The largest losses were in credit intermediation and related activities (down 3.5%) and monetary authorities—central bank (down 2.8%). These losses correspond with the economic problems associated with the subprime loan crisis.

The financial activities supersector employed over 8.2 million people in April 2008, down by 1% from the previous year. (See Table 5.4.) The unemployment rate in April 2008 was 3.4%, lower than the overall nonfarm unemployment rate of 5%. (See Table 5.5.) According to the BLS (December 18, 2007, http://www.bls.gov/oco/cg/cg1006.htm), employment projections for the financial industries between 2006 and 2016 are:

- Banking—4% increase

- Insurance—7.4% increase

- Securities, commodities, and other investments—46.1% increase

Projected growth rates in banking and insurance employment are lower than the overall expected average of 11%. The enormous increase projected for the investment job sector is tied to the aging U.S. population and associated management of retirement portfolios.

GOVERNMENT. The government sector encompasses all local, state, and federal government agencies as well as public schools and public hospitals. This includes law enforcement agencies, courts, and legislative assemblies, but, for the purposes of industry tracking, it does not include military personnel.

Richards notes that government employment increased by 0.8% to 1.1% per year between 2004 and 2007. (See Table 5.3.) Slight gains were spread across all three government sectors: local, state, and federal. The U.S. Postal Service reported the only employment losses (down 0.3 to 0.9% per year).

This supersector employed nearly 22.4 million people in April 2008, up 1% from the previous year. (See Table 5.4.) The government was the largest employer among all the supersectors in 2008. The government unemployment rate in April 2008 was 1.7%, which was much lower than the overall nonfarm unemployment rate of 5%. (See Table 5.5.) The BLS (December 18, 2007, http://www.bls.gov/oco/cg/cg10010.htm) predicts that federal government employment (excluding the U.S. Postal Service) will decrease by 4.6% between 2006 and 2016. Employment in state and local government (excluding hospitals and educational services) is expected to increase by 7.7% over the same period. These rates compare poorly to the 11% growth rate projected for industry overall.

INFORMATION. The production and distribution of information falls under the information supersector of the U.S. economy. This supersector includes book and software publishing, Internet service providers, and television broadcasting, as well as the motion picture and sound recording industries.

According to Richards, information employment decreased slightly by 0.5% to 0.8% per year between 2004 and 2007. (See Table 5.3.) Job losses in 2007 were most severe in non-Internet broadcasting (down 1.9%), non-Internet publishing (down 1.4%), and telecommunications (down 1.4%). By contrast, employment was up 3.4% for jobs in data processing, hosting, and related services and up 6.5% for other information services.

This supersector employed over three million people in April 2008, down by 0.8% from the previous year. (See Table 5.4.) The information unemployment rate in April 2008 was 4.4%, which was slightly lower than the overall nonfarm unemployment rate of 5%. (See Table 5.5.) According to the BLS (December 18, 2007, http://www.bls.gov/oco/cg/cg1005.htm), employment predictions from 2006 to 2016 for jobs within this supersector are:

- Broadcasting (excluding Internet)—9.4% increase

- Data Internet service providers, Web search portals, and data processing services—14% increase

- Motion picture and video industries—10.9% increase

- Publishing, except software—7.5% decrease

- Software publishing—32% increase

- Telecommunications—5% increase

LEISURE AND HOSPITALITY. The leisure and hospitality supersector contains businesses in the arts, entertainment, recreation, spectator sports, accommodation, and food service industries. This includes performance venues, gambling outlets, golf courses, amusement parks, arcades, hotels and other lodging sites, food service establishments, and privately funded exhibit spaces and historic sites.

Richards states that leisure and hospitality employment increased by 2.2% to 3% per year between 2004 and 2007. (See Table 5.3.) The largest gains in 2007 were in jobs in performing arts and spectator sports (up 6.5%) and museums, historical sites, zoos, and parks (up 4.1%). Employment at food services and drinking places was up by 3.1%.

This supersector employed nearly 13.7 million people in April 2008, up 2.4% from the previous year. (See Table 5.4.) The leisure and hospitality unemployment rate in April 2008 was 6.9%, which was higher than the overall nonfarm unemployment rate of 5%. (See Table 5.5.) The BLS (December 18, 2007, http://www.bls.gov/oco/cg/cg1009.htm) projects that employment in leisure and hospitality is anticipated to grow at or above the 11% growth rate for industry overall.

The projected employment growth rates for particular job sectors are:

- Arts, entertainment, and recreation—30.9% increase

- Food services and drinking places—10.9% increase

- Hotels and other accommodations—13.9% increase

MANUFACTURING. An organization is considered part of the manufacturing supersector if its primary business is to transform raw materials into new products through mechanical, physical, or chemical processes. Manufacturing covers many separate industries, including aerospace, apparel, computers, automobiles, pharmaceuticals, printing, steel, and textiles, among others, and provides products that contribute and support all other economic sectors.

According to Richards, manufacturing employment decreased by 0.6% from 2004 to 2005 and by 1.2% from 2005 to 2006. (See Table 5.3.) The number of manufacturing jobs fell by 1.9% from 2006 to 2007. The largest losses were in textile mills (down 11.3%), apparel (down 8.9%), and motor vehicles and parts (down 7.6%). Only two sectors—machinery (up 0.3%) and food manufacturing (up 0.9%)—posted job gains in 2007.

This supersector employed nearly 13.6 million people in April 2008, down by 2.3% from the previous year. (See Table 5.4.) The manufacturing unemployment rate in April 2008 was 4.8%, which was slightly lower than the overall nonfarm unemployment rate of 5%. (See Table 5.5.) According to the BLS (December 18, 2007, http://www.bls.gov/oco/cg/cg1002.htm), employment projections for various manufacturing sectors from 2006 to 2016 are as follows:

- Aerospace product and parts manufacturing—5.4% increase

- Chemical manufacturing, except pharmaceutical and medicine manufacturing—15.7% decrease

- Computer and electronic product manufacturing—12% decrease

- Food manufacturing—0.3% increase

- Machinery manufacturing—12.3% decrease

- Motor vehicle and parts manufacturing—14.3% decrease

- Pharmaceutical and medicine manufacturing—23.7% increase

- Printing—21.8% decrease

- Steel manufacturing—25.1% decrease

- Textile, textile product, and apparel manufacturing—35.4% decrease

Employment is expected to decrease dramatically or, at best, increase modestly for most sectors. The one exception is pharmaceutical and medicine manufacturing, which is expected to undergo tremendous job growth by 2016. This positive outlook is due in large part to the aging of the U.S. population and the associated need for more pharmaceutical goods.

NATURAL RESOURCES AND MINING. The natural resources and mining supersector includes all agriculture, forestry, fishing, hunting, and mining enterprises. Farms engaged in growing crops and raising animals are included in this sector, as are lumber and fishing operations, coal mining, petroleum and natural gas extraction, and other mining and quarrying activities.

Richards states that natural resources and mining employment (excluding farming) increased by 8.3% per year from 2004 to 2006 and by 4.7% from 2006 to 2007. (See Table 5.3.) Results were mixed across individual sectors during 2007—logging employment decreased by 2.9%, whereas oil and gas extraction and mining support activities were up 9.5% and 6.1%, respectively.

About 747,000 people were employed in natural resources and mining (excluding farming) in April 2008, a 4% increase from the previous year (See Table 5.4.) In April 2008 the unemployment rate for the mining industry was 3.6%, and for agricultural workers it was 8.6%. (See Table 5.5.) The overall nonfarm unemployment rate at that time was 5%.

The BLS (December 18, 2007, http://www.bls.gov/oco/cg/cg1001.htm) projects negative employment rates for industries in this supersector between 2006 and 2016. Mining employment is expected to fall by 1.6% and agriculture, forestry, and fishing employment by 8.6%. These rates compare poorly to the 11% growth rate expected for overall employment.

OTHER SERVICES. This supersector includes jobs such as repairing equipment and machinery, promoting or administering religious activities, operating dry cleaning and laundry services, conducting personal care, death care, and pet care services, and supplying photo processing services, temporary parking, and dating services. People who work in grant making and advocacy are also included in this category.

Employment in other services increased by 0.1% from 2004 to 2005 and by 1.1% from 2005 to 2006. (See Table 5.3.) From 2006 to 2007 employment increased by 0.8%.

This supersector employed more than 5.5 million people in April 2008, up by 0.7% from the previous year. (See Table 5.4.) The unemployment rate in April 2008 was 4%, which was lower than the overall nonfarm unemployment rate of 5%. (See Table 5.5.) The BLS (March 12, 2008, http://www.bls.gov/oco/cg/cgs054.htm#outlook) projects for only one job sector in other services: advocacy, grant making, and civic organizations. Employment in this sector is expected to grow by 12.8% between 2006 and 2016.

PROFESSIONAL AND BUSINESS SERVICES. Professional and business services include legal, accounting, architectural, engineering, advertising, marketing, translation, and veterinary services. This sector also includes those who manage companies and all the administrative support needed for a business to operate. In addition, security, surveillance, cleaning, and waste disposal services are tracked in this sector.

According to Richards, employment in this supersector increased by 4.1% from 2004 to 2005 and by 3.2% from 2005 to 2006. (See Table 5.3.) The number of jobs increased by 1.7% from 2006 to 2007. The largest gains were in management and technical consulting services (up 8.7%) and accounting and bookkeeping services (8.3% increase). The largest losses were in employment services (down 3.5%) and business support services (down 1.1%).

This supersector employed over eighteen million people in April 2008, up by 0.9% from the previous year (See Table 5.4.) The unemployment rate in April 2008 was 5.3%, only slightly higher than the overall nonfarm unemployment rate of 5%. (See Table 5.5.) The BLS (December 18, 2007, http://www.bls.gov/oco/cg/cg1007.htm) predicts that employment will increase for all job sectors in this supersector between 2006 and 2016:

- Advertising and public relations services—13.6% increase

- Computer systems design and related services—38.3% increase

- Employment services—18.9% increase

- Management, scientific, and technical consulting services—77.9% increase

- Scientific research and development services—9.4% increase

TRANSPORTATION, WAREHOUSING, AND UTILITIES. The transportation, warehousing, and utilities supersector includes businesses that transport passengers or cargo by air, rail, water, road, or pipeline. The sector also includes businesses that provide storage of goods and that support transportation activities. Also tracked in this sector are private enterprises that generate, transmit, or distribute utilities such as electric power, natural gas, and water.

Richards explains that transportation and warehousing employment increased between 0.3% and 2.8% per year from 2004 to 2007. The largest gains in 2007 were in scenic and sightseeing transportation (up 16.8%) and pipeline transportation (up 4.6%). The only losses were in truck transportation (down 1.8%) and couriers and messengers (down 0.4%). More than 4.5 million people were employed in transportation and warehousing in April 2008, up by 0.2% from the previous year. (See Table 5.4.)

Utilities employment decreased by 0.3% and 0.9% per year from 2004 to 2006, and increased by 1.5% from 2006 to 2007. (See Table 5.3.) Over 557,000 people were employed in this job sector in April 2008, up 1.1% from the previous year.

The unemployment rate for transportation and utilities in April 2008 was 4%, which was less than the overall nonfarm unemployment rate of 5%. (See Table 5.5.) The BLS (March 12, 2008, http://www.bls.gov/oco/cg/cg1004.htm) predicts that between 2006 and 2016 employment in air transportation will increase by 7.3% and in truck transportation and warehousing by 14.8%. For utilities employment, the BLS (March 4, 2008, http://www.bls.gov/oco/cg/cgs018.htm#outlook) projects that it will decrease by 5.7%. As noted earlier, the BLS projects an 11% growth rate over this period for industry overall.

WHOLESALE AND RETAIL TRADE. The wholesale and retail supersector encompasses private businesses that trade in products that they do not produce. Wholesalers buy large quantities of finished goods from manufacturers and sell the goods in smaller lots to businesses engaged in retail trade. Retailers then offer the goods for sale to consumers at an increased price, usually figured as a percentage of the wholesale cost. Goods in this sector are classified as durable (expected to last longer than three years) or nondurable (expected to need replacement within three years). Consumer goods in the durable sector include motor vehicles, furniture, household appliances, sporting goods, and toys. Durable goods are also sold to other businesses—for example, to the manufacturing or construction sector, including items such as machinery, equipment, metals, and construction materials. Examples of nondurable goods include paper products, drugs, apparel, groceries, books, flowers, and tobacco products. Even though the traditional notion of a retail establishment includes at least one store location, many retailers in the early twenty-first century operate via Internet and/or catalog sales without stores.

Wholesale trade employment increased by 1.7% to 2.5% per year from 2004 to 2007. (See Table 5.3.) Employment growth in 2007 was roughly even between durable and nondurable goods. More than six million people were employed in wholesale trade in April 2008, up 0.7% from the previous year. (See Table 5.4.)

Richards states that retail trade employment increased by 1.5% between 2004 and 2005 and then by only 0.4% to 0.5% per year over the following two years. (See Table 5.3.) The largest employment gains in 2007 were posted by health and personal care stores (up 2.7%) and sporting goods, hobby, book, and music stores (up 2%). The largest employment losses were in building material and garden supply stores (down 3.5%) and gasoline stations (down 1.4%). Nearly 15.4 million people were employed in retail

trade in April 2008, down 0.7% from the previous year. (See Table 5.4.)

The unemployment rate for the wholesale and retail trade supersector was 4.5% in April 2008, which was slightly below the overall nonfarm unemployment rate of 5%. (See Table 5.5.) The BLS (December 18, 2007, http://www.bls.gov/oco/cg/cg1003.htm) indicates that employment within the wholesale and retail trade between 2006 and 2016 is positive:

- Automobile dealers—11.3% increase

- Clothing, accessory, and general merchandise stores—7.5% increase

- Grocery stores—0.7% increase

- Wholesale trade—7.3% increase

These values are at or below the 11% increase projected by the BLS for employment growth overall over this period.

LABOR UNIONS

Even though many historians trace the origins of labor unions to medieval guilds (organized groups of tradespeople and artisans in the Middle Ages), the modern labor movement is more directly linked to the trade unions of the early Industrial Revolution, when working conditions in factories and mines were barely tolerable and employees began to join to demand reasonable work hours, safe conditions, and decent wages. Unions have often had tense relationships with both employers and government; at times they have been banned altogether, and the struggle between labor and employers has sometimes resulted in violence.

Labor unions have had a significant impact on the U.S. workforce and labor policy. Unions are often able to secure higher wages and increased benefits for their members. The BLS reports in *Union Members Summary* (January 25, 2008, http://www.bls.gov/news.release/union2.nr0.htm) that 15.7 million wage and salary workers were union members in 2007. This represented 12.1% of all wage and salary workers. The percentage was up slightly from 12% in 2006, but it was significantly lower than the rate of 20.1% reported in 1983 (the first year the BLS tracked union membership). According to the BLS, more than a third (35.9%) of government workers were unionized in 2007, compared to only 7.5% of private industry workers. Local governments have the most highly unionized employees, particularly teachers, police officers, and firefighters. The highest rates of union membership in the private industries are found in the transportation and utilities, telecommunications, and construction sectors.

Despite their successes on behalf of American workers, contemporary labor unions continue to face opposition from employers, and often from employees, who question whether the benefits of being associated with a union are worth the cost. Union members are required to go on strike when the union has an unresolved grievance against an employer, and striking union members receive only a fraction of their income in strike pay. Workers who are part of a union may also find themselves facing fines for not abiding by the union bylaws.

For employers, unions can pose other problems. Business operations can be greatly interrupted by unresolved negotiations, whether or not they lead to a strike. Furthermore, because of the increased expenses associated with employing union members, a company's products or services might become less competitively priced in the marketplace. If sales are lost to foreign or nonunion competitors, companies may be forced to lay off employees or even go out of business.

COMPENSATION OF AMERICAN WORKERS

Compensation has two components: pay and benefits. Pay includes wages (which is the term used primarily for pay made on an hourly, weekly, or monthly basis) and salaries (which is pay calculated yearly). Benefits provided by employers include paid time off from work, various insurance and retirement plans, and other programs designed to attract and keep employees.

Table 5.6 shows the wage and salary disbursements and supplements paid by employers in 2006, 2007, and calculated for 2008 based on first-quarter 2008 values. It is estimated that nearly $8.1 trillion was paid out in compensation in 2008, up from $7.4 trillion in 2006 and $7.9 trillion in 2007. In addition, more than $1.5 trillion in supplements was estimated to be contributed by

employers in 2008, primarily for employee pensions and insurance funds. In 2006 and 2007 these supplements totaled about $1.4 trillion and $1.5 trillion, respectively.

Income

In *Income, Poverty, and Health Insurance Coverage in the United States: 2006* (August 2007, http://www.census.gov/prod/2007pubs/p60-233.pdf), Carmen DeNavas-Walt, Bernadette D. Proctor, and Jessica Smith of the U.S. Census Bureau note that the median U.S. household income in 2006 was $48,201. Even though this value is higher than the median of $47,845 reported in 2005, there is actually no difference when inflation is considered.

According to DeNavas-Walt, Proctor, and Smith, incomes differed by householder characteristics, such as age, education, work experience, and race or ethnic origin. For example, the median annual income of householders aged fifteen to twenty-four years in 2006 was $30,937, compared to $64,874 for those aged forty-five to fifty-four years. White non-Hispanic householders had a median annual income of $52,423 in 2006. This was less than the median income of Asian householders ($64,238) but greater than that of African-American householders ($31,969).

Benefits

To attract and keep the best employees and earn a level of loyalty from them, many U.S. employers offer benefits and incentives. As of March 2007, a large majority of employees in private industry had access to unpaid family leave (83%) and paid holidays and vacations (77%). (See Table 5.7.) These were the most commonly offered benefits. Other benefits available to more than two-thirds of the workforce were medical care plans (71%), paid jury duty leave (71%), paid funeral leave

TABLE 5.6

Personal income, 2006–first quarter 2008

[Billions of dollars]

| | 2006 | 2007 | Seasonally adjusted at annual rates | | | | | |
| | | | 2006 | 2007 | | | | 2008 |
			IV	I	II	III	IV	I
Personal income	10,983.4	11,659.5	11,200.2	11,469.2	11,577.3	11,735.0	1,856.6	11,986.2
Compensation of employees, received	7,440.8	7,851.7	7,599.9	7,764.9	8701.9	7,882.7	7,957.2	8,064.9
Wage and salary disbursements	6,018.2	6,359.6	6,153.0	6,294.4	3618.9	6,382.7	6,442.4	6,526.8
Private industries	4,997.6	5,291.8	5,115.8	5,242.7	2556.9	5,309.8	5,357.7	5,422.6
Goods-producing industries	1,166.8	1,214.5	1,191.4	1,208.9	1,212.6	1,217.5	1,219.0	1,224.0
Manufacturing	731.0	754.5	743.3	755.4	754.1	754.7	753.6	67.95
Services-producing industries	3,830.8	4,077.3	3,924.4	4,033.9	4,044.3	4,092.3	4,138.7	4,198.6
Trade, transportation, and utilities	985.1	1,031.5	1,002.2	1,020.0	1,033.7	1,033.3	1,093.0	1,048.4
Other services-producing industries	2,845.7	3,045.8	2,922.2	3,013.8	3,010.6	3,059.0	3,099.7	3,150.2
Government	1,020.6	1,067.8	1,037.2	1,051.7	016,1.9	1,072.9	1,084.7	1,104.1
Supplements to wages and salaries	1,422.6	1,492.1	1,446.9	1,470.5	4183.0	1,500.0	1,514.8	1,538.1
Employer contributions for employee pension and insurances	970.7	1,016.8	986.7	999.2	010.9	1,022.7	1,034.3	1,048.3
Employer contributions for government social insurances	451.8	475.3	460.2	471.3	472.1	477.3	480.5	489.8

SOURCE: Adapted from "Table2. Personal Income and Its Disposition (Years and Quarters)," in *Personal Income and Outlays: March 2008*, U.S. Department of Commerce, Bureau of Economic Analysis, May 1,2008, http://www.bea.gov/newsreleases/national/pi/2008/pdf/pi0308.pdf (accessed May14, 2008)

TABLE 5.7

Percentage of private-industry workers with access to workplace benefits, March 2007

All workers	
Unpaid family leave	83
Paid holidays	77
Paid vacations	77
Medical care plans	71
Paid jury duty leave	71
Paid funeral leave	69
Prescription drug plan	68
Retirement benefits	61
Life insurance	58
Paid sick leave	57
Paid military leave	49
Work-related education assistance	49
Dental care plans	48
Employee assistance programs	42
Short-term disability	39
Paid personal leave	38
Health care reimbursement accounts	33
Long-term disability	31
Dependent care reimbursement accounts	31
Vision care plans	29
Wellness programs	25
Job-related travel accident insurance	22
Assistance for child care	15
Fitness centers	13
Long term care insurance	12
Adoption assistance	11
Paid family leave	8
Health savings accounts	8
Flexible workplace	5
Subsidized commuting	5
Employer-provided home PC	2

SOURCE: Adapted from "Table 5. Healthcare Benefits," "Table 6. Selected Health Benefits," "Table 13. Insurance Benefits," "Table 19. Leave Benefits," "Table 23. Quality of Life Benefits," "Table 24. Pretax Benefits," and "Table 25. Selected Benefits," in *National Compensation Survey: Employee Benefits in Private Industry in the United States, March 2007 (Summary 07–05)*, U.S. Department of Labor, Bureau of Labor Statistics, August 2007, http://www.bls.gov/ncs/ebs/sp/ebsm0006.pdf (accessed May 14, 2008)

(69%), and prescription drug plans (68%). More than half of employees also had access to retirement benefits, life insurance, and paid sick leave. Many other benefits were offered less frequently.

In general, employees working for larger companies— those with more than one hundred employees—and union members had the highest access to company benefits.

MEDICAL INSURANCE. Typically, the total cost of monthly health insurance coverage is split between employers and employees, with employers paying the largest portion. As shown in Figure 3.8 in Chapter 3, the price of medical care grew at a faster rate between 1998 and 2007 than the overall rate for the urban Consumer Price Index. Because of rising health-care costs, medical insurance has become a costly benefit for both employers and employees.

The BLS estimates that rising expenses for health insurance premiums are depressing wages. In other words, employers are paying lower wages than they otherwise would, because they are devoting so much money to

FIGURE 5.6

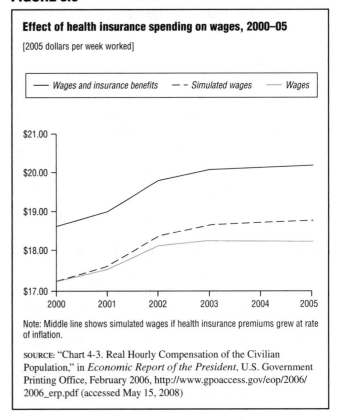

Effect of health insurance spending on wages, 2000–05

[2005 dollars per week worked]

— Wages and insurance benefits   – – Simulated wages   — Wages

Note: Middle line shows simulated wages if health insurance premiums grew at rate of inflation.

SOURCE: "Chart 4-3. Real Hourly Compensation of the Civilian Population," in *Economic Report of the President*, U.S. Government Printing Office, February 2006, http://www.gpoaccess.gov/eop/2006/2006_erp.pdf (accessed May 15, 2008)

providing health-care coverage. Paid hourly wages have remained relatively flat since 2002, whereas the price of insurance benefits has increased. (See Figure 5.6.) As a result, a disparity has developed between actual wages and the wages that could have been paid if health insurance premiums had grown at the same rate as inflation during this period.

NONTRADITIONAL WORK ARRANGEMENTS
Working from Home

The BLS states in *Work at Home Summary* (September 22, 2005, http://www.bls.gov/news.release/homey.nr0.htm) that in May 2004, 20.7 million people worked from home at least once per week. This represented approximately 15% of the total nonagricultural workforce, a value virtually unchanged from May 2001. The data were collected as part of a special supplement to the monthly Current Population Survey. Nearly two-thirds of the at-home workers in 2004 were wage and salary earners. The remainder were self-employed.

With technological advances such as Internet access, e-mail, and teleconferencing, working at home has become a viable option for many types of jobs. As employees conduct much of their daily work from home offices, employers are able to save on operating costs. Many employers will pay for computers, additional telephone lines, and even utilities to allow their employees to work from home offices. This allows them to reduce office space, one of the higher costs for an employer, especially in large metropolitan markets.

Self-Employment

Self-employed workers are not on the payroll of a company. They may own or operate small businesses or work under contract arrangements with companies. According to the BLS (April 14, 2008, http://www.bls.gov/cps/cpsaat12.pdf), 856,000 agricultural workers were self-employed in 2007, compared to approximately 1.2 million wage and salary workers in that field. Nearly 9.7 million people were self-employed in 2007 in nonagricultural industries, compared to 132.4 million wage and salary workers in that field.

FOREIGN WORKERS IN THE UNITED STATES

Relatively high wages and favorable working conditions have attracted workers from around the world to the United States. There are two broad categories of foreign workers: those who have entered the country legally with the proper paperwork to pursue work and those who have entered illegally. Legal workers are tracked by the U.S. Citizenship and Immigration Service (USCIS), formerly the U.S. Immigration and Naturalization Service.

Legal Foreign Workers

The U.S. Department of Labor (January 6, 2006, http://www.doleta.gov/Business/gw/guestwkr/) issues a limited number of certifications to foreign workers to work in the United States on a temporary or permanent basis under the following programs:

- Permanent Labor Certification—allows a foreign worker to work permanently in the United States

- H-1B Specialty (Professional) Workers—temporary certification for workers in occupations requiring highly specialized knowledge with at least a bachelor's degree or equivalent

- H-2A Temporary Labor Certification (Seasonal Agricultural)—for workers engaged in agricultural labor or services of a temporary or seasonal nature working for employers anticipating a shortage of U.S. workers

- H-2B Temporary Labor Certification (Nonagricultural)— for nonagricultural laborers working for employers anticipating a shortage of U.S. workers; the need can be a one-time occurrence, seasonal, peak load, or intermittent

- D-1 Crewmembers Certification—for longshoremen hired to work at U.S. ports; there are many restrictions, one of which is that there cannot be a strike or lockout ongoing that keeps U.S. longshoremen from working

According to the Department of Labor, "certification may be obtained in cases where it can be demonstrated that there are insufficient qualified U.S. workers avail-

able and willing to perform the work at wages that meet or exceed the prevailing wage paid for that occupation in the area of intended employment."

The U.S. Department of Homeland Security's Office of Immigration Statistics (OIS) tracks the number of foreign workers entering the United States and publishes related data in annual reports. The most recent report available on nonimmigrant (temporary) foreign workers is *Temporary Admissions of Nonimmigrants to the United States: 2006* (July 2007 (http://www.dhs.gov/xlibrary/assets/statistics/publications/NI_FR_2006_508_final.pdf). The OIS notes that approximately 821,000 temporary workers and trainees were admitted into the United States in 2006. Legal permanent residents are foreigners who have obtained "green cards" and have been granted permanent residency in the United States. According to the OIS, in *U.S. Legal Permanent Residents: 2007* (March 2008, http://www.dhs.gov/xlibrary/assets/statistics/publications/LPR_FR_2007.pdf), close to 162,000 foreigners were granted employment-based legal permanent residency during fiscal year 2007 (October 1, 2006 to September 30, 2007).

Temporary foreign workers maintain the citizenship of their native countries, and after fulfilling their contracts with U.S. employers they typically return to their own countries. Immigrant workers are people who have come to the United States through legal channels and intend to become citizens. They obtain jobs while waiting for their naturalization (the process of becoming a U.S. citizen) to be finalized.

Illegal Foreign Workers

The issue of illegal immigration has become a heated topic. Much of the debate centers on the economic effect of undocumented workers—foreign workers who have entered the United States illegally. Some people claim that undocumented workers take jobs away from Americans and place a large burden on government-provided social programs. Others believe that undocumented workers are willing to take jobs that Americans do not want—low paying, labor-intensive jobs with no benefits and little to no chance for advancement.

Jeffrey M. Jones of the Gallup Organization explains in *Hispanics, Whites, Blacks Not in Complete Agreement on Illegal Immigration* (July 10, 2006, http://www.gallup.com/poll/23620/Hispanics-Whites-Blacks-Complete-Agreement-Illegal-Immigration.aspx) that in 2006 nearly three-fourths (74%) of Americans believed illegal immigrants "mostly take low-paying jobs Americans don't want." Only 17% said illegal immigrants "mostly take jobs that American workers want."

Employers are required by law to verify that new hires are U.S. citizens or foreigners with legal working status who are eligible to work in the United States. Job applicants have to show identification and documentation, including a Social Security card. However, the authenticity of these documents cannot be verified immediately. Thus, well-meaning businesses may unknowingly hire and train illegal workers who use fake documentation to obtain jobs. According to the article "Jobs and Illegal Immigrants" (*Christian Science Monitor*, December 4, 2003), as of December 2003 the Social Security Administration had $374 billion in funds that could not be matched to valid Social Security numbers. It is believed that much of the money was paid into the system by illegal workers using fake Social Security numbers.

There is little doubt that some businesses purposely hire illegal workers or at least ignore questionable paperwork to get inexpensive labor. The article "Many Illegal Immigrants Have Jobs in U.S. before Crossing Border" (Associated Press, April 16, 2006) reports that there is "an underground employment network" in the United States that encourages and facilitates the employment of illegal immigrants from Mexico and Central and South America. The article notes that lax enforcement of laws prohibiting the hiring of illegal workers allows the network to flourish. Many critics maintain that the federal government's focus on terrorism and national security has diminished attention on issues related to undocumented workers. Others believe that businesses willing to hire the workers are to blame. Like many factors in the U.S. economy, the issue of undocumented workers is driven by supply and demand factors. As one analyst notes in the article, "It continues to become clear who controls immigration: It's not governments, but rather the market."

POLITICAL DEBATE AND PUBLIC PROTEST. The Department of Homeland Security indicates in *Estimates of the Unauthorized Immigrant Population Residing in the United States, January 2006* (August 2007, http://www.dhs.gov/xlibrary/assets/statistics/publications/ill_pe_2006.pdf) that there were around 11.6 million illegal immigrants in the United States at the beginning of 2006. Illegal immigration has become a politically charged and divisive issue. In late 2005 the U.S. House of Representatives and the U.S. Senate began drafting immigration reform bills designed to deal with the problem. Both bodies called for tighter border security. Some politicians advocated allowing many illegal immigrants already in the country the opportunity to obtain U.S. citizenship under certain conditions. This so-called amnesty provision has been harshly criticized, but it has been advocated by President George W. Bush (1946–).

In October 2007 Bush signed into law a bill calling for the building of a seven-hundred-mile fence along the U.S.-Mexican border. As of July 2008, more comprehensive legislation dealing with illegal immigration issues had not been finalized.

U.S. JOBS GOING TO FOREIGN COUNTRIES

One consequence of the globalization of U.S. business has been offshoring (the transfer of jobs from the United States to other countries). This can occur when an entire business establishment, such as a factory or service center, is relocated to another nation or when certain jobs within a business are transferred to a foreign company. The latter is also an example of outsourcing (a business practice in which certain tasks within a company are contracted out to another firm; outsourcing may or may not involve sending work to another country). During the 1990s outsourcing became a popular means of reducing costs for some companies. Noncore functions, such as payroll management or housekeeping, are common examples in which outsourcing can be cost effective. However, offshoring is controversial because jobs move outside of the United States, primarily to developing countries, where labor costs are much cheaper.

Critics say that offshoring harms the U.S. economy by putting Americans out of work. Others claim that relocation of some operations to foreign countries has a limited effect on domestic employment. They argue that offshoring leads to lower prices for consumer and investment goods, with the ultimate effect of raising real wages (wages that are adjusted for changes in the price of consumer goods) and living standards in the United States.

In 2004 the BLS published data on the relationship between extended mass layoffs and overseas job relocations. An extended mass layoff is defined as an event in which at least fifty initial claims for unemployment benefits are filed against an establishment during a five-week period. In the press release "Extended Mass Layoffs Associated with Domestic and Overseas Relocations, First Quarter 2004 Summary" (June 10, 2004, http://www.bls.gov/news.release/reloc.nr0.htm), the BLS notes that the layoffs of 4,633 workers during the first quarter of 2004 were associated with job relocations to other countries. This number represents just 1.9% of the total of 239,361 private-sector nonfarm workers who were separated from their jobs for at least thirty-one days during the quarter. Overseas relocations within the same company accounted for 2,976 lost jobs, and 1,657 jobs were lost to overseas workers employed by different companies.

The BLS states in *Extended Mass Layoffs in 2006* (April 2008, http://www.bls.gov/mls/mlsreport1004.pdf) that more than 936,000 workers in private nonfarm jobs were subjected to mass layoffs in 4,885 layoff events during 2006. There were 252 layoff events due to movement of work to other locations within the United States or out of the country. Another 349 work relocations were associated with these layoff events. (Note that multiple work relocations can be associated with one layoff event.) According to the BLS, employers were able to provide detailed information on 232 of these work relocations.

In nearly two-thirds (64%) of reported cases domestic relocation (relocation within the United States) was cited as the reason for the mass layoff.

In the press release "Fortune 500 Reap Early Cost Benefits from Offshoring Initiatives" (December 10, 2004, http://www.fuqua.duke.edu/admin/extaff/news/fortune_offshore_dec_2004.htm), Duke University's Fuqua School of Business in conjunction with Archstone Consulting report that offshoring is cost effective for large U.S. companies. Researchers studied the offshoring experiences of ninety large companies with average annual revenues of $21 billion. A large majority (72%) of offshore implementations had met or bettered expected costs savings. As a result, companies indicated great willingness to pursue additional offshoring opportunities. The functions most often offshored were information technology (66%), finance and accounting (60%), engineering services (44%), and research (32%). Eighty percent of offshored operations had been transferred to India. A combination of relatively low costs and many well-educated workers who speak English has made India a popular location to offshore work.

The article "Don't Blame Trade for U.S. Job Losses" (*McKinsey Quarterly*, February 2005) estimates that approximately 274,000 software and business-process jobs were moved from the United States to India between 2000 and 2003. The article notes that "although the costs were substantial for the displaced employees, a job shift of this size is small compared with the 2.1 million service jobs created every year during the 1990s and minor compared even with the net annual job increase of about 327,000 from 2000 to 2003."

PROTECTING AMERICAN WORKERS

The United States has enacted comprehensive labor laws to ensure that workplaces are operated safely and that workers are treated fairly. These include relatively strict laws to protect American workers from discrimination on the basis of gender, age, race, ethnicity, religion, sexual orientation, and other factors.

The Fair Labor Standards Act

The Fair Labor Standards Act (FLSA) offers protection for full- and part-time workers in private and government jobs, covering minimum wages, overtime pay, employer record keeping, and child labor. The FLSA also established the standard forty-hour workweek. Local fire and police employees are typically not covered by the FLSA. It was passed in 1938 and has been amended many times over the years.

THE MINIMUM WAGE. The FLSA established a federal hourly minimum wage that U.S. employers must honor for many nonsupervisory, nonfarm, private-sector, and government employees. Most states have their own

minimum wage as well. In states with minimum wages that differ from the federal minimum wage, the employer must pay the higher of the two. As of July 2008, the federal minimum wage was $6.55 per hour. Figure 5.7 shows previous minimum wages dating back to 1990 and the increase planned in 2009.

There are many exceptions to the minimum wage law. Employers may apply for subminimum wage certificates for disabled workers, full-time students, workers under age twenty who are in their first ninety days of employment, workers who receive tips, and student-learners (usually high school students). Lawmakers reason that exempting employers from paying the minimum wage to certain workers (e.g., the disabled and students) encourages them to hire more of those workers who may otherwise be at a disadvantage. Employers may not, however, displace other workers to hire those subject to the subminimum wage. Other workers exempt from the minimum wage include certain professional and administrative employees, certain workers in the fishing industry, certain seasonal employees, babysitters, and certain farm workers.

The BLS tracks the number of hourly wage earners in the United States based on the results of the Current Population Survey. In *Characteristics of Minimum Wage Workers: 2007* (March 25, 2008, http://www.bls.gov/cps/minwage2007.htm), the BLS indicates that there were 267,000 workers paid the federal minimum wage during 2007. Nearly 1.5 million workers earned less than the minimum wage. The total number of workers earning minimum wage or less accounted for 2.3% of the 75.9 million people earning hourly wages that year.

Women, people under age twenty-five, part-time workers, and those without a college degree were the groups most likely to earn the minimum wage or less in 2007. Jobs in the service sector—particularly those related to food service—had the highest rate (about 7% of the total) of workers making the federal minimum wage. In some cases, however, those who work in food and beverage service jobs also earn tips, which supplement their hourly wages.

The minimum wage policy is not without controversy. Advocates for low-income workers believe the minimum wage should be increased regularly to keep up with the effects of inflation. Opponents of the minimum wage assert that wage levels should be determined by market conditions and supply and demand factors. They argue that forcing businesses to pay a higher minimum wage discourages the hiring of low-income workers.

CHILD LABOR LAWS. In an agricultural economy, children typically begin working on the family farm or are apprenticed out to other farms at early ages. During the colonial period in North America, children as young

FIGURE 5.7

Federal minimum wage, 1990–2009

[Effective July 24, 2009]

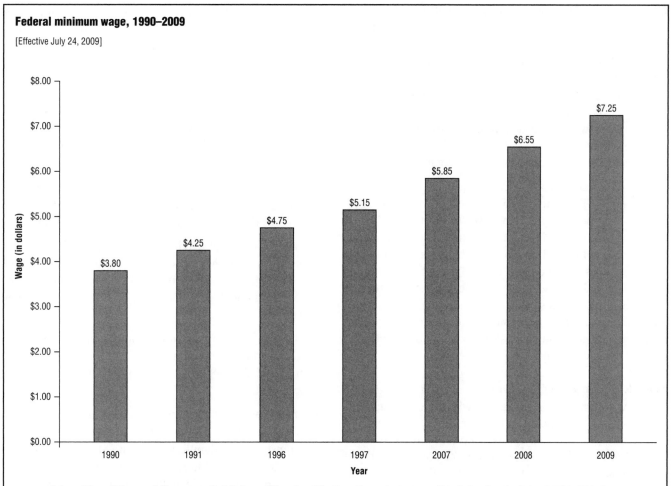

SOURCE: Adapted from "History of Changes to the Minimum Wage Law," in *Compliance Assistance—Fair Labor Standards Act (FLSA)*, U.S. Department of Labor, April 10, 2008, http://www.dol.gov/esa/minwage/coverage.htm (accessed April 10, 2008)

as three whose parents could not afford to support them were apprenticed out to work. This was the case in the United States until the early nineteenth century, when the Industrial Revolution permanently changed the U.S. economy and way of life. Because they were considered easier to manage, less likely to unionize, and could be paid far less than adults, children became desirable as workers in the industrial economy, particularly in factories, mines, cotton fields, and the textile industry.

With no laws to regulate children's work, and no mandatory school attendance, the use of children as a cheap labor source became a widely accepted practice. Children as young as six worked thirteen-hour days, six days per week. They frequently suffered from hunger and malnutrition, work-related injuries, and diseases. Even though social reformers began to campaign for child labor laws in the mid-nineteenth century, and the National Child Labor Committee was formed in 1904, it was not until the passage of the FLSA in 1938 that child labor in the United States was finally regulated by the federal government.

The FLSA prohibits employers from hiring children under the age of sixteen, although fourteen- and fifteen-year-olds are allowed to work at nonmining, nonmanufacturing jobs as long as the hours worked do not interfere with time spent in school and are not hazardous to the young person's health and well-being. The FLSA also prohibits anyone under age eighteen from working at jobs considered dangerous. Babysitting, delivering newspapers, and working in the entertainment industry are all specifically exempted from the provisions of the FLSA, and children of migrant farm workers often are not protected by the legislation because of the transient nature of their family's life.

Occupational Safety and Health Administration

The Occupational Safety and Health Administration (OSHA) was formed in 1971 to institute and monitor safety regulations in the workplace. Focusing mainly on industries with high rates of work-related injuries and illnesses, OSHA works directly with employers and employees to ensure that health and safety standards are followed.

According to the BLS, in the press release "National Census of Fatal Occupational Injuries in 2006" (August 9, 2007, http://www.bls.gov/news.release/pdf/cfoi.pdf), there were 5,703 fatal work injuries during 2006, a slight decrease from the 5,734 fatalities reported in 2005. The most frequent events blamed for the deaths were highway incidents, falls, being struck by objects, and workplace homicides. The industries with the highest number of fatal work injuries were construction; transportation and warehousing; mining; agriculture, forestry, fishing, and hunting; professional and business services; and manufacturing.

In the press release "Workplace Injuries and Illnesses in 2006" (October 16, 2007, http://www.bls.gov/news.release/pdf/osh.pdf), the BLS reports that there were 4.1 million nonfatal work injuries and illnesses in the private sector in 2006, down slightly from 4.2 million in 2005. Illnesses accounted for 228,000 of the cases in 2006. The industry sectors with the largest number of nonfatal work injuries were manufacturing, health care and social assistance, professional and business services, retail trade, leisure and hospitality, construction, and transportation and warehousing.

Whistleblower Protection Laws

A whistleblower is a person who reports unlawful activity in the workplace to the authorities. At one time whistleblowers were subject to demotion, threats, harassment, and firing if their reports were discovered by their employers, who wanted to prevent public scandals and avoid facing criminal and civil charges. However, in 1989 the federal government passed the Whistleblower Protection Act to protect employees who report evidence of criminal wrongdoing in the workplace. In May 2002 President Bush signed the Notification and Federal Employee Antidiscrimination and Retaliation Act, which strengthened protections for whistleblowers by requiring federal agencies to be accountable for violations of whistleblower laws. Some states have their own additional whistleblower protection laws.

Equal Employment Opportunity Commission

The Equal Employment Opportunity Commission (EEOC) enforces federal workplace discrimination laws. It is composed of a general counsel and five commissioners who are appointed by the U.S. president and approved by the Senate. Besides its enforcement role, the EEOC has a training institute to educate employers on workplace discrimination and help them comply with the laws. According to the EEOC (January 15, 1997, http://www.eeoc.gov/policy/laws.html), it enforces six federal antidiscrimination laws:

- The Equal Pay Act of 1963, which protects men and women who perform approximately equal work in the same workplace from gender-based wage discrimination

- Title VII of the Civil Rights Act of 1964, which prohibits employment discrimination based on race, color, religion, sex, or national origin, including sexual harassment and discrimination against pregnant women

- The Age Discrimination in Employment Act of 1967, which protects individuals who are forty years of age or older; this act applies to both employees and job applicants

- Titles I and V of the Americans with Disabilities Act of 1990, which prohibit employment discrimination against qualified individuals with disabilities in the private sector and in state and local governments (the act applies to people with both physical and mental impairments)

- Sections 501 and 505 of the Rehabilitation Act of 1973, which prohibit discrimination against qualified individuals with disabilities who work in the federal government

- The Civil Rights Act of 1991, which, among other things, provides monetary damages in cases of intentional employment discrimination

CHAPTER 6
U.S. BUSINESSES

The chief business of the American people is business.

—President Calvin Coolidge, 1925

Businesses are diverse in the United States. They range in size from the huge multinational corporation employing thousands of people to the self-employed individual. They include large and small businesses, home-based businesses, Internet-based businesses, and corporate and family farms. Businesses are a vital part of the American economic engine. They supply goods and services to the world. The consumption of business output is the primary driver behind the growth of the nation's gross domestic product (GDP; the total market value of final goods and services produced within an economy in a given year). Businesses also provide opportunities for employment, wealth-building, and investment.

Capitalism encourages business growth. However, businesses can become so large and powerful that they trigger concern about the lack of competition within an industry. Corporate fraud and accounting scandals have eroded the public's trust in the integrity of "big business." American society also has certain expectations regarding the effects of business on the environment, local development, and public welfare and well-being.

HISTORICAL DEVELOPMENTS

When the first colonists arrived in North America, they traded in furs and food with the native peoples and exchanged North American resources for goods from other countries. The primary industries were agriculture, timber harvesting, and shipbuilding. Manufacturing gradually grew in importance as the United States became an independent country and underwent the Industrial Revolution. Agriculture accounted for 22% of the national income in 1869. (See Figure 1.2 in Chapter 1.) Other major sectors were trade and manufacturing (15% each), services (14%), and finance, insurance, and real estate

(12%). The U.S. Census Bureau reports in *Historical Statistics of the United States, Colonial Times to 1970, Bicentennial Edition, Part 1* (September 1975, http://www2.census .gov/prod2/statcomp/documents/CT1970p1-07.pdf) that by 1929 the contribution of agriculture to the national income had shrunk to only 12%, whereas manufacturing had grown to 22%. By the mid-1950s agriculture accounted for only 5% of the national income, whereas manufacturing had grown to 31%. (See Figure 1.8 in Chapter 1.)

Over the next half-century, the United States underwent a gradual change from dependence on manufacturing as its primary business to reliance on service industries. Services accounted for only 10% of national income in the mid-1950s. (See Figure 1.8 in Chapter 1.) By the beginning of the twenty-first century, service industries dominated the American business world.

LEGAL STRUCTURES OF BUSINESSES

For legal and tax purposes, all businesses must be structured as one of several legally defined forms: sole proprietorships, business partnerships, corporations, or limited liability companies. Each offers both advantages and disadvantages to the business owner.

Sole Proprietorships

In a sole proprietorship one person owns and operates the whole business. Because the business and its owner are considered a single entity under the law, the owner assumes all the risk but also reaps all the benefits of the business. If the business fails, the sole proprietor may have to cover the losses from his or her personal assets, but if the business succeeds, he or she keeps all the profits. Sole proprietors can pay lower taxes than those who head corporations or other forms of small businesses. Still, because almost all credit decisions are based on the owner's assets and credit history, it is often difficult for businesses set up under this structure to borrow enough money to expand as rapidly as other kinds of businesses.

Business Partnerships

A business partnership has two or more co-owners. As in a sole proprietorship, members of a business partnership are legally recognized as one and the same with their company, meaning that they are personally responsible for the company's debts and other liabilities. Most partnerships start with the partners signing agreements that specify their duties in the business. Many states allow for silent partners, who invest start-up capital but have little role in the company's day-to-day affairs. (Start-up capital is the money used to start a new business.) A significant drawback of this form of business is that each of the partners is responsible for every other partner's actions. If a partner loses or steals money from the company, the other partners will have a legal responsibility to pay that debt.

There are three kinds of business partnerships: A general partnership is the simplest form, in which profits and liability are equally divided among partners or divided according to the terms of the signed agreement; a limited partnership allows partners to have limited liability for the company but also limited decision-making rights; and a joint venture, while similar legally to a general partnership, is used only for single projects or short periods of time.

Corporations

A corporation is an entity recognized by the state and federal government as entirely separate from its owner or owners. As such, a corporation can be taxed and sued, and it can enter into contractual agreements. Because it is an individual legal entity, a corporation allows its owners to have less personal liability for debts and lawsuits than a sole proprietorship or partnership. Owners of corporations are considered shareholders, and they may elect a board of directors to oversee management of the company.

Even though corporations are commonly thought of as large companies with hundreds or thousands of employees and publicly traded stock, this is not always the case. Owners of small businesses frequently incorporate as their business expands. All corporate owners must file "articles of incorporation" with their state government. For smaller businesses these forms are simple to fill out and file. One option is to file with the Internal Revenue Service as a subchapter S corporation. In an S corporation the owner must pay him- or herself wages like any other employee, but the structure also offers substantial tax flexibility. All corporations that are publicly traded have C corporation status. This means they have nearly unrestricted ownership and they are subject to corporate taxes, paying at both the corporate and stockholder levels.

Limited Liability Company

The limited liability company is a combination of a corporation and a partnership in which the owners (or shareholders) have less personal liability for the company's debts and legal issues and have the benefit of simpler tax filings and more control over management issues.

THE ROLE OF SMALL BUSINESS IN A COMPLEX ECONOMY

Many people perceive the U.S. economy as being dominated by large businesses, such as McDonald's and Microsoft. Even though it is true that many of the world's largest companies are headquartered in the United States, small businesses exert enormous influence on the U.S. economy.

The Small Business Administration (SBA) is a federal agency created in 1953 with the passage of the Small Business Act. The SBA's purpose is to support small businesses by offering financial and counseling assistance and ensuring that small businesses can compete against large companies in receiving government contracts.

The size of what is considered a small business varies by industry, and official size standards are determined by the SBA's Office of Size Standards, which issues standards according to a business's number of employees or its average annual receipts. However, the more generally accepted definition of a small business is one that employs fewer than five hundred people at any one time. Of the 5,983,546 firms in business in 2005, 5,966,069 had less than 500 employees. (See Table 6.1.) These small businesses employed 6.4 million of the nearly 7.5 million workers employed by businesses. In addition, small businesses accounted for $2 trillion in payroll in 2005 out of nearly $4.5 trillion in total business payrolls. As such, small businesses accounted for 99.7% of the number of business firms, 50.4% of total business employment, and 44.9% of total business annual payroll. (See Figure 6.1.)

Of the nearly 6 million small businesses in operation in 2005, the vast majority (5.4 million, or 89.5%) were firms that employed less than twenty people each. (See Table 6.2.) Close to 3.7 million (61.5%) of all small business firms had four or less employees each.

Small business employment is not evenly distributed among all industry sectors. The construction industry accounted for the largest percentage (86.1%) of small business employment in 2005. (See Table 6.3.) In other words, 86.1% of people employed in construction in 2005 worked in small businesses. The industry dubbed "other services" was also dominated by small business employment. More than 85% of employees in this industry worked in small businesses. As noted in Chapter 5, "other services" includes jobs such as repairing

TABLE 6.1

Business sizes, number of establishments, employment, and annual payrolls, 2005

Employment size of firm	Firms	Establishments	Employment	Annual payroll ($1,000)
Total	5,983,546	7,499,702	116,317,003	4,482,722,481
0*	823,832	824,952	—	42,182,002
1–4	2,854,047	2,859,095	5,936,859	177,827,102
5–9	1,050,062	1,062,907	6,898,483	206,178,084
10–14	415,989	432,470	4,865,539	153,325,562
15–19	213,957	229,727	3,588,315	116,091,356
20–24	131,514	147,060	2,870,060	94,111,977
25–29	88,097	101,840	2,365,072	78,099,071
30–34	63,260	76,225	2,016,475	67,807,561
35–39	47,373	60,241	1,746,960	59,433,250
40–44	36,656	48,154	1,535,517	52,703,860
45–49	29,143	39,773	1,366,993	47,040,730
50–74	84,607	130,095	5,095,569	178,105,960
75–99	40,247	75,994	3,447,703	123,150,994
100–149	38,694	93,959	4,673,931	169,007,646
150–199	18,538	61,697	3,189,340	115,639,275
200–299	17,383	82,949	4,208,878	153,071,046
300–399	7,999	52,447	2,756,388	103,080,535
400–499	4,671	40,947	2,082,503	75,725,730
500–749	5,823	67,664	3,539,488	135,660,216
750–999	2,878	43,464	2,478,859	95,138,017
1,000–1,499	2,845	56,614	3,456,833	139,104,676
1,500–2,499	2,314	75,406	4,435,321	185,189,876
2,500–4,999	1,787	111,752	6,199,781	276,630,183
5,000–9,999	918	123,808	6,438,639	297,593,815
10,000+	912	600,462	31,123,497	1,340,823,957
<20	5,357,887	5,409,151	21,289,196	695,604,106
<50	5,753,930	5,882,444	33,190,273	1,094,800,555
<100	5,878,784	6,088,533	41,733,545	1,396,057,509
<500	5,966,069	6,420,532	58,644,585	2,012,581,741

*Employment is measured in March, thus some firms (start-ups after March, closures before March, and seasonal firms) will have zero employment and some annual payroll. Excludes farms.

SOURCE: "Employer Firms, Establishments, Employment, and Annual Payroll, Small Firm Size Classes, 2005," in *Firm Size Data*, U.S. Small Business Administration, Office of Advocacy, 2005, http://www.sba.gov/advo/research/us_05ss.pdf (accessed April 18, 2008)

FIGURE 6.1

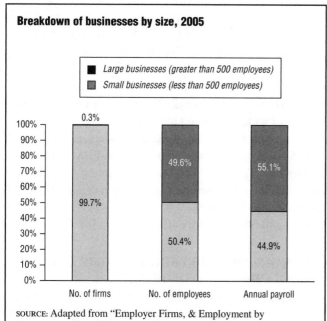

Breakdown of businesses by size, 2005

■ Large businesses (greater than 500 employees)
▨ Small businesses (less than 500 employees)

SOURCE: Adapted from "Employer Firms, & Employment by Employment Size of Firm by NAICS Codes, 2005," in *Firm Size Data*, Small Business Administration, Office of Advocacy, 2005, http://www.sba.gov/advo/research/us05_n6.pdf (accessed May 17, 2008)

equipment and machinery, promoting or administering religious activities, operating dry cleaning and laundry services, conducting personal care, death care, and pet care services, and supplying photo processing services, temporary parking, dating services, grant making, and advocacy services.

Every year since 1982 the SBA has prepared a report for the U.S. president that summarizes the economic status and impact of small businesses. In *The Small Business Economy for Data Year 2006: A Report to the President* (December 2007, http://www.sba.gov/advo/research/sb_econ2007.pdf), the SBA indicates that small businesses accounted for all the net new jobs in the United States in 2004 (the most recent year for which data were available). Small businesses (i.e., those with less than five hundred employees each) added 1.8 million net jobs that year, whereas larger firms suffered a net loss of 181,000 jobs.

Katherine Kobe of the Economic Consulting Services examines in *The Small Business Share of GDP, 1998–2004* (April 2007, http://www.sba.gov/advo/research/rs299tot.pdf) the contribution of small businesses to the

TABLE 6.2

Number of small businesses by major industry and employment size, 2005

Industry		Firms		
			Employment size	
	Total	0*–4	<20	<500
Major industries				
Total	5,983,546	3,677,879	5,357,887	5,966,069
Forestry, fishing, hunting & agriculture support	23,447	16,060	21,957	23,352
Mining	19,406	11,040	16,308	19,091
Utilities	6,660	3,589	5,301	6,459
Construction	777,664	510,965	714,441	776,663
Manufacturing	288,568	114,265	213,652	284,536
Wholesale trade	336,736	190,516	288,828	333,706
Retail trade	736,940	434,707	667,955	734,636
Transportation & warehousing	169,086	108,339	148,386	166,946
Information	75,261	44,693	63,970	74,147
Finance & insurance	259,983	184,094	238,433	258,310
Real estate & rental & leasing	300,525	235,283	285,853	299,302
Professional, scientific, & technical services	757,174	549,175	708,772	754,274
Management of companies & enterprises	26,513	4,056	5,860	19,540
Administrative & support & waste management & remediation services	320,252	203,934	280,721	316,766
Educational services	72,410	35,670	55,723	71,293
Health care & social assistance	599,392	307,428	523,312	595,641
Arts, entertainment, & recreation	114,145	70,415	98,465	113,495
Accommodation & foodservices	462,983	203,627	371,557	461,168
Other services (except public administration)	676,400	428,283	630,210	675,026
Unclassified	23,986	22,645	23,890	23,986

*Employment is measured in March, thus some firms (start-ups after March, closures before March, and seasonal firms) will have zero employment.

SOURCE: Adapted from "Employer Firms, & Employment by Employment Size of Firm by NAICS Codes, 2005," in *Firm Size Data*, Small Business Administration, Office of Advocacy, undated, http://www.sba.gov/advo/research/us05_n6.pdf (accessed May 17, 2008)

TABLE 6.3

Small business employment percentage by major industry sector, 2005

[Millions]

	Percent small business
Goods-producing industries	**57.88**
Natural resources and mining	61.93
Construction	86.14
Manufacturing	44.18
Service-producing industries	**48.72**
Trade, transportation and utilities	45.27
Wholesale trade	60.94
Retail trade	41.12
Information	26.16
Financial activities	41.88
Professional and business services	43.88
Education and health services	47.84
Leisure and hospitality	60.89
Other services	85.57
Government	0

Notes: Seasonally adjusted. The small business percentage by sector is based on 2005 firm size data. Trends may reflect rounding error.

SOURCE: Adapted from "Employment by Major Sector," in *First Quarter 2008: The Economy and Small Business*, Small Business Administration, Office of Advocacy, May 8, 2008, http://www.sba.gov/advo/research/sbqei0801.pdf (accessed May 17, 2008)

nation's GDP. Kobe notes that U.S. businesses with less than five hundred employees were responsible for approximately 48% to 51% of the nation's nonfarm, private

industry GDP between 1998 and 2004. Thus, small businesses produce roughly half of the nation's nonfarm, private industry GDP.

Home-Based Businesses

Small businesses operated out of a person's home may be organized as any of the legal business structures. The latest comprehensive data on home-based businesses were collected in 2002 by the Census Bureau in its Survey of Business Owners (SBO; May 16, 2008, http://www.census.gov/csd/sbo/cbsummaryoffindings.htm). Approximately 16.7 million businesses participated in the SBO, representing nearly three-fourths (72.6%) of the nation's total nonfarm businesses operating at that time. Over eight million firms reported being home-based businesses. Nearly all (99.8%) were small businesses with less than five hundred employees. The four industries accounting for the most home-based businesses were professional, scientific, and technical services (19%), construction (16%), retail trade (11%), and other services (10%).

THE ROLE OF BIG BUSINESS IN THE U.S. AND GLOBAL ECONOMIES

Big businesses (i.e., those with five hundred or more employees) accounted for only 0.3% of all nonfarm firms in the United States in 2005. (See Figure 6.1.) However, these 17,477 big firms employed almost 58 million people (nearly half of the nation's total nonfarm workforce) and provided $2.5 trillion in payroll (just over 55% of the total annual payroll).

The business magazine *Forbes* publishes an annual list of the world's two thousand largest companies, with the most recent being "The Global 2000" (April 2, 2008, http://www.forbes.com/2008/04/02/worlds-largest-companies-biz-2000 global08-cx_sd_0402global_land.html). *Forbes* ranks public companies using a composite score based on sales, assets, profits, and market value. The top-ten-ranked companies in the 2008 report and their primary areas of business were:

- HSBC Holdings (banking)
- General Electric (conglomerate)
- Bank of America (banking)
- JP Morgan Chase (banking)
- Exxon Mobil (oil and gas)
- Royal Dutch Shell (oil and gas)
- BP (oil and gas)
- Toyota Motor (consumer durables)
- ING Group (insurance)
- Berkshire Hathaway (diversified financials)

Five of the top ten companies—General Electric, Bank of America, JP Morgan Chase, Exxon Mobil, and Berkshire Hathaway—are based in the United States. Together, the two thousand top-ranked public companies in the world employed seventy-two million people, had $119 trillion in assets, $30 trillion in revenues, $2.4 trillion in profits, and $39 trillion in market value.

Multinational Corporations

Many large businesses operate in more than one country, through subsidiaries or part ownership of foreign companies. These companies are called multinational or transnational corporations. Generally through mergers and acquisitions, a large company can grow beyond the boundaries of a single nation, buying and taking over companies in other countries to form a global network of subsidiaries. For example, Exxon Mobil, which was formed in 1999 by the merger of the two oil companies Exxon and Mobil, is headquartered in Irving, Texas, but it operates affiliated companies in at least forty countries on six continents.

BUSINESS AND POLITICS

Large companies often have strong ties to the government. They have the resources to be able to donate millions of dollars to political campaigns to elect sympathetic lawmakers and to otherwise encourage the passage of pro-business legislation. Likewise, lawmakers, eager to have companies locate facilities in their constit-

uencies to boost local economies, may support policies that favor business interests to the detriment of other programs. Members of Congress may be more inclined to pass pro-business laws if their region has benefited from a large corporation's presence, or if they or their party have received campaign contributions from such a company. This raises concerns that big businesses may be able to convince the government to favor their interests at the expense of the interests of other businesses, or even the population as a whole.

ECONOMIC PERFORMANCE

U.S. businesses produce goods and provide services that are purchased by consumers. The consumption of business output is the major driving force behind the nation's GDP growth.

The U.S. Department of Commerce's Bureau of Economic Analysis (BEA) compiles data on the contributions made to the GDP by various industries. One measure of output is called real value added. This is defined as gross output minus the consumption of intermediate inputs. For example, the real value added to the economy by a manufacturer is calculated using the market value of the goods sold minus the cost of producing the goods.

Figure 6.2 shows the BEA breakdown of GDP growth per year by industry category from 2004 through 2007. In 2004 goods-producing and service-producing industries contributed almost equally to the annual GDP growth rate

FIGURE 6.2

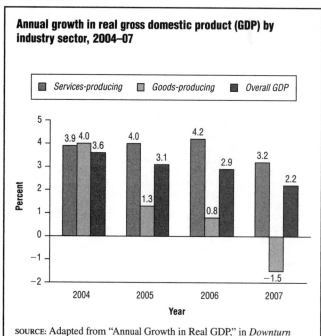

Annual growth in real gross domestic product (GDP) by industry sector, 2004–07

SOURCE: Adapted from "Annual Growth in Real GDP," in *Downturn in Finance and Insurance Restrains Real GDP Growth in 2007*, U.S. Department of Commerce, Bureau of Economic Analysis, April 29, 2008, http://www.bea.gov/newsreleases/industry/gdpindustry/2008/pdf/gdpind07.pdf (accessed April 29, 2008)

of 3.6%. Over the next two years the contribution of services-producing industries increased slightly, whereas that of the goods-producing industries dropped dramatically to 1.3% in 2005 and to 0.8% in 2006. In 2007 the goods-producing sector had negative GDP growth. The services-producing sector experienced GDP growth of 3.2% in 2007, contributing to the overall rate of 2.2%.

The growth in the service-providing industry during 2007 was due to strong performance by information services (with a 9% increase) and professional and business services (with a 4.6% increase). (See Table 6.4.) The leading performer in the goods-producing sector was manufacturing of durable goods (with a 4.9% increase). Declines were reported in the construction industry (down 12.1%), manufacturing of nondurable goods (down 1.1%), and finance and insurance (down 0.3%).

Agriculture

The U.S. Department of Agriculture's National Agricultural Statistics Service (NASS) performs a census of agriculture every five years. The most recent census was conducted in 2002 (http://www.agcensus.usda.gov/Publi cations/2002/index.asp). According to the results, there were just over two million farms and ranches operating in 2002. The NASS (http://www.agcensus.usda.gov/Help/ FAQs/2002_Census/index.asp#1) defines a farm/ranch as an establishment from which at least $1,000 in agricultural products is produced or sold (or normally would be produced or sold) during a year. Even though less than 10% of farm/ranch establishments were owned by corporations or business partnerships in 2002, these farms accounted for nearly half of all sales and government payments.

The number of U.S. farms declined dramatically during the twentieth century, from 5.7 million in 1900 to 2.1 million in 2000. (See Table 6.5.) Likewise, farming's share of the nation's workforce decreased from 41% to only 2%. However, the average farm size increased from 146 acres to 441 acres. This growth, combined with advances in agricultural science and technology, has resulted in an increase in farm output, even as farming's contribution to the nation's GDP has diminished. (See Figure 6.3.)

Nonagricultural Businesses

The Census Bureau conducts an economic census every five years. Table 6.6 shows results from the 2002 economic census. (Note that the results from the 2007 economic census were not available as of July 2008). This table provides an economic overview of nonagricultural industry sectors with employee payrolls. The sectors are listed from largest to smallest in terms of value of sales, receipts, or shipments. Also included for each sector are the number of establishments, the number of paid employees, and the annual payroll.

TABLE 6.4

Percent change in real value added by industry group, 2007

[Percent change]

	2007
Gross domestic product	**2.2**
Private industries	**2.1**
Agriculture, forestry, fishing, and hunting	1.4
Mining	0.0
Utilities	5.3
Construction	−12.1
Manufacturing	2.3
Durable goods	4.9
Nondurable goods	−1.1
Wholesale trade	0.9
Retail trade	4.9
Transportation and warehousing	3.1
Information	9.0
Finance, insurance, real estate, rental, and leasing	1.2
Finance and insurance	−0.3
Real estate and rental and leasing	2.1
Professional and business services	4.6
Professional, scientific, and technical services	5.4
Management of companies and enterprises	0.9
Administrative and waste management services	4.9
Educational services, health care, and social assistance	3.5
Educational services	3.3
Health care and social assistance	3.5
Arts, entertainment, recreation, accommodation, and food services	1.9
Arts, entertainment, and recreation	1.0
Accommodation and food services	2.2
Other services, except government	2.1

Note. The industry estimate for 2007 is based in part on data from the Census Bureau's accelerated November 2007 release of the Annual Survey of Manufactures (ASM). These data were unavailable for the July 2007 release of the National Income and Product Accounts (NIPAs).

SOURCE: Adapted from "Table 1. Percent Changes in Real Value Added by Industry Group," in *Downturn in Finance and Insurance Restrains Real GDP Growth in 2007*, U.S. Department of Commerce, Bureau of Economic Analysis, April 29, 2008, http://www.bea.gov/newsreleases/industry/gdpindustry/2008/pdf/gdpind07.pdf (accessed April 29, 2008)

TABLE 6.5

Historical changes in agriculture sector, selected years, 1900–2000

	1900	1930	1945	1970	2000
Number of farms (millions)	5.7	6.3	5.9	2.9	2.1
Average farm size (acres)	146	151	195	376	441
Average number of commodities produced per farm	5.1	4.5	4.6	2.7	1.3
Farm share of population (percent)	39	25	17	5	1
Rural share of population (percent)	60	44	36[b]	26	21
Farm share of workforce (percent)	41	22	16	4	2
Farm share of GDP (percent)	na	8	7	2	1[c]
Off-farm labor[a]	na	100 days	27%	54%	93%

na = Not available.
[a]Off-farm labor measures the extent to which members of farm households work in other sectors besides farming: 1930, average number of days worked off-farm; 1945, percent of farmers working off-farm; 1970 and 2000, percent of farm households with off-farm income.
[b]Data for 1950.
[c]Data for 2002.

SOURCE: "Table 8-1. 100 Years of Structural Change in U.S. Agriculture," in *Economic Report of the President*, U.S. Government Printing Office, February 2006, http://www.gpoaccess.gov/eop/2006/2006_erp.pdf (accessed June 10, 2008)

FIGURE 6.3

Farming output and share of gross domestic product, 1950–2002

Legend:
— Farming share of U.S. GDP (left axis)
--- Physical farm output (right axis)

SOURCE: "Chart 8-2. Farming Output and Share of U.S. GDP," in *Economic Report of the President*, U.S. Government Printing Office, February 2006, http://www.gpoaccess.gov/eop/2006/2006_erp.pdf (accessed June 10, 2008)

Wholesale trade had $4.6 trillion in sales, receipts, or shipments during 2002. (See Table 6.6.) Wholesalers buy large quantities of finished goods from manufacturers and sell the goods in smaller lots to businesses engaged in retail trade. Retailers then offer the goods for sale to consumers at an increased price. There were over 1.1 million retail establishments operating in 2002. Even though the traditional notion of a retail establishment includes at least one store location, many retailers operate via the Internet and/or catalog sales, instead of or besides their physical locations.

The manufacturing sector had the highest annual payroll in 2002 at $576 billion. (See Table 6.6.) Nearly 14.7 million people were employed in this sector, the second-highest number of the sectors listed. The health care and social assistance sector was the top employer with nearly 15.1 million paid employees.

Corporate Profits

One of the economic indicators tracked by the BEA is corporate profits. This is a measure of the income generated by corporations from the current production of goods and services. Because only current production is counted, corporate profits do not include capital gains, such as inventory profits.

Table 6.7 lists the corporate profits by industry from 2005 through 2007 and the change from 2006 to 2007. Corporate profits totaled almost $1.6 trillion in 2007, up by $41.5 billion from 2006. Domestic industries accounted for $1.3 trillion (79%) of the total in 2007. These values include adjustments for inventory valuation and capital consumption.

Among domestic industries, corporations engaged in financial services had the highest corporate profits in 2007. These businesses had profits of $498.5 billion (including only the inventory valuation adjustment). (See Table 6.7.) Similarly, the manufacturing sector had

TABLE 6.6

Economic statistics by industry, 2002

NAICS code	Description	Establishments	Sales, receipts or shipments ($1,000)	Annual payroll ($1,000)	Paid employees
42	Wholesale trade	435,521	4,634,755,112	259,653,080	5,878,405
31–33	Manufacturing	350,828	3,916,136,712	576,170,541	14,699,536
44–45	Retail trade	1,114,637	3,056,421,997	302,113,581	14,647,675
52	Finance & insurance	440,268	2,803,854,868	377,790,172	6,578,817
62	Health care & social assistance	704,526	1,207,299,734	495,845,829	15,052,255
23	Construction	710,307	1,196,555,587	254,292,144	7,193,069
51	Information	137,678	891,845,956	194,670,163	3,736,061
54	Professional, scientific, & technical services	771,305	886,801,038	376,090,052	7,243,505
72	Accommodation & food services	565,590	449,498,718	127,554,483	10,120,951
56	Administrative & support & waste management & remediation service	350,583	432,577,580	206,439,329	8,741,854
22	Utilities	17,103	398,907,044	42,417,830	663,044
48–49	Transportation & warehousing	199,618	382,152,040	115,988,733	3,650,859
53	Real estate & rental & leasing	322,815	335,587,706	60,222,584	1,948,657
81	Other services (except public administration)	537,576	307,049,461	82,954,939	3,475,310
21	Mining	24,087	182,911,093	21,173,895	477,840
71	Arts, entertainment, & recreation	110,313	141,904,109	45,169,117	1,848,674
55	Management of companies & enterprises	49,308	107,064,264	178,996,060	2,605,292
61	Educational services	49,319	30,690,707	10,164,378	430,164

Notes: Table includes only establishments of firms with payroll. Nonemployers are shown separately.

SOURCE: Adapted from "Summary Statistics by 2002 NAICS, United States: All Sector Totals," in *2002 Economic Census*, U.S. Census Bureau, November 7, 2005, www.census.gov/econ/census02/data/us/US000.HTM (accessed June 10, 2008)

TABLE 6.7

Level of corporate profits and change from preceding period, by industry, 2005–07

[Billions of dollars]

	Level			Change from preceding period	
	2005	2006	2007	2006	2007
Corporate profits with inventory valuation and capital consumption adjustments	1,372.8	1,553.7	1,595.2	180.9	41.5
Domestic industries	1,154.6	1,296.4	1,257.7	141.8	−38.7
Financial	405.5	482.2	473.4	76.7	−8.8
Nonfinancial	749.1	814.3	784.3	65.2	−30.0
Rest of the world	218.2	257.3	337.6	39.1	80.3
Receipts from the rest of the world	358.7	419.8	491.0	61.1	71.2
Less: Payments to the rest of the world	140.6	162.5	153.4	21.9	−9.1
Corporate profits with inventory valuation adjustment	1,543.4	1,769.5	1,830.5	226.1	61.0
Domestic industries	1,325.2	1,512.2	1,493.0	187.0	−19.2
Financial	423.6	505.3	498.5	81.7	−6.8
Federal Reserve banks	26.6	33.8	38.4	7.2	4.6
Other financial	397.1	471.4	460.1	74.3	−11.3
Nonfinancial	901.6	1,006.9	994.5	105.3	−12.4
Utilities	28.4	35.7	44.4	7.3	8.7
Manufacturing	251.2	293.4	305.7	42.2	12.3
Durable goods	85.1	95.9	121.9	10.8	26.0
Fabricated metal products	17.3	20.3	25.2	3.0	4.9
Machinery	16.0	19.3	21.8	3.3	2.5
Computer and electronic products	10.1	7.7	8.0	−2.4	.3
Electrical equipment, appliances, and components	−3.7	−1.9	2.0	1.8	3.9
Motor vehicles, bodies and trailers, and parts	.1	−1.1	9.4	−1.2	10.5
Other durable goods	45.3	51.7	55.5	6.4	3.8
Nondurable goods	166.0	197.5	183.8	31.5	−13.7
Food and beverage and tobacco products	27.8	29.2	33.4	1.4	4.2
Petroleum and coal products	89.8	110.4	86.5	20.6	−23.9
Chemical products	29.7	37.6	43.9	7.9	6.3
Other nondurable goods	18.7	20.3	20.0	1.6	−.3
Wholesale trade	95.2	97.0	98.7	1.8	1.7
Retail trade	114.4	124.5	137.5	10.1	13.0
Transportation and warehousing	28.2	41.9	47.1	13.7	5.2
Information	74.8	85.4	103.4	10.6	18.0
Other nonfinancial	309.5	329.0	257.5	19.5	−71.5
Rest of the world	218.2	257.3	337.6	39.1	80.3

SOURCE: Adapted from "Table 12. Corporate Profits by Industry: Level and Change from Preceding Period," in *Gross Domestic Product: Fourth Quarter 2007 (Final); Corporate Profits: Fourth Quarter 2007*, U.S. Department of Commerce, Bureau of Economic Analysis, March 27, 2008, http://www.bea.gov/newsreleases/national/gdp/2008/pdf/gdp407f.pdf (accessed April 24, 2008)

corporate profits of $305.7 billion during 2007. Corporate profits were positive for all subsectors.

Figure 6.4 shows the percentage change in year-over-year growth in corporate profits for the first quarter of 2004 through the fourth quarter of 2007. Corporate profits for each quarter of 2007 were down, compared to the same quarter in 2006, indicating a general slowdown in the overall U.S. economy.

Industry Outlook

Table 6.8 lists the industries expected to undergo the greatest growth or decline in output through 2016. This list was compiled by the U.S. Bureau of Labor Statistics (BLS). The BLS expects phenomenal growth (a 20.5% increase) from businesses engaged in the manufacture of computers and peripheral equipment. This industry is expected to increase its output by $732.5 billion between 2006 and 2016. Strong performance is also expected from

manufacturers of semiconductors and other electronic components, with an increase in output of $380.8 billion. Likewise, software publishers are expected to increase output by $266.5 billion during this period.

Industries expected to suffer the largest declines in output between 2006 and 2016 include footwear manufacturers (down 8.4%), cut and sew apparel manufacturers (down 5.9%), and tobacco manufacturers (down 5.6%). (See Table 6.8.)

FEDERAL REGULATION OF BUSINESS

Historically, U.S. economic philosophy has been to let the market operate with a minimum of government interference. This does not mean, however, that U.S. businesses go unregulated. Many local, state, and federal laws exist to protect the public and the economy from dangerous, unfair, or fraudulent activities by businesses. Major federal programs that oversee business activities are:

FIGURE 6.4

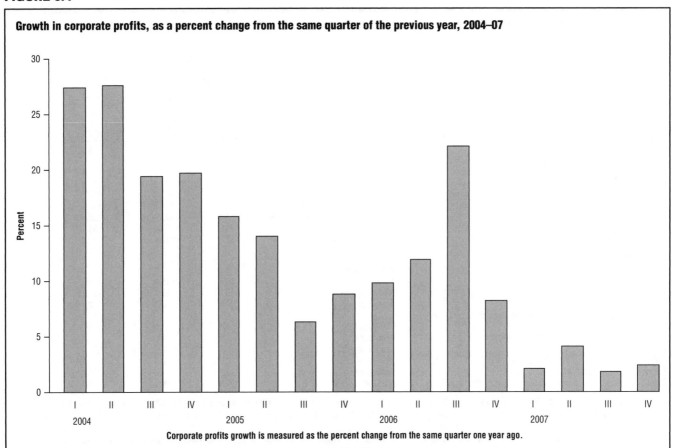

Growth in corporate profits, as a percent change from the same quarter of the previous year, 2004–07

Corporate profits growth is measured as the percent change from the same quarter one year ago.

Note: The "advance" estimate of GDP for the first quarter of 2008 will be released on April 30, 2008.

SOURCE: "Year-over-Year Growth in Corporate Profits," in *Growth Slows in the Fourth Quarter*, U.S. Department of Commerce, Bureau of Economic Analysis, March 27, 2008, http://www.bea.gov/newsreleases/national/gdp/2008/pdf/gdp407f_fax.pdf (accessed April 24, 2008)

• Federal Trade Commission (FTC)—created in 1914 with the passage of the Federal Trade Commission Act. Originally intended to combat the rise of business monopolies, the FTC grew to become the U.S. government's consumer protection agency, addressing consumer issues such as identity theft, false advertising, telemarketing and Internet scams, and anticompetition moves by businesses.

• Consumer Product Safety Commission (CPSC)—established in 1973 to protect the American public from unreasonable risks of serious injury or death from consumer products. Through a combination of voluntary and mandatory safety standards, the CPSC tries to prevent dangerous products from entering the market. If a product is found to be dangerous after it has already been sold to consumers, the CPSC has the duty to inform the public and the power to force a recall of the product if it is deemed necessary.

• Equal Employment Opportunity Commission (EEOC)—established in 1965, the EEOC is the primary federal agency responsible for preventing discrimination in the workplace. Its original purpose was to investigate viola-

tions of the Civil Rights Act of 1964, which prohibited discrimination in the workplace on the basis of race, color, national origin, sex, and religion. Over the years its powers have been expanded and it has been given responsibility to enforce other antidiscrimination laws.

• Employment Standards Administration (ESA)—one of the largest branches of the U.S. Department of Labor, the ESA is charged with enforcing a wide variety of labor laws dealing with minimum wage requirements, overtime pay standards, child labor protections, and unpaid leaves of absence. It also provides oversight of federal contractors about employment issues.

• The U.S. Environmental Protection Agency (EPA)—develops and enforces federal environmental regulations. The EPA keeps track of industrial pollutants and regularly updates its compliance codes for individual sectors and industries.

• The U.S. Food and Drug Administration (FDA)—works to ensure that the food, drugs, and cosmetics sold in the United States are safe and effective. It establishes safety and sanitation standards for manufacturers of these goods, as well as quality standards that the goods

TABLE 6.8

Ten industries with the fastest growing and most rapidly declining output growth, 2006–16

| Industry description | Sector | Billions of chained 2000 dollars | | Change | Average annual rate of change |
		2006	2016	2006–16	2006–16
Fastest growing					
Computer and peripheral equipment manufacturing	Manufacturing	134.5	867.0	732.5	20.5
Semiconductor and other electronic component manufacturing	Manufacturing	162.6	543.4	380.8	12.8
Software publishers	Information	153.3	419.8	266.5	10.6
Securities, commodity contracts, and other financial investments and related activities	Financial activities	351.2	958.3	607.1	10.6
Internet and other information services	Information	109.4	248.2	138.8	8.5
Lessors of nonfinancial intangible assets (except copyrighted works)	Financial activities	138.6	278.4	139.8	7.2
Management, scientific, and technical consulting services	Professional and business services	171.0	317.8	146.8	6.4
Office administrative services	Professional and business services	73.7	128.7	55.0	5.7
Home health care services	Healthcare and social assistance	48.2	83.4	35.2	5.6
Scientific research and development	Professional and business services	126.8	216.1	89.3	5.5
Most rapidly declining					
Footwear manufacturing	Manufacturing	1.8	.7	−1.0	−8.4
Cut and sew apparel manufacturing	Manufacturing	27.6	15.1	−12.5	−5.9
Tobacco manufacturing	Manufacturing	39.2	22.1	−17.1	−5.6
Apparel knitting mills	Manufacturing	5.4	3.3	−2.1	−4.8
Leather and hide tanning and finishing, and other leather and allied product manufacturing	Manufacturing	3.4	2.1	−1.2	−4.5
Apparel accessories and other apparel manufacturing	Manufacturing	2.6	1.8	-.8	−3.8
Fabric mills	Manufacturing	15.0	10.6	−4.4	−3.4
Textile and fabric finishing and fabric coating mills	Manufacturing	8.6	6.4	−2.2	−3.0
Fishing, hunting and trapping	Agriculture	5.7	4.2	−1.5	−2.9
Pesticide, fertilizer, and other agricultural chemical manufacturing	Manufacturing	20.8	16.7	−4.1	−2.1

SOURCE: Adapted from Eric B. Figueroa and Rose A. Woods, "Table 5. Industries with the Fastest Growing and Most Rapidly Declining Output Growth, 2006–16," in "Employment Outlook: 2006–2016, Industry Output and Employment Projections to 2016," *Monthly Labor Review*, vol. 130, no. 11, November 2007, http://www.bls.gov/opub/mlr/2007/11/art4full.pdf (accessed April 29, 2008).

themselves must meet. FDA scientists must prove that certain products, especially drugs, are safe and effective before they can be sold in the United States, and it can force products off the market if they are later discovered to be dangerous. In addition, the FDA ensures that the labeling of food, drugs, and cosmetics is complete and truthful.

- The Occupational Safety and Health Administration (OSHA)—establishes and enforces workplace safety standards. One or more OSHA standards covers almost every workplace in the United States.

Other Agencies

Besides the previously mentioned agencies, there are a number of other government agencies that regulate specific industries or aspects of the economy. Some of them are well known, whereas many others may be virtually unknown to people outside the fields they regulate. A few examples are:

- The Federal Communications Commission regulates the telecommunications industry, including all television, radio, satellite, cable, and wire services in the United States and its territories.

- The Federal Energy Regulatory Commission regulates the national transmission network for oil, natural gas, and electricity.

- The Federal Maritime Commission regulates the waterborne foreign commerce of the United States.

- The National Highway Traffic Safety Administration regulates automobile design and safety.

- The Office of Surface Mining regulates surface coal mining.

- The Securities and Exchange Commission (SEC) regulates the stock market.

Government Regulation and Deregulation

Since the late 1970s the federal and many state governments have lessened their restrictions on certain industries. Called deregulation, this process allows industries to set their own standards and control their own systems of pricing and other business functions. For example, beginning in 1938 the airline industry was regulated by a federal body called the Civil Aeronautics Board, which controlled airlines' schedules, flying routes, and prices. To stimulate competition in the industry, Congress passed the Airline Deregulation Act of 1978. The industry experienced a flood of new airlines offering low fares to compete with the established airlines. Even though deregulation has actually caused some problems with larger airlines having too much control (or monopolizing) of the industry and with overly crowded flight routes, most economists agree that the result has been an air transportation system that offers some of the lowest costs and safest flights in its one-hundred-year history. Other industries that have experienced some degree of deregulation include electric utilities, telephone services, trucking, railroads, and banking.

MARKET POWER: MONOPOLIES AND MONOPSONIES

One of the foundations of a capitalistic economy is competition. Competition for customers among sellers theoretically ensures that buyers receive the lowest price. If an industry becomes dominated by one seller, the lack of competition allows that entity to set prices in the marketplace—a situation known as monopolization. The federal government has long fought against monopolization in most U.S. industries. In 1890 Congress passed the Sherman Antitrust Act to strengthen competitive forces in the economy. Section 2 of the law states: "Every person who shall monopolize, or attempt to monopolize, or combine or conspire with any other person or persons, to monopolize any part of the trade or commerce among the several States, or with foreign nations, shall be deemed guilty of a felony."

A monopsony is a different situation, in which the power lies with one buyer. This arrangement can occur if one company wields enormous power over the suppliers in that industry. The lack of other customers forces the suppliers to meet the price and quota demands of the monopsonist. Monopsony is an obscure economic concept to most Americans. However, changing market forces in the retail industry are drawing attention to the possible existence and consequences of monopsony in some business sectors.

The Microsoft Monopoly?

In 1993 the U.S. Department of Justice began an investigation of the software company Microsoft based on allegations that the company was engaging in unfair competition. Microsoft's Windows program already dominated the operating systems market. By bundling Web browsers and other applications with Windows, Microsoft made it difficult for other companies to compete in the market for these other applications as well.

In 1994 Microsoft reached an agreement with the Department of Justice, and the company agreed to stop bundling other products with Windows. In 1998 Microsoft was accused of violating its agreement, and the Department of Justice and the attorneys general of twenty states brought an antitrust suit against it. Microsoft reached a settlement in the case but still faced a number of class-action lawsuits. (A class-action lawsuit is one that is filed by a large group of people, all of whom accuse a single company of engaging in the same illegal acts against them.)

During the early 2000s Microsoft fought and lost antitrust cases brought against it in Japan, South Korea,

and Europe. In 2004 a European court ordered Microsoft to pay a fine of $613 million for violating the European Union's competition law. The company was also ordered to offer for sale a modified version of Windows that does not include a media player and to share certain communications protocols with competitors. In July 2006 the European Commission levied a $357 million fine against Microsoft for failing to fully comply with the 2004 ruling. Microsoft appealed the fine, but lost in September 2007. In February 2008 the European Commission claimed that Microsoft had failed to fully comply with the original ruling, so it levied an additional $1.3 billion fine against the company. In May 2008 the company announced that it would appeal the latest fine.

The Wal-Mart Monopsony?

During the early 2000s the mega-retailer Wal-Mart became the subject of much media attention for its business practices. In November 2003 the *Los Angeles Times* published a three-part series on Wal-Mart. In part two, Nancy Cleeland, Evelyn Iritani, and Tyler Marshall describe in "Scouring the Globe to Give Shoppers an $8.63 Polo Shirt" the relentless push at Wal-Mart for suppliers to lower costs. One textile producer summed up Wal-Mart's power: "They control so much of retail that they can put someone into business or take someone out of business if they choose to."

In November 2004 the Public Broadcasting System (PBS) series *Frontline* aired the episode "Is Wal-Mart Good for America?" (http://www.pbs.org/wgbh/pages/frontline/shows/walmart/). The episode traces the rise of Wal-Mart as a major force in the retail industry and describes the power that the company developed over its suppliers. Sam Hornblower notes in "Always Low Prices" (November 23, 2004, http://www.pbs.org/wgbh/pages/frontline/shows/walmart/secrets/pricing.html) that "Wal-Mart used its buying power and its information about consumer buying habits to force vendors into squeezing their costs and keeping their profit margins low. Over time, some suppliers—especially middle-sized and smaller firms—were bankrupted."

In 2004 Wal-Mart employed 1.2 million employees and served 100 million shoppers per week at more than 3,000 stores around the country. The company had sales of $256 billion in 2003 and accounted for approximately 8% of total U.S. retail sales (excluding automobiles).

Wal-Mart's relatively small share of retail sales is one factor that helps the company avoid antitrust charges. In "Discount Nation: Is Wal-Mart Good for America?" (*New York Times*, December 7, 2003), Steve Lohr asserts that Wal-Mart's emphasis on low prices to consumers is another factor. Peter J. Solomon states in "A Lesson from Wal-Mart" (*Washington Post*, March 28, 2004) that "federal regulators have refrained from pursuing monopsony antitrust action against Wal-Mart for putting the squeeze on its suppliers, because of the price benefits to consumers."

CORPORATE BEHAVIOR AND RESPONSIBILITY

Businesses play a vital role in the economic well-being of the United States. Besides economic performance, Americans also expect businesses to behave in a legally and socially responsible manner. There is no public or political consensus on the exact social responsibilities of businesses. However, it is recognized that the decisions and practices of company officials, particularly of large corporations, affect not only employees and investors but also the communities in which businesses are located. Fraud and corruption at the corporate level can adversely affect large numbers of people. Likewise, poor performance by businesses in meeting environmental, health, or consumer-protection standards has detrimental effects on society at large.

Corporate Scandals

ENRON. Based in Houston, Texas, Enron was an international broker of commodities such as natural gas, water, coal, and steel. In August 2000 Enron's stock rose to an all-time high of $90 per share. However, the company was incurring more and more debt because its contracts outstripped its ability to deliver. To hide its liabilities, Enron created a web of partnerships; the idea was to transfer debt so it would not show on the company's books. Enron's accounting firm, Arthur Andersen, helped the company hide its debts and shredded key documents. With debts transferred to other entities, Arthur Andersen and Enron could overstate the value of the company, and its stock continued to perform well.

Enron eventually had to pay the debts either with cash or with stock, which would create a huge loss that the company could not hide. Sherron Watkins (1959–), the vice president of Enron, discovered the accounting discrepancy in the summer of 2001, and she became the key whistleblower when she sent a memo about the problem to the chief executive officer (CEO) Kenneth Lay (1942–2006). In October 2001 Enron announced part of the loss—$638 million in the third quarter of 2001, with a loss in shareholder equity of $1.2 billion—and its stock price plummeted. The company announced that it was being investigated by the SEC for possible conflicts of interest with its many partnerships. In November 2001 Enron stock dropped to less than a dollar per share, and in December the company filed for bankruptcy. Four thousand employees were laid off at that time.

Shortly before announcing the income overstatement, Enron executives took two additional steps. First, some of them sold their stock so they could get their money out before the stock lost all its value. Second, the company imposed a freeze on employee sales of the stock shares in their 401(k) plans. So when the news broke and employees tried to sell their stock to save what they could of their retirement savings funds, they found that they were stuck with worthless stock in a bankrupt company. Thousands of people lost their jobs, along with their health care, retirement funds, and, in many cases, life savings. Even though investors both in and outside the company lost tens of billions of dollars, Enron wrote $55 million in bonus checks for company executives the day before it declared bankruptcy.

In 2002 Arthur Andersen, Enron's accounting firm, was found guilty of obstruction of justice charges; two years later the company also lost its appeal of the original ruling.

In December 2005 the former accounting officer Richard Causey (1960–) pleaded guilty to securities fraud and agreed to cooperate with authorities in exchange for a plea deal that included a five- to seven-year prison term and a $1.3 million fine. In May 2006, after a long trial, Lay and the former CEO Jeffrey Skilling (1953–) were found guilty on various counts of fraud and conspiracy. Lay died six weeks later from a heart attack. In October 2006 Skilling was sentenced to more than twenty-four years in prison and was fined $45 million. As of July 2008, his case was under appeal. Dozens of other people were charged in the Enron scandal, including three British bankers who were sentenced in February 2008 to thirty-seven-month prison terms.

WORLDCOM. In 2002 the federal government began investigating the accounting practices of WorldCom, the second largest long-distance telephone company in the United States and the world's largest Internet service provider. Eventually, an $11 billion scandal was uncovered. The company filed for bankruptcy—the largest such filing in U.S. history to date. The stock held by investors was worthless, and thousands of former employees lost their jobs, pensions, benefits, and severance pay.

Company executives were indicted on fraud charges; several agreed to testify against the former CEO Bernard J. Ebbers (1941–) in exchange for lighter sentences. In March 2005 Ebbers was convicted of all nine charges against him. He received a sentence of twenty-five years in prison.

TYCO. In 2002 Tyco International became embroiled in a series of scandals centered on L. Dennis Kozlowski (1946–), the company's CEO, and Mark H. Swartz (1960–), the company's chief financial officer (CFO). Both men resigned and were sued by Tyco in connection with $600 million in loans, salary, and fringe benefits they allegedly took from the company without board approval. The government indicted the men for grand larceny and securities fraud, among other criminal charges.

Kozlowski and Swartz were first tried in September 2003. Particularly at issue during the trial was Kozlowski's extravagant lifestyle. Prosecutors told of Kozlowski throwing his wife a $2.1 million birthday party paid for in part by Tyco, living in a $19 million Manhattan duplex bought for him by the company, and purchasing a $6,000 shower curtain, all while Tyco investors lost millions because of his stock manipulations. The case was declared a mistrial in April 2004 when a juror, suspected of communicating with defense attorneys, was named in the media and subsequently received threatening letters and phone calls. In 2005 the men were retried, found guilty, and sentenced to up to twenty-five years in prison.

QWEST COMMUNICATIONS. In 2001 federal officials began investigating an accounting scandal at Qwest Communications International. The government ultimately found that the company had overstated its earnings by more than $2 billion. By the time the scandal became public in 2002, top Qwest executives had sold millions of dollars in company stock, even though they knew the company was in serious financial trouble. In 2006 Robin Szeliga (1961–), Qwest's former CFO, was sentenced to two years' probation, with the first six months home detention, and fined $250,000 for her role in the scandal. She received a light sentence in exchange for testifying against other top executives, including the CEO Joseph P. Nacchio (1949–). In July 2007 Nacchio was sentenced to six years in federal prison, fined $19 million, and ordered to forfeit $52 million he made from illegal stock sales. In March 2008 Nacchio's lawyers won an appeal for a retrial.

Big Tobacco: An Industry under Attack

In the 1990s many state governments brought lawsuits against the nation's major tobacco firms to recoup taxpayer money spent treating sick smokers under state Medicaid programs. In 1998 a settlement was reached in which the companies agreed to pay a total of $246 billion spread among the governments of all fifty states. The payments are to be made over a twenty-five-year period. The settlement also required the tobacco companies to change their advertising methods and reduce their political lobbying efforts.

In 1999 the federal government filed its own lawsuit, *United States v. Philip Morris* (116 F. Supp. 2d 131), against the tobacco companies, alleging that the defendants had engaged in a decades-long scheme to "defraud the American public" regarding the safety of cigarette smoking. The case centered on internal documents obtained from tobacco companies that seemed to demonstrate that the companies were well aware that nicotine was addictive and cigarette smoking caused lung cancer. The trial began in 2004 and lasted for nine months.

In August 2006 Judge Gladys Kessler (1938–) of the U.S. District Court for the District of Columbia ruled that the cigarette companies had committed civil violations of the Racketeer Influenced and Corrupt Organizations (RICO) Act. However, rulings by other courts during 2005 meant that the government could not receive billions of dollars in penalty fines that it had sought from the tobacco companies. Kessler did order the companies to remove terms such as *light* and *ultra light* from cigarette packaging. That order was stayed (delayed) several months later when the companies appealed the case. In 2007 the federal government began filing legal briefs indicating its intent to also appeal the case. As of July 2008, those appeals had not been heard in court.

The lawsuits represent an unusual occurrence in U.S. history, because the government has brought financial pressure on an entire industry. Rising costs of doing business in an unfavorable climate have led tobacco companies to raise prices. Price inflation for tobacco products has outpaced the general inflation rate over this period, particularly since 1999. On the flip side of the supply-demand relationship, the consumption of cigarettes has dropped dramatically. This is likely due to a combination of price pressure and greater public awareness about the dangers of smoking. The total U.S. consumption of cigarettes peaked in the 1980s at around 640 billion cigarettes per year. (See Figure 6.5.) Since then, consumption has plummeted; only 378 billion cigarettes were purchased in 2005, based on preliminary estimates.

Gregory N. Connolly and Hillel R. Alpert report in "Trends in the Use of Cigarettes and Other Tobacco Products, 2000–2007" (*Journal of the American Medical Association*, vol. 299, no. 21, June 11, 2008) that U.S. sales of cigarette packs decreased from 21.1 billion in 2000 to 17.4 billion in 2007, an 18% decline.

Public Perception of Big Business

In June 2007 the Gallup Organization conducted a poll to gauge public confidence in various institutions.

FIGURE 6.5

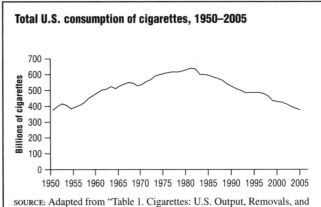

Total U.S. consumption of cigarettes, 1950–2005

SOURCE: Adapted from "Table 1. Cigarettes: U.S. Output, Removals, and Consumption, 1950–2005," in *Tobacco Yearbook 2005*, U.S. Department of Agriculture, Economic Research Service, January 2006, http://usda.mannlib.cornell.edu/usda/ers/92015/Tab01.xls (accessed June 10, 2008)

FIGURE 6.6

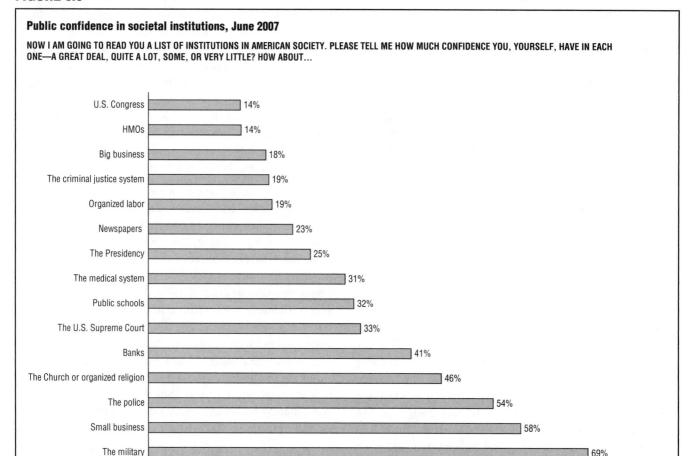

Public confidence in societal institutions, June 2007

NOW I AM GOING TO READ YOU A LIST OF INSTITUTIONS IN AMERICAN SOCIETY. PLEASE TELL ME HOW MUCH CONFIDENCE YOU, YOURSELF, HAVE IN EACH ONE—A GREAT DEAL, QUITE A LOT, SOME, OR VERY LITTLE? HOW ABOUT...

Institution	Percent
U.S. Congress	14%
HMOs	14%
Big business	18%
The criminal justice system	19%
Organized labor	19%
Newspapers	23%
The Presidency	25%
The medical system	31%
Public schools	32%
The U.S. Supreme Court	33%
Banks	41%
The Church or organized religion	46%
The police	54%
Small business	58%
The military	69%

SOURCE: Adapted from "Question qn11. Now I Am Going To Read You a List of Institutions in American Society. Please Tell Me How Much Confidence You, Yourself, Have in Each One—a Great Deal, Quite a Lot, Some, or Very Little? How about…," in *June Wave 2*, The Gallup Organization, June 11–14, 2007, http://brain.gallup.com/documents/questionnaire.aspx?STUDY=P0706021 (accessed May 19, 2008). Copyright © 2007 by The Gallup Organization. Reproduced by permission of The Gallup Organization.

The military garnered the highest rating, with 69% of those asked expressing a great deal or quite a lot of confidence in the military. (See Figure 6.6.) Small business also fared well with 58% of respondents providing a favorable opinion. Big business received a much lower rating. Only 18% of respondents had a great deal or quite a lot of confidence in big business.

CHAPTER 7
SAVING AND INVESTING

If you would be wealthy, think of saving as well as of getting.

—Benjamin Franklin, *The Way to Wealth* (1779)

Saving and investing are two sides of the same coin. The purpose of saving is to put aside money for use in the future. Saved money can actually make money if it is put into a bank account that earns interest. This is basically a low-risk investment with a low rate of return, but it does preserve the money for the future. Investing is another matter. It means exchanging money for assets that may or may not go up in value over time. Investments that go up in value reap profits for the investor, and those profits can be modest or extravagant. Investments that go down in value are another story. Some or even all the original money invested is lost. Thus, investing entails risk, particularly in a market-driven economy where fluctuations in supply and demand determine the profitability of investments. At a macroeconomic level, the U.S. economy thrives on investing—it provides money for business growth and government expenses. From a microeconomic standpoint, Americans are urged to save and/or gainfully invest some of their earnings to ensure that they have a safety net in the event of a personal financial crisis and to sustain them after they retire.

PERSONAL SAVING RATE

The personal saving rate is a government-measured rate that tracks how much money Americans have available for saving and investing. It is calculated by the U.S. Department of Commerce's Bureau of Economic Analysis (BEA) using data from many sources on income, taxes, government revenues and expenses, and personal expenses. The rate is actually a ratio of two BEA measures: personal saving and disposable personal income (DPI). The DPI is defined as personal income (e.g., wages and salaries) minus tax and nontax payments made to the government. Personal saving is determined by subtracting personal

outlays (which are 97% personal consumption expenditures) from DPI. Thus, personal saving is the money left over. This value is divided by the DPI to show what percentage of DPI is available for saving and investing.

Because the personal saving rate is based on so many other calculated variables, any small errors in the dependent variables will be exaggerated in the rate itself. In addition, the BEA excludes from its definition of income certain wealth components such as capital gains (which is an increase in the value of an asset). As a result, the agency admits that the personal saving rate gives an incomplete picture of household savings behavior. However, it is useful for tracking changes over time.

Table 7.1 shows the amounts and derivations of personal saving from 1959 to the third quarter of 2007. Personal saving was $56.7 billion in 2007, based on a seasonally adjusted annual rate calculated using data for the third quarter of 2007. Personal saving peaked in 1992 at $366 billion and then began to decline dramatically. Figure 7.1 shows the personal saving rate for the first quarter of 2000 to the first quarter of 2008. The rate is calculated by dividing personal saving by DPI. The rate was positive through the second quarter of 2005 and negative in the subsequent quarter. A negative amount of personal saving indicates that Americans spent more than their disposable income. From the fourth quarter of 2005 through the first quarter of 2008 the saving rate was positive, with the exception of the third quarter of 2006, when it was slightly less than zero.

DEFINING INVESTMENTS

In the broadest sense, any money expenditure that returns a profit is considered an investment. Thus, the cost of a college education would be considered an investment, because it will likely increase earnings potential in the future. In this discussion, investments are limited to tangible

TABLE 7.1

Disposition of personal income, 1959–third quarter 2007

[Billions of dollars, quarterly data at seasonally adjusted annual rates]

Year or quarter	Personal income	Less: personal current taxes	Equals: disposable personal income	Less: personal outlays				Equals: personal saving
				Total	Personal consumption expenditures	Personal interest payments*	Personal current transfer payments	
1959	392.8	42.3	350.5	323.9	317.6	5.5	0.8	26.7
1960	411.5	46.1	365.4	338.8	331.7	6.2	.8	26.7
1961	429.0	47.3	381.8	349.6	342.1	6.5	1.0	32.2
1962	456.7	51.6	405.1	371.3	363.3	7.0	1.1	33.8
1963	479.6	54.6	425.1	391.8	382.7	7.9	1.2	31.3
1964	514.6	52.1	462.5	421.7	411.4	8.9	1.3	40.8
1965	555.7	57.7	498.1	455.1	443.8	9.9	1.4	43.0
1966	603.9	66.4	537.5	493.1	480.9	10.7	1.6	44.4
1967	648.3	73.0	575.3	520.9	507.8	11.1	2.0	54.4
1968	712.0	87.0	625.0	572.2	558.0	12.2	2.0	52.8
1969	778.5	104.5	674.0	621.4	605.2	14.0	2.2	52.5
1970	838.8	103.1	735.7	666.2	648.5	15.2	2.6	69.5
1971	903.5	1017	801.8	721.2	701.9	16.6	2.8	80.6
1972	992.7	1236	869.1	791.9	770.6	18.1	3.1	77.2
1973	1,110.7	132.4	978.3	875.6	852.4	19.8	3.4	102.7
1974	1,222.6	151.0	1,071.6	958.0	933.4	21.2	3.4	113.6
1975	1,335.0	1476	1,187.4	1,061.9	1,034.4	23.7	3.8	125.6
1976	1,474.8	172.3	1,302.5	1,180.2	1,151.9	23.9	4.4	122.3
1977	1,633.2	197.5	1,435.7	1,310.4	1,278.6	27.0	4.8	125.3
1978	1,837.7	229.4	1,608.3	1,465.8	1,428.5	31.9	5.4	142.5
1979	2,062.2	268.7	1,793.5	1,634.4	1,592.2	36.2	5.9	159.1
1980	2,307.9	298.9	2,009.0	1,807.5	1,757.1	43.6	6.8	201.4
1981	2,591.3	345.2	2,246.1	2,001.8	1,941.1	49.3	11.4	244.3
1982	2,775.3	354.1	2,421.2	2,150.4	2,077.3	59.5	13.6	270.8
1983	2,960.7	352.3	2,608.4	2,374.8	2,290.6	69.2	15.0	233.6
1984	3,289.5	377.4	2,912.0	2,597.3	2,503.3	77.0	16.9	314.8
1985	3,526.7	417.4	3,109.3	2,829.3	2,720.3	90.4	18.6	280.0
1986	3,722.4	437.3	3,285.1	3,016.7	2,899.7	96.1	20.9	268.4
1987	3,947.4	489.1	3,458.3	3,216.9	3,100.2	93.6	23.1	241.4
1988	4,253.7	505.0	3,748.7	3,475.8	3,353.6	96.8	25.4	272.9
1989	4,587.8	566.1	4,021.7	3,734.5	3,598.5	108.2	27.8	287.1
1990	4,878.6	592.8	4,285.8	3,986.4	3,839.9	116.1	30.4	299.4
1991	5,051.0	586.7	4,464.3	4,140.1	3,986.1	118.5	35.6	324.2
1992	5,362.0	610.6	4,751.4	4,385.4	4,235.3	111.8	38.3	366.0
1993	5,558.5	646.6	4,911.9	4,627.9	4,477.9	107.3	42.7	284.0
1994	5,842.5	690.7	5,151.8	4,902.4	4,743.3	112.8	46.3	249.5
1995	6,152.3	744.1	5,408.2	5,157.3	4,975.8	132.7	48.9	250.9
1996	6,520.6	832.1	5,688.5	5,460.0	5,256.8	150.3	52.9	228.4
1997	6,915.1	926.3	5,988.8	5,770.5	5,547.4	163.9	59.2	218.3
1998	7,423.0	1,027.0	6,395.9	6,119.1	5,879.5	174.5	65.2	276.8
1999	7,802.4	1,107.5	6,695.0	6,536.4	6,282.5	181.0	73.0	158.6
2000	8,429.7	1,235.7	7,194.0	7,025.6	6,739.4	204.7	81.5	168.5
2001	8,724.1	1,237.3	7,486.8	7,354.5	7,055.0	212.2	87.2	132.3
2002	8,881.9	1,051.8	7,830.1	7,645.3	7,350.7	196.4	98.2	184.7
2003	9,163.6	1,001.1	8,162.5	7,987.7	7,703.6	182.5	101.5	174.9
2004	9,727.2	1,046.3	8,680.9	8,499.2	8,195.9	191.3	112.1	181.7
2005	10,301.1	1,209.1	9,092.0	9,047.4	8,707.8	217.7	121.8	44.6
2006	10,983.4	1,354.3	9,629.1	9,590.3	9,2241.5	238.0	127.8	38.8
2007:I	11,469.2	1,454.7	10,014.5	9,917.5	9,540.5	243.3	133.7	97.0
II	11,577.3	1,477.6	10,099.7	10,069.2	9,6741.0	259.5	135.7	30.5
III	11,746.7	1,489.2	10,257.5	10,200.9	9,785.7	275.8	139.3	56.7

*Consists of nonmortgage interest paid by households.

SOURCE: Adapted from "Table B-30. Disposition of Personal Income, 1959–2007," in *Economic Report of the President*, U.S. Government Printing Office, February 2008, http://www.gpoaccess.gov/eop/2008/2008_erp.pdf (accessed May 23, 2008)

assets (such as cash or real estate) and intangible financial assets (such as stocks, bonds, and other securities).

SAVINGS ACCOUNTS

Savings accounts are accounts held at financial institutions in which customers can deposit money for safe-keeping. Deposits up to $100,000 per customer are insured at most financial institutions by the Federal Deposit Insurance Corporation (FDIC), an independent government agency. FDIC insurance ensures depositors that their money will be repaid even if the financial institution goes out of business.

FIGURE 7.1

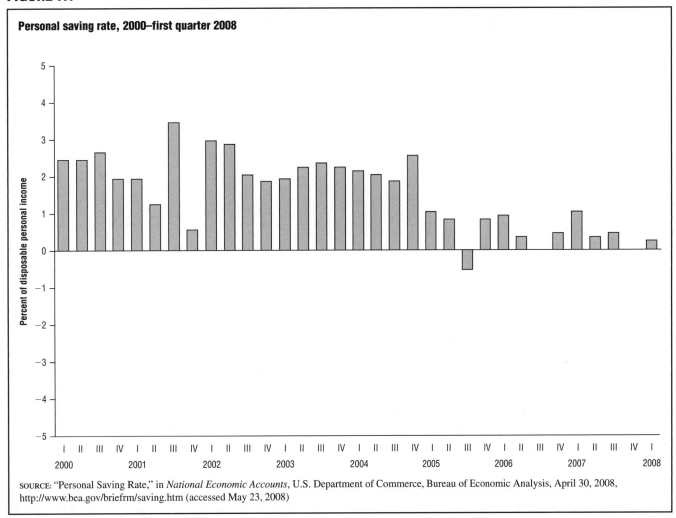

Personal saving rate, 2000–first quarter 2008

SOURCE: "Personal Saving Rate," in *National Economic Accounts*, U.S. Department of Commerce, Bureau of Economic Analysis, April 30, 2008, http://www.bea.gov/briefrm/saving.htm (accessed May 23, 2008)

The Survey of Consumer Finances (SCF) is a survey conducted every three years by the Federal Reserve Board, the national bank of the United States, in cooperation with the Internal Revenue Service, to collect detailed financial information on American families. The most recent SCF was conducted in 2007; however, those results had not been published as of July 2008. Thus, this discussion relies on 2004 SCF data.

According to Brian K. Bucks, Arthur B. Kennickell, and Kevin B. Moore of the Federal Reserve, in "Recent Changes in U.S. Family Finances: Evidence from the 2001 and 2004 Survey of Consumer Finances" (*Federal Reserve Bulletin*, February 2006), less than half (47.1%) of American families had a savings account in 2004.

Variations on savings accounts include money market deposit accounts (which allow limited withdrawals in some circumstances) and certificates of deposit (CDs). CDs are savings accounts in which money is placed for a predetermined amount of time, commonly one to five years, in exchange for payment of a set interest rate throughout that time period. There are penalties for early withdrawal of the money.

GOVERNMENT SECURITIES

The government issues a variety of securities with the purpose of earning revenue. Local and state governments sell bonds to raise funds for public projects, such as road improvement or school construction. A bond is basically an IOU from the government that promises to pay back the borrowed amount plus interest at a specified future date (the maturity date). The federal government also sells bonds (called savings bonds) through the U.S. Department of Treasury.

Savings bonds are not marketable securities. They can only be sold or redeemed by the Department of Treasury. Treasury bills (T-bills) are short-term securities that mature within a few days or up to twenty-six weeks. The customer purchases a T-bill for less than its face value and then receives face value at maturity. For example, a customer might pay $90 upfront for a $100 T-bill. When the T-bill matures, the customer will receive the $100. T-bills can be bought and sold in other markets. Treasury notes (T-notes) have maturity periods lasting two, three, five, and ten years. They earn a fixed rate of

FIGURE 7.2

Yield on 10-year Treasury notes, 1995–2008

SOURCE: Adapted from "Market Yield on U.S. Treasury Securities at 10-Year Constant Maturity, Quoted on Investment Basis," in *H.15 Selected Interest Rates: Treasury Constant Maturities*, U.S. Federal Reserve, May 2008, http://www.federalreserve.gov/releases/h15/data/Monthly/H15_TCMNOM_Y10 .txt (accessed May 23, 2008)

interest every six months. T-notes can be sold by the customer before the maturity date.

Figure 7.2 shows the annual percent yield between 1995 and 2008 on a ten-year T-note. The interest paid on the ten-year T-note decreased during the late 1990s, rebounded in 2000, and then declined through 2003. After rising for several years, the rate took another drop beginning in early 2007.

HOMEOWNERSHIP AS AN INVESTMENT

One of the largest investments made by most Americans is the purchase of a home. Because real estate tends to appreciate in value, buying a home is considered a relatively low-risk investment. During the mid-1980s interest rates began a downward trend in response to rate cuts by the Federal Reserve. The result was a boom in home purchases and refinancings that lasted into the middle of the first decade of the 2000s. In 2005 the housing market began a sharp market downturn that had not subsided as of July 2008. Figure 7.3 shows the sales rate for newly built and existing single-family homes from 1997 through the spring of 2008. Annual sales of newly built homes peaked above 1.4 million units in 2005 and then plummeted to 530,000 units by March 2008. (Note that these are seasonally adjusted annual rates). Annual sales

of existing homes exceeded six million units in 2005 and early 2006 before declining sharply. As of March 2008, annual sales were estimated at 4.3 million units.

Table 7.2 shows the vacancy rates for owner homes and rental units between 1995 and early 2008. The vacancy rate of owner homes was less than 2% through 2005, and then it began to rise. The homeowner vacancy rate for the first quarter of 2008 was 2.9%. In contrast, the rental vacancy rate soared to 10.4% in the early 2000s and remained high in the first quarter of 2008 by historical standards. Economists agree that high vacancy rates are generally an indicator of a sluggish economy.

The Housing Bubble Bursts

A housing bubble is a condition in which homes become overvalued due to overconfidence by exuberant investors. As described in Chapter 1, a stock market bubble in Internet-based companies grew and then burst in 2000, causing major losses for some investors. A bubble is only obvious after the fact, when investments suddenly plummet in value and it becomes apparent that they were overvalued.

Appreciating home prices and decreasing interest rates combined to make the housing market attractive to investors during the 1990s and early 2000s. Flipping is a practice in which a home is purchased as a short-term

FIGURE 7.3

Number of single-family homes sold, 1997–March 2008

[Millions of units, seasonally adjusted annual rate]

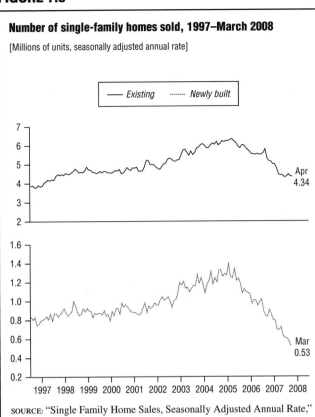

SOURCE: "Single Family Home Sales, Seasonally Adjusted Annual Rate," in *National Economic Indicators: Housing Investment*, Federal Reserve Bank of New York, May 23, 2008, http://www.ny.frb.org/research/directors_charts/ibcd_04.pdf (accessed May 23, 2008)

TABLE 7.2

Vacancy rates for rental units and owned homes, 1995–2008

[In percent]

Year	Rental vacancy rate				Homeowner vacancy rate			
	First quarter	Second quarter	Third quarter	Fourth quarter	First quarter	Second quarter	Third quarter	Fourth quarter
2008	10.1				2.9			
2007	10.1	9.5	9.8	9.6	2.8	2.6	2.7	2.8
2006	9.5	9.6	9.9	9.8	2.1	2.2	2.5	2.7
2005	10.1	9.8	9.9	9.6	1.8	1.8	1.9	2.0
2004	10.4	10.2	10.1	10.0	1.7	1.7	1.7	1.8
2003	9.4	9.6	9.9	10.2	1.7	1.7	1.9	1.8
2002*	9.1	8.4	9.0	9.3	1.7	1.7	1.7	1.7
2002	9.1	8.5	9.1	9.4	1.7	1.7	1.7	1.7
2001	8.2	8.3	8.4	8.8	1.5	1.8	1.9	1.8
2000	7.9	8.0	8.2	7.8	1.6	1.5	1.6	1.6
1999	8.2	8.1	8.2	7.9	1.8	1.6	1.6	1.6
1998	7.7	8.0	8.2	7.8	1.7	1.7	1.7	1.8
1997	7.5	7.9	7.9	7.7	1.7	1.6	1.5	1.7
1996	7.9	7.8	8.0	7.7	1.6	1.5	1.7	1.7
1995	7.4	7.7	7.7	7.7	1.5	1.6	1.5	1.6

*Revised in 2002 to incorporate information collected in Census 2000.
Note: The estimates in this report are based on responses from a sample of the population and may differ from actual values because of sampling variability or other factors. As a result, apparent differences between the estimates for two or more groups may not be statistically significant. The data in this report are from the monthly samples of the Housing Vacancy Survey, which is a supplement to the Current Population Survey. The populations represented (the population universe) are all housing units (vacancy rates) and the civilian noninstitutional population of the United States (homeownership rate).

SOURCE: Robert R. Callis and Linda B. Cavanaugh, "Table 1. Rental and Homeowner Vacancy Rates for the United States: 1995 to 2008 (in Percent)," in *Census Bureau Reports on Residential Vacancies and Homeownership*, U.S. Department of Commerce, U.S. Census Bureau, April 28, 2008, http://www.census.gov/hhes/www/housing/hvs/qtr108/q108press.pdf (accessed May 23, 2008)

investment, rather than for living purposes. During a housing boom homes can be bought and resold quickly for a handsome profit. Likewise, homeowners who want to move may wait for a boom to peak before selling or sell quickly and rent in anticipation of lower home prices after the bubble bursts. The gamble for all parties involved is the difficulty of predicting when a boom will end and prices will fall.

Cynthia Angell and Norman Williams of the FDIC conducted a study to quantify housing booms and busts that have occurred since 1978 and reported their findings in "U.S. Home Prices: Does Bust Always Follow Boom?" (February 10, 2005, http://www.fdic.gov/bank/analytical/fyi/2005/021005fyi.html). The researchers define a boom as occurring when inflation-adjusted home prices in an area increase by 30% or more during any three-year period. Using this criterion, Angell and Williams identify dozens of metropolitan areas around the country that have experienced temporary housing booms that could be described as unsustainable bubbles. Geographically, they were concentrated in California and the Northeast.

Housing Price Index

The Office of Federal Housing Enterprise Oversight (OFHEO) is a federal financial regulator. It was estab-

lished as an independent entity within the U.S. Department of Housing and Urban Development by the Federal Housing Enterprises Financial Safety and Soundness Act of 1992. The OFHEO House Price Index (HPI) provides an indicator of home appreciation (increase in home value) by measuring average price changes in repeat sales of the same properties over time.

In *Decline in House Prices Accelerates in First Quarter* (May 22, 2008, http://www.ofheo.gov/media/hpi/1q08hpi.pdf), the OFHEO explains that, nationwide, home prices appreciated dramatically during the late 1990s and early 2000s. (See Figure 7.4.) Appreciation peaked in 2005 and then plummeted. The HPI was actually negative from the third quarter of 2007 through the first quarter of 2008. The HPI decline of 1.7% in the first quarter of 2008 was the largest quarterly decrease recorded by OFHEO since the index began in 1991.

From 1997 through 2006 the OFHEO reports strong appreciation rates. (See Figure 7.5.) During 2004 and 2005 home prices appreciated by 8% to 9% per year. A definite turndown in the housing market is apparent between the first quarter of 2006 and the first quarter of 2007, when the HPI increased by only 3.2%. Between the first quarter of 2007 and the first quarter of 2008 home

FIGURE 7.4

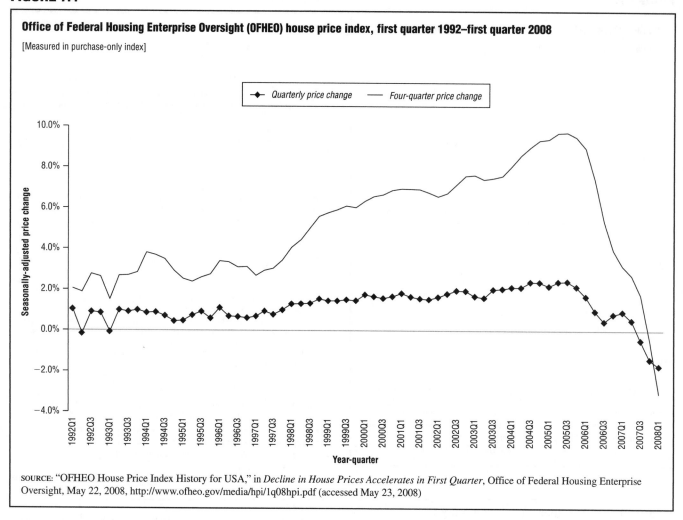

Office of Federal Housing Enterprise Oversight (OFHEO) house price index, first quarter 1992–first quarter 2008

[Measured in purchase-only index]

SOURCE: "OFHEO House Price Index History for USA," in *Decline in House Prices Accelerates in First Quarter*, Office of Federal Housing Enterprise Oversight, May 22, 2008, http://www.ofheo.gov/media/hpi/1q08hpi.pdf (accessed May 23, 2008)

prices fell by 3.1%. According to the OFHEO, the states with the sharpest depreciation levels for this period were:

- California—down 10.6%

- Nevada—down 10.3%

- Florida—down 8.1%

- Arizona—down 5.5%

- Michigan—down 3.1%

Nationwide, the OFHEO reports declines during the first quarter of 2008 in forty-three states.

Some analysts believe the OFHEO index values do not completely capture the seriousness of the housing slump, because the OFHEO only tracks conforming mortgages (i.e., mortgages that conform, or meet, loan limits set by the Federal Home Loan Mortgage Corporation [Freddie Mac] and the Federal National Mortgage Association [Fannie Mae]). Thus, the OFHEO does not track mortgages in the high-end of the market (e.g., greater than approximately $400,000).

Another index, the Standard & Poor's Case-Shiller HPI, does include high-end mortgages and is frequently reported in financial publications. Actually, dozens of indices are reported for different geographical regions. A national index tracks single-family home resales around the country and is reported quarterly. Standard & Poor's reports in the press release "National Trend of Home Price Declines Continued into the First Quarter of 2008 According to S&P/Case-Shiller Home Price Indices" (May 27, 2008, http://www2.standardandpoors.com/spf/pdf/index/CSHomePrice_Release_052703.pdf) that the Case-Shiller HPI for the first quarter of 2008 was down 14.1%, compared to the first quarter of 2007. Since early 2006 the index has experienced a continuous quarterly decline in value.

Home Mortgages

The Federal Reserve compiles home mortgage data on a quarterly and annual basis. These values are published in tabular form in "L.218 Home Mortgages" as part of the *Federal Reserve Statistical Release Z.1: Flow of Funds Accounts of the United States* (http://www.federalreserve.gov/releases/z1/). The Federal Reserve only includes mortgages secured by one-to-four family properties, including owner-occupied condominium units. Mortgage types include first and second mortgages, home equity lines of credit,

FIGURE 7.5

Office of Federal Housing Enterprise Oversight (OFHEO) house price appreciation over previous four quarters, first quarter 1998–first quarter 2008

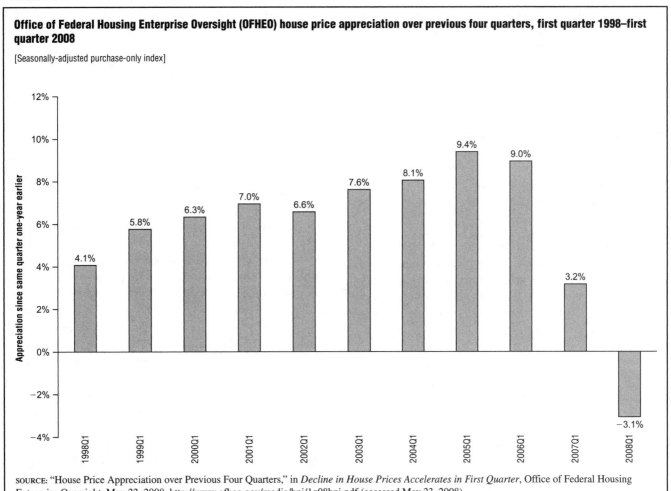

[Seasonally-adjusted purchase-only index]

SOURCE: "House Price Appreciation over Previous Four Quarters," in *Decline in House Prices Accelerates in First Quarter*, Office of Federal Housing Enterprise Oversight, May 22, 2008, http://www.ofheo.gov/media/hpi/1q08hpi.pdf (accessed May 23, 2008)

TABLE 7.3

Amounts of home mortgages for 1–4 family properties, 2003–fourth quarter 2007

[Billions of dollars; amounts outstanding end of period, not seasonally adjusted]

	2003	2004	2005	2006				2007				
				Q1	Q2	Q3	Q4	Q1	Q2	Q3	Q4	
Total liabilities	7,227.8	8,270.5	9,374.3	9,690.7	10,012.9	10,269.1	10,444.0	10,626.8	10,835.6	11,012.5	11,135.8	1
Household sector	6,882.4	7,837.6	8,866.2	9,157.7	9,456.5	9,693.1	9,854.0	10,024.9	10,223.4	10,392.4	10,508.8	2
Nonfinancial corporate business	18.8	23.5	31.1	33.7	35.9	37.9	39.4	40.4	40.3	41.1	41.4	3
Nonfarm noncorporate business	326.7	409.4	477.0	499.3	520.4	538.1	550.6	561.5	571.8	579.1	585.6	4

Note: Mortgages on 1–4 family properties includes mortages on farm houses.

SOURCE: Adapted from "Table L.218. Home Mortgages," in *Federal Reserve Statistical Release Z.1: Flow of Funds Accounts of the United States, Flow and Outstandings, Fourth Quarter 2007*, The Federal Reserve, March 6, 2008, http://www.federalreserve.gov/releases/z1/20080306/z1.pdf (accessed May 23, 2008)

mortgages held by households under seller-financing arrangements, and construction and land development loans associated with one-to-four family residences.

Table 7.3 lists outstanding mortgage amounts reported by the Federal Reserve as annual amounts from 2003 through 2005 and on a quarterly basis from 2006 and

2007. As of the end of the fourth quarter of 2007, there was more than $11.1 trillion in outstanding mortgages. The vast majority of this amount—$10.5 trillion, or 95% of the total—was devoted to the household sector. Another $586 billion in mortgages was attributed to nonfarm, non-corporate businesses. Just over $41 billion was devoted to nonfinancial corporate businesses.

SECURITIES AND COMMODITIES

Securities markets (stocks, bonds, and mutual funds) and commodities markets (raw materials and foreign currencies and securities) in the United States are used by corporations to raise money for their business operations and by individuals and banks to build wealth and, in some cases, pay for retirement. These markets have fueled periods of astounding economic growth (called bull markets), but they have also been at the center of downturns (called bear markets) and disastrous economic crashes, creating the need for an extensive regulatory system. Despite regulations, however, the markets occasionally see high-profile scandals involving major figures in the business world.

Securities are financial assets that give holders ownership or creditor rights in a particular organization. The word usually refers to stocks (also sometimes called equities), but there are other types of securities that can be bought and sold on the open market, including bonds and mutual funds. Commodities are tangible products—usually raw materials—that are bought and sold in bulk, as well as financial instruments such as foreign currencies and securities of the U.S. and foreign governments. Commodities can refer either to the material itself or to a contract to buy the item in the future.

Stocks

To raise money to operate and expand a company, its owners will often sell part of the company. A company that wants to raise money this way must first organize itself as a legal corporation. At that time, it creates shares of stock, which are small units of ownership in the company. These shares of stock can then be sold to raise funds for the company. Those who own them are called shareholders in the company. They have the right to attend shareholder meetings, inspect corporate documents, and vote on certain matters that affect the company. Shareholders may also have preemptive rights, which means they are able to buy new shares before they are offered to the public so that existing shareholders can maintain their percentage of ownership in a company.

Not all corporations offer their shares for sale to the public. When a company chooses to do so, its first sale of shares is called an initial public offering (IPO). IPO stock is purchased by investors at a price set by the company. The money paid for each share of stock is then available to the company for its business operations. In return, shareholders can receive benefits in two forms: dividends and appreciation. Dividends are a portion of the company's profits distributed to shareholders. Not all companies that issue stock pay dividends. Those that do usually pay them every quarter (a quarter is three consecutive months of the year; there are four quarters in a fiscal year), and, even though each share of stock might earn

only a few pennies in dividends, the total amounts to individual or institutional investors who hold large amounts of shares can be enormous. Appreciation is a gradual increase in the value of a share over time. If a corporation prospers, a shareholder can sell his or her share to someone else for a higher price than he or she originally paid for it. There is no guarantee that a stock will appreciate; however, it is quite possible that it will depreciate (decrease in value) over time.

TYPES OF SHAREHOLDERS. Corporations can offer different types of shares, called either common or preferred shares, with each type providing the shareholder a different set of rights. According to TD Ameritrade (2003, http://www.ameritradefinancial.com/educationv2/fhtml/stocksfunds/prevscom.fhtml), owners of common stock shares can be paid dividends in cash, property, or more stock. Cash dividends are investment earnings that are paid to the shareholder in the form of cash; they are taxed in the year in which they are paid out by a corporation to the shareholder. Property dividends are earnings usually paid in the form of the issuing company's products or services. Stock dividends are earnings paid in more shares of a company's stock. Even though cash dividends are the type of stock earning most often issued to common shareholders, a corporation may decide to stop paying dividends on a temporary basis if it is experiencing financial instability. Additionally, if a company files for bankruptcy, owners of common stock are the last to be paid, after all creditors and owners of preferred stock. Regardless, common stock shareholders do have certain rights within a company, such as the right to vote for board members and officers, which preferred stock owners do not have.

Preferred stock shareholders do earn guaranteed dividends, the values of which are set in advance and pay indefinitely unless the stock is retired or recalled. There are four different kinds of preferred stock. Cumulative preferred stock accumulates whether or not a company has suspended paying dividends, and the preferred shareholder is paid the accumulated earnings once the company begins paying dividends again. Cumulative preferred stock owners receive their dividends before common stock owners receive theirs. Noncumulative preferred stock does not accumulate over temporary dividend suspensions, and its owners do not receive dividend earnings before common stock shareholders. Participating preferred stocks allow shareholders to earn additional dividends when a company's profits exceed expectations. Convertible preferred stock can be changed into common stock if its owner wants to take advantage of common stock appreciation.

Even though both common and preferred shareholders can lose the money that they paid for their shares, as well as whatever money the shares may have earned since the initial purchase, they have what is called limited liability, meaning they cannot be held financially responsible for any lawsuits filed against the company. This limited liability is one of the most important characteristics of stock ownership. Without limited liability, people would not want to become part owners of the corporation, and the corporation would therefore have trouble raising the money it needs to operate and expand.

PRICING SHARES. When a corporation creates shares, it determines the price per share for the initial public offering. From then on the price of each share depends on the public's perception of how well the corporation is doing. The more profit a corporation makes, the higher the price per share is likely to be. The challenge for investors is that they cannot predict the future, and stock prices tend to fluctuate up and down over time. A variety of events can influence a stock's price, from the release of a popular new product to news that a company's chief executive officer is being investigated for fraud.

The market for stocks sold by shareholders to other shareholders is called the secondary stock market. It would be almost impossible for all shareholders to find buyers for their shares on their own when they choose to sell. To make it easier for shareholders to buy and sell shares, companies affiliate with a particular stock exchange that handles share transactions. The two most prominent exchanges in the United States are the New York Stock Exchange (NYSE) and the National Association of Securities Dealers Automated Quotations (NASDAQ). The NYSE and NASDAQ are themselves publicly traded companies. The United States also hosts the American Stock Exchange in New York City, the Boston Stock Exchange, the Philadelphia Stock Exchange, the Chicago Stock Exchange, and the Pacific Exchange in San Francisco, California. Additionally, there are stock exchanges in most countries throughout the world.

Bonds

Another way for a company to raise money is to borrow it. Companies can borrow from banks, just like individuals, but they can also borrow by issuing bonds, which are written promises to pay the bondholder back with interest. Bonds have a face value, called par, and that amount defines the amount of the debt.

A bond offers returns to holders in two ways. The organization that issued the bond pays interest to the holder, and the holder can redeem the bond after a certain period. That is, the holder can sell the bond back to the organization for its face value. The issuing organization will either make regular interest payments on the bond or initially sell the bond at a much lower price than the face value. After a certain amount of time (often many years), the holder can redeem the bond for face value.

Bonds differ from shares of stock in several important respects. First, any organization can issue bonds, whereas only corporations can issue stock. For that reason, unincorporated businesses and federal, state, and local governments use bonds to raise money. Second, bonds provide no ownership interest in the company. The organization's only obligation to the bondholder is to pay the debt and interest. Bonds are usually less risky for the purchaser than stocks, because the organization is legally obligated to pay the debt, whereas if a corporation has financial difficulties, it is not permitted to pay anything to shareholders until it has paid off its creditors. However, the rate of return on investment for stocks is generally higher than on bonds to compensate for the higher risk factor. Like stocks, though, bonds are traded by investors for prices that may be different from the par value. Investors who buy bonds are buying the right to receive the interest payments and to redeem the bond.

The price of a bond depends on a number of factors, including the organization's creditworthiness and the interest rate. Generally, the better the organization's credit rating, the higher the price of the bond. If the organization begins to have financial problems that could affect its ability to repay the bonds, the price of those bonds will go down. One of the best-known rating companies for bonds is Standard & Poor's, which rates issuing organizations on a scale ranging from AAA to D.

Bonds may be short term or long term. Long-term bonds are riskier than short-term bonds, and therefore tend to pay higher interest rates.

Mutual Funds

Most investors try to diversify investments; that is, they put money into a number of different types of investments, rather than just one or two (a person's total investments are called his or her portfolio). That way, even if one investment loses money, another may make enough profit to compensate for the loss.

However, for small investors it can be difficult to diversify. It takes time to evaluate different investments, and small investors may only be able to afford to buy one or two shares of each stock. Most brokers have a minimum purchase requirement that is higher than what the average investor can afford. Mutual funds were developed to solve such problems for small investors. In a mutual fund, the money of multiple investors is pooled and then invested in stocks, bonds, or both. The managers of the mutual fund then buy and sell the stocks and bonds on behalf of the investors. By combining their money, small investors are able to diversify.

Unlike the prices of stocks and bonds, the price of a mutual fund is determined by the fund manager, rather than by the open market. This price, called the net asset value, is based on the fund manager's estimation of the fund's value at a particular time. Mutual funds may be purchased either directly from the fund manager or through a broker or other intermediary. The latter is more expensive, because the investor will be required to pay fees. Mutual funds provide income to investors in two ways. First, if the mutual fund sells stocks or bonds at a profit or receives dividends or interest payments on bonds, these gains can be paid to investors as distributions. Second, the price of the mutual fund itself may go up, in which case investors can sell their mutual funds for more than they paid.

Some people are willing to take a fair amount of risk when they invest, hoping that they will make more money. Usually, the riskier the investment is, the higher the potential return on it is. Others would rather get a smaller return but know that their money is invested in a safer vehicle. Different types of mutual funds have been developed to meet the needs of these different types of investors. Mutual funds differ just as investors do in how much risk they want to take. Some mutual funds invest more conservatively than others. The safest type of mutual fund—and the one that pays the lowest interest—is a money-market fund, which invests in short-term bonds such as T-bills.

Commodities

The term *commodity*, in the narrow sense used here, means a contract to buy or sell something that will be available in the future. (In a broader sense, anything that can be bought or sold is a commodity.) These sorts of agreements are traded in commodities exchanges. Two important exchanges in the United States are the Chicago Board of Trade and the Kansas City Board of Trade.

There are two basic types of commodities. Futures are standardized contracts in which the seller promises to deliver a particular good to the buyer at a specified time in the future, at which point the buyer will pay the seller the price called for in the contract. Options on futures (which are usually simply called options) are more complicated. Depending on their exact terms, they establish the right of the buyer of the option to either buy or sell a futures contract for a specified price. Options that establish the right to buy a futures contract are call options. Those that establish the right to sell a futures contract are put options. In either case, the buyer of the option only has a limited time in which he or she can exercise his or her right, but the buyer is also free not to exercise the right at all.

The meaning of a commodities contract has changed over the years. Raw materials and agricultural commodities have been traded through commodities exchanges since the mid-nineteenth century. More recently, commodities markets have expanded to include trading in foreign currencies, U.S. and foreign government securities, and U.S. and foreign stock indexes.

Because contracts are made before the goods are actually available, commodities are by their very nature speculative. Buyers purchase commodities because they think their value may increase over time, whereas the sellers think their value may decrease. For example, the seller of a grain futures contract may believe there will be a surplus of grain that will drive down prices, whereas the buyer thinks a shortage of grain will drive up prices. It is the speculative nature of commodities that makes them interesting to investors. Even if they have no need for the goods that the commodities contracts represent, speculative investors can make a profit by buying the commodities contracts at low prices and then selling them to others when prices rise. Commodities respond differently than stocks and bonds to market forces such as inflation; therefore, they can be a valuable part of a diversified portfolio. However, they are riskier and more difficult to understand.

INVESTMENT OPTIONS

Thanks to retirement investment options including 401(k) plans (funds that workers can contribute to on a before-tax basis and that grow tax-free until the money is withdrawn), a large percentage of Americans are now stock market investors. Given that Social Security retirement benefits are relatively low compared to a person's career income, and that the long-term solvency (the state of having enough money to pay all debts) of Social Security continues to be in question, retirement funds are essential to the baby-boom and later generations as they approach retirement age.

Historically, stocks have appreciated faster than inflation has increased, allowing people to build greater wealth than if they attempted to save money in traditional accounts. Investments can also serve as collateral for certain loans. Therefore, even though Wall Street might seem far away, it provides small investors the opportunity to build wealth and prepare for retirement far more effectively than they otherwise could.

The stock market has also made it easier for employers to contribute to their employees' retirement funds. This is because many employers contribute company stock, instead of cash, to their employees' retirement accounts.

Retirement accounts are the most commonly held type of financial asset. Nearly half (49.7%) of all families surveyed in 2004 had a retirement account. (See Table 7.4.) Another 20.7% held stocks, 17.6% had savings bonds, and 1.8% had bonds of other types.

According to the Investment Company Institute (ICI), in *2008 Investment Company Fact Book* (2008, http://www.icifactbook.org/pdf/2008_factbook.pdf), retirement assets were greater than $17.6 trillion in 2007, up 7% from 2006. The ICI notes that the largest types of retirement

TABLE 7.4

Family holdings of financial assets, 2004

Family characteristic	Transaction accounts	Certificates of deposit	Savings bonds	Bonds	Stocks	Pooled investment funds	Retirement accounts	Cash value life insurance	Other managed assets	Other	Any financial asset
					Percentage of families holding asset						
All families	**91.3**	**12.7**	**17.6**	**1.8**	**20.7**	**15.0**	**49.7**	**24.2**	**7.3**	**10.0**	**93.8**
Percentile of income											
Less than 20	75.5	5.0	6.2	*	5.1	3.6	10.1	14.0	3.1	7.1	80.1
20–39.9	87.3	12.7	8.8	*	8.2	7.6	30.0	19.2	4.9	9.9	91.5
40–59.9	95.9	11.8	15.4	*	16.3	12.7	53.4	24.2	7.9	9.3	98.5
60–79.9	98.4	14.9	26.6	2.2	28.2	18.6	69.7	29.8	7.8	11.2	99.1
80–89.9	99.1	16.3	32.3	2.8	35.8	26.2	81.9	29.5	12.1	11.4	99.8
90–100	100.0	21.5	29.9	8.8	55.0	39.1	88.5	38.1	13.0	13.4	100.0
Age of head (years)											
Less than 35	86.4	5.6	15.3	*	13.3	8.3	40.2	11.0	2.9	11.6	90.1
35–44	90.8	6.7	23.3	.6	18.5	12.3	55.9	20.1	3.7	10.0	93.6
45–54	91.8	11.9	21.0	1.8	23.2	18.2	57.7	26.0	6.2	12.1	93.6
55–64	93.2	18.1	15.2	3.3	29.1	20.6	62.9	32.1	9.4	7.2	95.2
65–74	93.9	19.9	14.9	4.3	25.4	18.6	43.2	34.8	12.8	8.1	96.5
75 or more	96.4	25.7	11.0	3.0	18.4	16.6	29.2	34.0	16.7	8.1	97.6
Race or ethnicity of respondent											
White non-Hispanic	95.5	15.3	21.1	2.5	25.5	18.9	56.1	26.8	9.2	10.2	97.2
Nonwhite or Hispanic	80.6	6.0	8.5	*	8.0	5.0	32.9	17.4	2.1	9.4	85.0
Current work status of head											
Working for someone else	92.2	9.8	20.1	.8	19.6	13.5	57.1	21.8	5.4	9.5	94.5
Self-employed	94.4	14.2	18.7	4.3	31.6	22.3	54.6	29.8	7.6	15.1	96.1
Retired	90.4	20.2	11.4	3.5	19.0	16.2	32.9	29.7	12.8	8.4	93.6
Other not working	76.2	7.9	14.5	*	14.3	10.2	24.9	10.7	*	11.5	79.6
Housing status											
Owner	96.0	15.9	21.2	2.6	25.8	19.2	60.2	30.1	9.6	9.6	97.5
Renter or other	80.9	5.6	9.5	.2	9.1	5.7	26.2	11.0	2.0	10.9	85.5
Percentile of net worth											
Less than 25	75.4	2.2	6.2	*	3.6	2.0	14.3	7.7	*	6.9	79.8
25–49.9	92.0	6.5	13.2	*	9.3	7.2	43.1	19.3	2 3	9.5	96.1
50–74.9	98.0	16.0	22.7	*	21.0	12.5	61.8	30.1	8.8	10.2	99.4
75–89.9	99.7	24.2	28.5	3.2	39.1	32.4	77.6	36.7	15.6	11.2	100.0
90–100	100.0	28.8	28.1	12.7	62.9	47.3	82.5	43.8	21.0	16.4	100.0
					Median value of holdings for families holding asset (thousands of 2004 dollars)						
All families	**3.8**	**15.0**	**1.0**	**65.0**	**15.0**	**40.4**	**35.2**	**6.0**	**45.0**	**4.0**	**23.0**
Percentile of income											
Less than 20	.6	10.0	.4	*	6.0	15.3	5.0	2.8	22.0	2.5	1.3
20–39.9	1.5	14.0	.6	*	8.0	25.0	10.0	3.9	50.0	2.0	4.9
40–59.9	3.0	10.0	.8	*	12.0	23.0	17.2	5.0	36.0	2.5	15.5
60–79.9	6.6	18.0	1.0	80.0	10.0	25.5	32.0	7.0	35.0	4.0	48.5
80–89.9	11.0	20.0	.8	26.7	15.0	33.5	70.0	10.0	50.0	5.0	108.2
90–100	28.0	33.0	2.0	160.0	57.0	125.0	182.7	20.0	100.0	20.0	365.1
Age of head (years)											
Less than 35	1.8	4.0	.5	*	4.4	8.0	11.0	3.0	5.0	1.0	5.2
35–44	3.0	10.0	.5	10.0	10.0	15.9	27.9	5.0	18.3	3.5	19.0
45–54	4.8	11.0	1.0	30.0	14.5	50.0	55.5	8.0	43.0	5.0	38.6
55–64	6.7	29.0	2.5	80.0	25.0	75.0	83.0	10.0	65.0	7.0	78.0
65–74	5.5	20.0	3.0	40.0	42.0	60.0	80.0	8.0	60.0	10.0	36.1
75 or more	6.5	22.0	5.0	295.0	50.0	60.0	30.0	5.0	50.0	22.0	38.8
Race or ethnicity of respondent											
White non-Hispanic	5.0	16.0	1.0	80.0	18.0	45.0	41.0	7.0	45.0	5.0	36.0
Nonwhite or Hispanic	1.5	12.0	.6	*	5.3	18.0	16.0	5.0	40.0	2.5	5.0
Current work status of head											
Working for someone else	3.1	10.0	.7	25.0	10.0	25.0	30.0	5.4	50.0	3.0	20.5
Self-employed	10.0	20.0	1.9	130.0	25.0	60.0	60.0	10.5	42.0	6.0	53.2
Retired	4.2	25.0	3.0	90.0	45.0	75.0	47.0	5.0	45.0	10.0	26.5
Other not working	2.0	8.0	2.0	*	5.0	15.9	31.0	8.4	*	3.0	5.0
Housing status											
Owner	6.0	20.0	1.0	65.0	20.0	50.0	46.0	7.0	45.0	6.0	47.9
Renter or other	1.1	7.0	.7	130.0	4.5	10.0	11.0	3.0	42.0	2.0	3.0

TABLE 7.4

Family holdings of financial assets, 2004 [CONTINUED]

Family characteristic	Transaction accounts	Certificates of deposit	Savings bonds	Bonds	Stocks	Pooled investment funds	Retirement accounts	Cash value life insurance	Other managed assets	Other	Any financial asset
	Median value of holdings for families holding asset (thousands of 2004 dollars)										
Percentile of net worth											
Less than 25	5	2.0	.3	*	1.9	2.0	2.9	.8	*	.7	1.0
25–49.9	2.0	5.8	.5	*	3.5	7.4	11.8	4.0	9.4	2.0	9.9
50–74.9	5.8	10.4	1.0	*	8.0	16.0	33.5	5.0	22.0	5.0	47.2
75–89.9	15.8	31.0	2.0	25.0	20.0	50.0	95.7	10.0	50.0	7.0	203.0
90–100	43.0	46.0	2.5	111.1	110.0	160.0	264.0	20.0	135.0	40.0	728.8
Memo											
Mean value of holdings for families holding asset	27.1	54.9	5.8	547.0	160.3	184.0	121.3	23.1	207.0	39.5	200.7

*Ten or fewer observations.

Note: For questions on income, respondents were asked to base their answers on the calendar year preceding the interview. For questions on saving, respondents were asked to base their answers on the twelve months preceding the interview. Percentage distributions may not sum to 100 because of rounding. Dollars have been converted to 2004 values with the current-methods consumer price index for all urban consumers.

SOURCE: Brian K. Bucks, Arthur B. Kennickell, and Kevin B. Moore, "Table 5. Family Holdings of Financial Assets, by Selected Characteristics of Families and Type of Asset, 2001 and 2004 Surveys. B. 2004 Survey of Consumer Finances," in "Recent Changes in U.S. Family Finances: Evidence from the 2001 and 2004 Survey of Consumer Finances," *Federal Reserve Bulletin*, vol. 92, February 2006, http://www.federalreserve.gov/pubs/oss/oss2/2004/bull0206.pdf (accessed May 23, 2008)

assets were individual retirement accounts ($4.7 trillion) and employer-sponsored defined contribution plans ($4.5 trillion). Seventy-one percent of U.S. households reported in May 2007 that they had assets in individual retirement accounts and/or employer-sponsored retirement plans.

GOVERNMENT REGULATION OF THE MARKET SYSTEM

Prices of stocks, bonds, and commodities fluctuate naturally, which generally is not cause for concern. However, when fluctuations are created as a result of greed or corruption, or by the creation of artificial and unsustainable conditions, the results can be disastrous. Such was the case in 1929, when the stock market crashed and ushered in the period known as the Great Depression. The exact causes of the 1929 crash and the ensuing depression are complex and reach far beyond U.S. borders. However, certain conditions related to the U.S. stock market were significant contributors to the economic disaster. The federal government under President Franklin D. Roosevelt (1882–1945), who served from 1933 to 1945, passed a number of laws designed to prevent the sort of abuses of the market that led to the Great Depression, laws that form the basis for the modern market regulatory system.

An Unregulated System

At the time of the 1929 crash, the stock market was largely unregulated. In the months before the crash, there were signs that the system was beginning to collapse under its own weight, but the industrialists who owned most of the real wealth fed millions of dollars into the market to stabilize it. They were successful for a time, but at last the artificial conditions created through margin buying (the buying of many market shares at a deflated value) and wild speculation brought the whole system down. Most people lost all, or nearly all, of the money they had invested in the stock market.

Regulation of Securities

Beginning in 1933, Congress enacted a series of laws designed to regulate the securities markets. The Securities Act of 1933 (sometimes referred to as the Truth in Securities law) was a reaction against the events that led up to the stock market crash of 1929. Its purpose was relatively simple: to protect investors by ensuring that they receive full information on the securities offered for sale to the public, and to prohibit fraud in such sales. The Securities Act set up a system whereby most corporations that wanted to offer shares for sale to the public had to register their securities; the registration information was then made available to the public for review. The required registration forms (which are still in use today) contained information on the company's management and business structure and the securities it was offering for sale, as well as financial statements drafted by independent accountants. This system was intended to protect investors by making available any information they needed to make informed decisions about their investments, although the truth or accuracy of the information was not guaranteed.

With the passage of the Securities Exchange Act in 1934, Congress established the Securities and Exchange Commission (SEC), which regulates the entire U.S. securities industry. The SEC expanded the Securities Act of

1933 to require more stringent reporting of publicly traded companies and all other entities involved in securities transactions, including stockbrokers, dealers, transfer agents, and exchanges. Additionally, large companies with more than $10 million in assets and five hundred shareholders are required to file regular reports with the SEC detailing their finances and business dealings. The Securities Exchange Act of 1934 also explicitly outlawed illegal insider trading.

Additional legislation that regulates the securities industry includes:

- Public Utility Holding Company Act of 1935—this act oversees interstate holding companies that sell or provide gas and electric utilities.

- Trust Indenture Act of 1939—this act requires a trust indenture (a formal agreement between a bondholder and an issuer of bonds) when debt securities such as bonds are offered for public sale.

- Investment Company Act of 1940—this act requires investment and trading companies, such as those that handle mutual funds, to divulge their financial and management information to the public, as well as information about the funds they offer for sale.

- Investment Advisers Act of 1940 (amended in 1996)—when this act was originally passed, it required most investment advisers to register with the SEC and abide by laws designed to protect investors. In its amended form, the act applies only to advisers who manage at least $25 million in assets or work with a registered investment company.

- Sarbanes-Oxley Act of 2002—this act is the strongest legislation since the 1940s to impose reforms on the securities industry. Intended to combat fraud and encourage corporate accountability, it also established the Public Company Accounting Oversight Board. Under Sarbanes-Oxley, companies that trade in the U.S. markets must perform audits of their fraud-prevention and accounting procedures, as well as annual examinations by management of their internal controls. One of the most significant reforms instituted by Sarbanes-Oxley is the provision that bankrupt companies must compensate investors before paying creditors. This provision was largely the result of the WorldCom scandal.

The Commodities Futures Trading Commission

The trading of commodities futures and options in the United States is regulated by the Commodities Futures Trading Commission (CFTC). Established by Congress in 1974, the CFTC is responsible for ensuring integrity in the commodities markets. Like the securities markets, commodities exchanges are not immune to corruption in the form of fraud, misrepresentation, and price manipulation. The most recent update to the Commod-

ities Exchange Act was the Commodity Futures Modernization Act of 2000.

In "About the CFTC" (May 6, 2008, http://www.cftc .gov/cftc/cftcabout.htm?from=home&page=aboutcftcleft), the CFTC notes that the sitting U.S. president appoints the five commissioners of the commission, who serve staggered five-year terms, as well as a chairman. Under the chairman's administration are the Office of the Inspector General, which is responsible for the internal audits of the CFTC; the Office of International Affairs, which handles the CFTC's involvement in the global markets; and the Office of External Affairs, which serves as the CFTC's media liaison. The CFTC has offices in all U.S. cities that have commodities exchanges: New York, Chicago, Kansas City, and Minneapolis.

WEAKNESSES IN THE MARKET SYSTEM

Even with careful oversight, fraudulent activities can occur in the securities industry. Securities fraud and the ensuing scandals are devastating to investors and to the markets as a whole. There were many high-profile instances of accounting scandals and securities fraud in the early twenty-first century.

Illegal Insider Trading

Insider trading is the buying or selling of stock by someone who has information about the company that other stockholders do not have. Most often, it refers to directors, officers, or employees buying or selling their own company's stock. Insider trading alone is not illegal, but insiders must report their stock transactions to the SEC. Insider trading becomes illegal when it is unreported to the SEC and breaches a fiduciary duty to the corporation; that is, when it violates a duty to act in the corporation's best interests. Most often, this happens when someone in the company has confidential information and uses it as the basis for a stock transaction. For example, if a company officer knows that the company is going to file for bankruptcy the next day and sells the company's stock because he or she knows the stock price is going to plummet, the trading is illegal. The same goes for someone who gives the information to an outside stockholder so he or she can act on it.

The best-known case of illegal insider trading in the early twenty-first century involved the company ImClone Systems, the media mogul Martha Stewart (1941–), and the stockbroker Peter Bacanovic (1962–). The SEC alleged that Bacanovic passed confidential information to Stewart and that she sold her stock in ImClone because of that information. The SEC also accused Stewart and Bacanovic of trying to cover up the matter afterward by lying to federal investigators. The insider trading charge against Stewart was dropped, but she was convicted of lying to investigators and obstruction of justice.

Bacanovic was convicted of most of the charges against him. Stewart entered prison to serve a five-month sentence in October 2004 and was released to house arrest in March 2005.

Overvaluing and Accounting Scandals

Overvaluing is the overstatement of income by companies with the assistance of their accountants to create an inflated impression of financial success among investors, thereby increasing the value of stock. In the early twenty-first century, Wall Street experienced many scandals concerning such accounting practices at major corporations. The most egregious and notorious breaches of regulations occurred at three companies: Enron, WorldCom, and Tyco (see Chapter 6). All three became targets of SEC investigations, with company executives brought up on criminal fraud charges and investors losing billions of dollars.

CHAPTER 8
WEALTH IN THE UNITED STATES

All communities divide themselves into the few and the many. The first are the rich and the well-born; the other, the mass of the people.

—Alexander Hamilton, 1787

Wealth is collected assets—cash, commodities, stocks, bonds, businesses, and properties. In the United States a small percentage of people have enormous wealth and the rest of the population has far less wealth. Is this a natural and acceptable result of capitalism or an economic injustice that must be righted for the good of society? This is a debate that has raged since the nation was founded. Some people believe the accumulation of great wealth is possible for anyone in the United States as the reward for hard work, ingenuity, and wise decision making. Other people believe American political, business, and social systems are unfairly structured so as to limit wealth building by certain segments of the population.

THE COMPONENTS OF WEALTH

The components of wealth can be divided into two broad categories: tangible assets and intangible assets. Tangible assets are things that have value in and of themselves. Examples include gold, land, houses, cars, boats, artwork, jewelry, and all other durable consumer goods with recognizable value in the marketplace. These are material possessions. Intangible assets are financial devices that have worth because they have perceived value. The most obvious examples are stocks and bonds. Other devices often counted as intangible assets include pensions (which are promises of future income), life insurance policies with cash value, and insurance policies on tangible assets, because they protect valuable resources.

The federal government does not measure the overall wealth of individual Americans or the population as a whole. It does compile data on related economic indica-

tors that include wealth assets. These measures are called net worth and personal income.

Net Worth

Net worth is the sum of all assets minus the sum of all liabilities (such as debts). The Federal Reserve Board, the national bank of the United States, computes the aggregate net worth of households and nonprofit organizations (NPOs) on a quarterly and annual basis. These values are published in tabular form in "B.100 Balance Sheet of Households and Nonprofit Organizations" as part of the *Federal Reserve Statistical Release Z.1: Flow of Funds Accounts of the United States* (http://www.federalreserve.gov/releases/z1/). Table 8.1 shows the net worth data available as of March 2008 for the fourth quarter of 2007.

ASSETS. Overall, U.S. households and NPOs had assets of $72 trillion in the fourth quarter of 2007; of this, nearly $26.7 trillion was in tangible assets and $45.3 trillion was in financial assets. (See Table 8.1.) Between 1996 and 2007 tangible assets increased from roughly one-third of total assets to nearly 40%. (See Figure 8.1.) The Federal Reserve includes only three components in tangible assets: real estate, NPO equipment and software, and consumer durable goods. Real estate holdings of $22.5 trillion made up 84% of total tangible assets in the fourth quarter of 2007. (See Figure 8.2.) Consumer durable goods at $4 trillion accounted for 15% of the total, and NPO equipment and software at $240.8 billion encompassed only 1% of the total.

Financial assets were much more diverse. The largest components were pension fund reserves ($12.8 trillion, or 28% of the total), equity in noncorporate businesses ($7.9 trillion, or 17% of the total), and deposits and currency ($7.4 trillion, or 16% of the total). (See Figure 8.3.) Deposits include monies in checking and saving accounts and in money market funds.

TABLE 8.1

Balance sheet of households and nonprofit organizations, fourth quarter 2007

[Billions of dollars; amounts outstanding end of period, not seasonally adjusted]

		2007 Q4	
1	**Assets**	**72,092.5**	1
2	Tangible assets	26,759.5	2
3	Real estate	22,483.3	3
4	Households[a, b]	20,154.7	4
5	Nonprofit organizations	2,328.6	5
6	Equipment and software owned by nonprofit organizations[c]	240.8	6
7	Consumer durable goods[c]	4,035.3	7
8	**Financial assets**	**45,333.0**	8
9	Deposits	7,388.5	9
10	Foreign deposits	86.4	10
11	Checkable deposits and currency	78.4	11
12	Time and savings deposits	5,880.1	12
13	Money market fund shares	1,343.5	13
14	Credit market instruments	3,977.0	14
15	Open market paper	159.7	15
16	Treasury securities	308.8	16
17	Savings bonds	196.4	17
18	Other Treasury	112.4	18
19	Agency- and GSE-backed securities	946.7	19
20	Municipal securities	916.0	20
21	Corporate and foreign bonds	1,504.7	21
22	Mortgages	141.2	22
23	Corporate equities[a]	5,446.6	23
24	Mutual fund shares[d]	5,081.9	24
25	Security credit	853.5	25
26	Life insurance reserves	1,204.8	26
27	Pension fund reserves	12,779.5	27
28	Equity in noncorporate business[e]	7,891.9	28
29	Miscellaneous assets	709.3	29
30	**Liabilities**	**14,374.5**	30
31	Credit market instruments	13,825.4	31
32	Home mortgages[f]	10,508.8	32
33	Consumer credit	2,550.6	33
34	Municipal securities[g]	250.2	34
35	Bank loans n.e.c.	130.7	35
36	Other loans and advances	128.4	36
37	Commercial mortgages[g]	256.7	37
38	Security credit	324.8	38
39	Trade payables[g]	200.3	39
40	Deferred and unpaid life insurance premiums	24.0	40
41	**Net worth**	**57,718.0**	41

LIABILITIES. Assets alone do not provide an indication of the nation's wealth status. Debts and other obligations, known as liabilities, must be subtracted. These liabilities totaled $14.4 trillion during the fourth quarter of 2007. (See Table 8.1.) Credit market instruments accounted for the vast majority of this total, at $13.8 trillion. Home mortgages ($10.5 trillion) were the single largest credit market instrument, followed by consumer credit ($2.6 trillion).

TRENDS IN NET WORTH. The net worth of U.S. households and NPOs totaled $57.7 trillion in the fourth quarter of 2007. (See Table 8.1.) Figure 8.4 compares this value to net worth values calculated by the Federal Reserve from 2003 to the fourth quarter of 2007. Net worth has increased slightly each year during this period.

TABLE 8.1

Balance sheet of households and nonprofit organizations, fourth quarter 2007 [CONTINUED]

[Billions of dollars; amounts outstanding end of period, not seasonally adjusted]

		2007 Q4	
	Memo:		
	Replacement-cost value of structures:		42
42	Residential	14,326.9	43
43	Households	13,832.5	44
44	Farm households	303.2	45
45	Nonprofit organizations	191.2	46
46	Nonresidential (nonprofits)	1,324.1	47
47	Disposable personal income	10,341.3	
48	Household net worth as percentage of disposable personal income	558.1	48
49	Owners' equity in household real estate[h]	9,646.0	49
50	Owners' equity as percentage of household real estate[i]	47.9	50

Note: Sector includes farm households. GSE = Government sponsored enterprise.
[a]At market value.
[b]All types of owner-occupied housing including farm houses and mobile homes, as well as second homes that are not rented, vacant homes for sale, and vacant land.
[c]At replacement (current) cost.
[d]Value based on the market values of equities held and the book value of other assets held by mutual funds.
[e]Net worth of noncorporate business (table B.103, line 31) and owners' equity in farm business and unincorporated security brokers and dealers.
[f]Includes loans made under home equity lines of credit and home equity loans secured by junior liens, shown on table L.218, line 22.
[g]Liabilities of nonprofit organizations.
[h]Line 4 less line 32.
[i]Line 49 divided by line 4.

SOURCE: Adapted from "Table B.100. Balance Sheet of Households and Nonprofit Organizations," in *Federal Reserve Statistical Release Z.1: Flow of Funds Accounts of the United States, Flow and Outstandings, Fourth Quarter 2007*, The Federal Reserve, March 6, 2008, http://www.federalreserve.gov/releases/z1/20080306/z1.pdf (accessed May 23, 2008)

Personal Income

The U.S. Department of Commerce's Bureau of Economic Analysis (BEA) collects data on the personal income of Americans. In 2007 more than half (54%) of personal income was from wages and salaries. (See Figure 8.5.) Another 13% was attributed to employer-provided benefits. Interest income accounted for 10% of the total. Proprietors' income (the income earned by sole proprietorships, partnerships, and tax-exempt cooperatives) encompassed 9% of the total. The remainder of personal income was from dividends (7%), net transfer receipts (6%), and rental income (1%). Net transfer receipts are mostly government social benefits such as old-age, survivors, disability, and health insurance; unemployment insurance; veterans benefits; and family assistance funds.

DEMOGRAPHICS OF UNEMPLOYMENT. According to the BEA, in *Personal Income and Outlays: March 2008* (May 1, 2008, http://www.bea.gov/newsreleases/national/pi/2008/pdf/pi0308.pdf), in 2007 compensation (e.g., wages, salaries, and employer-provided benefits) amounted to over $7.8 trillion and accounted for more than two-thirds of total personal income. Historically, compensation has been the

FIGURE 8.1

Total assets of households and nonprofit organizations, 1996–2007

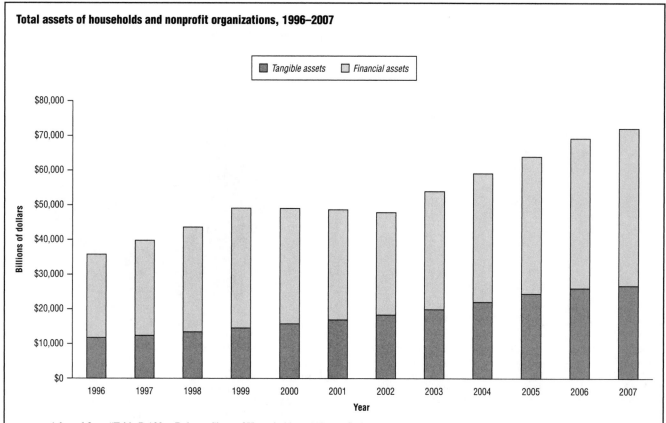

SOURCE: Adapted from "Table B.100.e. Balance Sheet of Households and Nonprofit Organizations with Equity Detail," in *Federal Reserve Statistical Release Z.1: Flow of Funds Accounts of the United States, Flow and Outstandings, Fourth Quarter 2007*, The Federal Reserve, March 6, 2008, http://www .federalreserve.gov/releases/z1/20080306/z1.pdf (accessed May 23, 2008)

single largest component of total personal income. Thus, employment factors are extremely important to a discussion of wealth and its distribution. Table 8.2 shows unemployment data and rates by demographic characteristics for 2007. The highest rates of unemployment were 15% for single (never married) African-American men aged sixteen years and older and 10.8% for single (never married) African-American women aged sixteen years and older. The overall unemployment rates for men and women aged sixteen years and older in 2007 were 4.7% and 4.5%, respectively. The lowest unemployment rates recorded were for married Asian-American men aged twenty-five years and older with the spouse present in the household (2.2%) and married white women aged twenty-five years and older with the spouse present in the household (2.5%).

In February 2008 the overall unemployment rate was around 5%. (See Figure 8.6.) The rate was 17% for teenagers, 8% for African-Americans, 6% for Hispanics, and 4% for whites. Unemployment rates were roughly equal for men and women.

POVERTY IN THE UNITED STATES

Poverty is defined and measured in different ways by different government entities. At the federal level it is meas-

ured using two methods: poverty thresholds and poverty guidelines. Poverty thresholds are set by the U.S. Census Bureau, which also tracks poverty populations in the United States. The thresholds specify minimum income levels for different sizes and categories of families. For example, the Census Bureau (January 29, 2008, http://www.census.gov/ hhes/www/poverty/threshld/thresh07.html) notes that in 2007 the poverty threshold for a family of four including two related children in the household was $21,027 per year.

Poverty guidelines are published by the U.S. Department of Health and Human Services (HHS) for the fifty states and Washington, D.C. According to the HHS, the poverty guidelines are a "simplification" of the poverty thresholds and are used for administrative purposes, such as determining eligibility for specific federal programs. The most recent guidelines were published in "Annual Update of the HHS Poverty Guidelines" (*Federal Register*, vol. 72, no. 15, January 24, 2007).

The Poverty Rate

The Census Bureau calculates the number of people in poverty and the poverty rate using the poverty thresholds. The most recent data were collected in 2006 as part of the Current Population Survey, Annual Social and Economic

FIGURE 8.2

FIGURE 8.3

Tangible assets of households and nonprofit organizations as of fourth quarter 2007

[Total: $26.8 trillion]

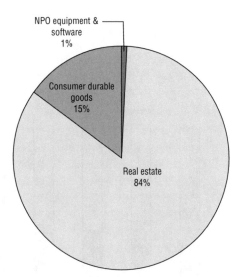

SOURCE: Adapted from "Table B.100. Balance Sheet of Households and Nonprofit Organizations," in *Federal Reserve Statistical Release Z. 1: Flow of Funds Accounts of the United States, Flow and Outstandings, Fourth Quarter 2007*, The Federal Reserve, March 6, 2008, http://www.federalreserve.gov/releases/z1/20080306/z1.pdf (accessed May 23, 2008)

Financial assets of households and nonprofit organizations as of fourth quarter 2007

[Total: $45.3 trillion]

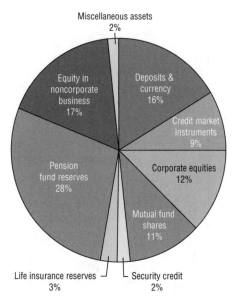

SOURCE: Adapted from "Table B.100. Balance Sheet of Households and Nonprofit Organizations," in *Federal Reserve Statistical Release Z.1: Flow of Funds Accounts of the United States, Flow and Outstandings, Fourth Quarter 2007*, The Federal Reserve, March 6, 2008, http://www.federalreserve.gov/releases/z1/20080306/z1.pdf (accessed May 23, 2008)

Supplement—a sample survey of approximately one hundred thousand households around the United States. The data are presented and analyzed by Carmen DeNavas-Walt, Bernadette D. Proctor, and Jessica Smith of the Census Bureau in *Income, Poverty, and Health Insurance Coverage in the United States: 2006* (August 2007, http://www.census.gov/prod/2007pubs/p60-233.pdf).

According to DeNavas-Walt, Proctor, and Smith, 36.5 million Americans lived at or below the federal poverty level in 2006. This represents 12.3% of the population and is down slightly from 12.6% in 2005. The number of people in poverty has varied widely over the past few decades. In 1960, 39.9 million Americans lived in poverty. This value dropped to fewer than twenty-five million people in the 1970s and then began increasing, reaching near the forty million mark during the early 1990s. The number declined to around thirty-one million in 2000 and then rose throughout the early 2000s.

The poverty rate was around 22% in the early 1960s, and then it dropped to around 11% in the early 1970s. It topped 15% during the early 1990s and then decreased to around 12% in 2000, before it began to rise again.

There were dramatic demographic differences in the U.S. poverty rate in 2006. The differences by race and ethnicity were:

- African-Americans—24.3%
- Hispanics—20.6%
- Asian-Americans—10.3%
- Non-Hispanic whites—8.2%

The poverty rates for non-Hispanic whites, African-Americans, and Asian-Americans were virtually unchanged from 2005. The rate for Hispanics decreased slightly, from 21.8% in 2005.

Other demographic differences were also significant. The poverty rate in 2006 for those under age eighteen was 17.4%, compared to 10.8% for people aged eighteen to sixty-four, and 9.4% for people aged sixty-five and older. Among family types, the highest poverty rate was experienced by families headed by unmarried females (28.3%). By contrast, the poverty rate for families headed by unmarried males was 13.2%, and for those headed by married couples it was only 4.9%.

The Working Poor

The U.S. Bureau of Labor Statistics (BLS) notes in *A Profile of the Working Poor, 2005* (September 2007, http://www.bls.gov/cps/cpswp2005.pdf) that in 2005, 7.7 million people were classified as "working poor"—those

FIGURE 8.4

Net worth of households and nonprofit organizations, 2003–fourth quarter 2007

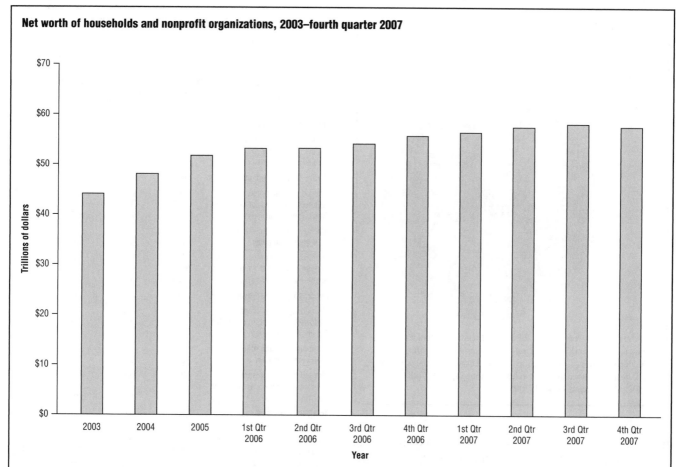

SOURCE: Adapted from "Table B.100. Balance Sheet of Households and Nonprofit Organizations," in *Federal Reserve Statistical Release Z.1: Flow of Funds Accounts of the United States, Flow and Outstandings, Fourth Quarter 2007*, The Federal Reserve, March 6, 2008, http://www.federalreserve.gov/releases/z1/20080306/z1.pdf (accessed May 23, 2008)

people who are in the workforce at least twenty-seven weeks per year but whose income still falls below the poverty level. Just over 6% of American women were among the working poor, compared to 4.8% of men. Rates differed between women and men in two racial categories: white and African-American. Five percent of white women were among the working poor, compared to 4.4% of white men. Thirteen percent of African-American women were classified as working poor, compared to 7.7% of African-American men. Asian-American and Hispanic women were just as likely as their male counterparts to be among the working poor.

The BLS indicates that even though most of the working poor were white (approximately 70%), a greater proportion of African-American and Hispanic workers were among the working poor (10.5% each of African-Americans and Hispanics, versus 4.7% each of whites and Asian-Americans). Around 10.5% of all working teenagers aged sixteen to nineteen were among the working poor.

According to the BLS, poverty rates varied greatly by educational attainment and occupation. Just over 14% of

those in the labor force with less than a high school diploma were among the working poor, compared to only 1.7% of college graduates with a bachelor's degree or higher. However, the BLS notes that African-Americans and Hispanics were more likely to be among the working poor than whites or Asian-Americans at nearly every level of educational attainment. In general, management and professional occupations, which tended to require higher levels of education, saw lower amounts of poverty among workers (1.8% were classified as working poor). Occupations in industries such as services and natural resources tended to have more workers living in poverty: 10.8% of service workers were poor in 2005, as were 13.7% of those who did farming, fishing, or forestry work and 8.1% of workers engaged in construction occupations.

Analysts consider three continuing problems in the labor market to be responsible for most poverty among working people: low wages, periodic unemployment, and involuntary part-time work. (Involuntary part-time workers are described by the BLS as "persons who, in at least 1 week of the year, worked fewer than 35

FIGURE 8.5

Personal income sources, 2007

[Total: $11.66 trillion]

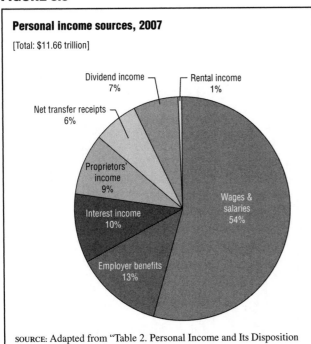

SOURCE: Adapted from "Table 2. Personal Income and Its Disposition (Years and Quarters)," in *Personal Income and Outlays: March 2008*, U.S. Department of Commerce, Bureau of Economic Analysis, May 1, 2008, http://www.bea.gov/newsreleases/national/pi/2008/pdf/pi0308.pdf (accessed May 14, 2008)

TABLE 8.2

Unemployed persons by demographic group, 2007

Marital status, race, Hispanic or Latino ethnicity, and age	Men Thousands of persons	Men Un-employment rates	Women Thousands of persons	Women Un-employment rates
	2007	2007	2007	2007
Total, 16 years and over	**3,882**	**4.7**	**3,196**	**4.5**
Married, spouse present	1,206	2.5	1,049	2.8
Widowed, divorced, or separated	544	5.3	724	5.0
Single (never married)	2,132	8.8	1,422	7.2
White, 16 years and over	**2,869**	**4.2**	**2,274**	**4.0**
Married, spouse present	965	2.4	830	2.6
Widowed, divorced, or separated	421	4.9	547	4.9
Single (never married)	1,483	7.8	897	6.3
Black or African American, 16 years and over	**752**	**9.1**	**693**	**7.5**
Married, spouse present	156	4.3	123	4.3
Widowed, divorced, or separated	92	7.5	135	5.7
Single (never married)	504	15.0	435	10.8
Asian, 16 years and over	**119**	**3.1**	**110**	**3.4**
Married, spouse present	54	2.2	61	3.1
Widowed, divorced, or separated	9	3.0	12	2.7
Single (never married)	56	5.2	37	4.4
Hispanic or Latino ethnicity, 16 years and over	**695**	**5.3**	**525**	**6.1**
Married, spouse present	247	3.5	191	4.7
Widowed, divorced, or separated	85	5.1	110	6.0
Single (never married)	363	8.3	224	8.3
Total, 25 years and over	**2,538**	**3.6**	**2,198**	**3.6**
Married, spouse present	1,152	2.5	959	2.7
Widowed, divorced, or separated	515	5.1	683	4.9
Single (never married)	871	6.3	556	5.2
White, 25 years and over	**1,907**	**3.3**	**1,579**	**3.3**
Married, spouse present	919	2.3	756	2.5
Widowed, divorced, or separated	401	4.8	516	4.7
Single (never married)	587	5.5	307	4.3
Black or African American, 25 years and over	**457**	**6.6**	**453**	**5.8**
Married, spouse present	149	4.1	113	4.1
Widowed, divorced, or separated	85	7.3	129	5.5
Single (never married)	222	10.5	211	7.7
Asian, 25 years and over	**92**	**2.7**	**87**	**3.0**
Married, spouse present	53	2.2	59	3.0
Widowed, divorced, or separated	9	2.8	12	2.7
Single (never married)	30	4.0	17	3.1
Hispanic or Latino ethnicity, 16 years and over	**455**	**4.2**	**355**	**5.1**
Married, spouse present	234	3.5	166	4.3
Widowed, divorced, or separated	77	4.9	100	5.7
Single (never married)	144	5.8	89	6.1

Note: Estimates for the above race groups (white, black or African American, and Asian) do not sum to totals because data are not presented for all races. Persons whose ethnicity is identified as Hispanic or Latino may be of any race. Updated population controls are introduced annually with the release of January data.

SOURCE: Adapted from "Table 24. Unemployed Persons by Marital Status, Race, Hispanic or Latino Ethnicity, Age, and Sex," in *Current Population Survey: Tables Created by BLS*, U.S. Department of Labor, Bureau of Labor Statistics, May 2008, http://www.bls.gov/cps/cpsaat24.pdf (accessed May 24, 2008)

hours because of slack work or business conditions, or because they could not find full-time work.") Approximately 80% of the working poor who typically worked full time experienced at least one of these conditions in 2005. Low earnings was reported as the most common problem.

WEALTH DISTRIBUTION

In "Currents and Undercurrents: Changes in the Distribution of Wealth, 1989–2004" (January 30, 2006, http://www.federalreserve.gov/Pubs/FEDS/2006/200613/200613pap.pdf), Arthur B. Kennickell of the Federal Reserve relies on data collected during the 2004 Survey of Consumer Finances (SCF). The SCF is a survey conducted every three years by the Federal Reserve in cooperation with the Internal Revenue Service to collect detailed financial information on American families. Kennickell traces changes in wealth distribution between 1989 and 2004 based on computed net worth values. Table 8.3 shows the distribution of net worth across this period. All values were computed using 2004 dollars to compensate for the effects of inflation between 1989 and 2004.

In 1989, 26.5% of families had a net worth of less than $10,000. (See Table 8.3.) At the other end of the spectrum, 10.8% had a net worth of at least $500,000. In 2004 the portion of families with a net worth of less than $10,000 was 22.7%, down 3.8 percentage points from

1989. By contrast, the percentage of families in 2004 with a net worth of at least $500,000 had risen by more than half, up 6.9 percentage points to 17.7%.

FIGURE 8.6

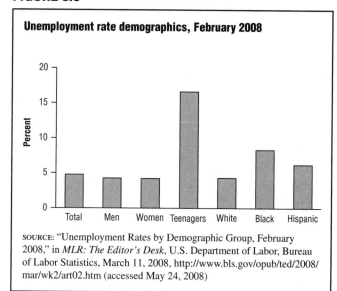

Unemployment rate demographics, February 2008

SOURCE: "Unemployment Rates by Demographic Group, February 2008," in *MLR: The Editor's Desk*, U.S. Department of Labor, Bureau of Labor Statistics, March 11, 2008, http://www.bls.gov/opub/ted/2008/mar/wk2/art02.htm (accessed May 24, 2008)

TABLE 8.3

Percent distribution of net worth in 2004 dollars, selected years, 1989–2004

	1989	1992	1995	1998	2001	2004
<0	.2	7.2	7.1	8.0	6.9	7.1
=0	.9	3.2	2.6	2.5	2.6	1.7
1–999	4.0	3.0	2.4	3.2	2.7	2.3
1K–2.49K	3.1	3.6	2.5	2.4	2.3	3.2
2.5K–4.9K	4.3	3.4	3.4	3.2	3.3	4.0
5K–9.9K	4.0	4.9	5.5	4.7	4.6	4.4
10K–24.9K	8.0	9.2	9.2	7.9	7.9	7.8
25K–49.9K	9.3	10.5	10.0	9.4	9.0	8.8
50K–99.9K	13.3	14.2	15.8	12.5	12.2	11.9
100K–249.9K	20.8	21.5	22.2	21.9	19.1	18.6
250K–499.9K	11.3	10.0	9.9	12.5	13.5	12.4
500K–999.9K	5.6	5.2	5.5	6.5	8.4	9.6
>=1M	5.2	4.2	3.8	5.3	7.5	8.1

SOURCE: Adapted from Arthur B. Kennickell, "Table 2. Percent Distribution of Net Worth in 2004 Dollars, 1989–2004," in *Currents and Undercurrents: Changes in the Distribution of Wealth, 1989–2004*, Federal Reserve Board, January 30, 2006 (corrected June 22, 2006), http://www.federalreserve.gov/pubs/oss/oss2/papers/concentration.2004.4.pdf (accessed June 10, 2008)

Gini Coefficients

The Gini coefficient is a mathematically derived value used to describe the inequality in a data distribution. It was developed during the early 1900s by the Italian statistician Corrado Gini (1884–1965). The Federal Reserve uses the Gini coefficient to measure the extent of the inequality in the distribution of wealth among American families. When used to compute wealth inequality, a value of zero indicates perfect equality, whereas a value of one indicates that all wealth is held by only one family. Kennickell calculates a Gini coefficient of 0.7863 for net worth in 1989 and a value of 0.8047 for net worth in 2004. This indicates that a greater amount of wealth became concentrated in the hands of families at the upper end of the spectrum. In other words,

TABLE 8.4

Proportions of total net worth and of gross assets held by various percentile groups, selected years, 1989–2004

	Net worth percentile group				
	0–50	50–90	90–95	95–99	99–100
	Proportion of total net worth held by group				
1989	3.0	29.9	13.0	24.1	30.1
1992	3.3	29.6	12.5	24.4	30.2
1995	3.6	28.6	11.9	21.3	34.6
1998	3.0	28.4	11.4	23.3	33.9
2001	2.8	27.4	12.1	25.0	32.7
2004	2.5	27.9	12.0	24.1	33.4
	Proportion of total gross assets held by group				
1989	5.4	32.5	12.6	22.3	27.1
1992	6.6	32.1	12.0	22.6	26.7
1995	7.5	31.2	11.4	19.5	30.4
1998	6.7	30.8	10.9	21.7	29.9
2001	5.6	29.9	11.7	23.4	29.5
2004	5.8	31.0	11.4	22.2	29.5

SOURCE: Adapted from Arthur B. Kennickell, "Table 5. Proportions of Total Net Worth and of Gross Assets Held by Various Percentile Groups, 1989–2004," in *Currents and Undercurrents: Changes in the Distribution of Wealth, 1989–2004*, Federal Reserve Board, January 30, 2006 (corrected June 22, 2006), http://www.federalreserve.gov/pubs/oss/oss2/papers/concentration.2004.4.pdf (accessed June 10, 2008)

the Gini coefficients suggest the rich got richer, and the poor got poorer during this period.

Concentration Ratios

Economists use concentration ratios to show the proportion of wealth held by certain groups within a population. Table 8.4 tabulates the proportion of total net worth and total gross assets held by specific percentile groups as calculated by Kennickell. The ratios shown in the upper table indicate that in 2004 just over one-third (33.4%) of total net worth was held by the wealthiest 1% of families (the families at the 99 to 100 percentile). The other two-thirds of total net worth was held by the other 99% of families. Another way to look at the data is that the poorest half of the families (those in the 0 to 50 percentile) held only 2.5% of all net worth in 2004. This value is down from a high of 3.6% in 1995—a decline deemed "significantly different" by Kennickell.

The lower table in Table 8.4 shows the concentration ratios for total gross assets. In 2004 the wealthiest 1% of families held 29.5% of total gross assets. The poorest 50% of families held only 5.8% of total gross assets. This marked a decline from the assets they held in 1992, 1995, and 1998.

WEALTH DEMOGRAPHICS

In "Recent Changes in U.S. Family Finances: Evidence from the 2001 and 2004 Survey of Consumer Finances" (*Federal Reserve Bulletin*, vol. 92, February 2006), Brian K. Bucks, Arthur B. Kennickell, and Kevin B. Moore of the Federal Reserve examine changes in

TABLE 8.5

Family net worth, selected years, 1995–2004

[Thousands of 2004 dollars]

Family characteristic	1995		1998		2001		2004	
	Median	Mean	Median	Mean	Median	Mean	Median	Mean
All families	**70.8**	**260.8**	**83.1**	**327.5**	**91.7**	**421.5**	**93.1**	**448.2**
	(2.4)	(6.4)	(3.2)	(10.7)	(3.3)	(7.1)	(4.3)	(9.7)
Percentile of income								
Less than 20	7.4	54.7	.8	55.4	.4	56.1	.5	72.6
20–39.9	41.3	97.4	38.4	111.5	39.6	121.8	34.3	122.0
40–59.9	57.1	126.0	61.9	146.6	66.5	171.4	71.6	193.8
60–79.9	93.6	198.5	130.2	238.3	150.7	311.3	160.0	342.8
80–89.9	157.7	316.8	218.5	377.1	280.3	486.6	311.1	485.0
90–100	436.9	338.0	524.4	1,793.9	887.9	2,406.7	924.1	2,534.4
Age of head (years)								
Less than 35	14.8	53.2	10.6	74.0	12.3	96.6	14.2	73.5
35–44	64.2	176.8	73.5	227.6	82.6	276.4	69.4	299.2
45–54	116.8	364.8	122.3	420.2	141.6	517.6	144.7	542.7
55–64	141.9	471.1	148.2	617.0	193.3	775.4	248.7	843.8
65–74	136.6	429.3	169.8	541.1	187.8	717.9	190.1	690.9
75 or more	114.5	317.9	145.6	360.3	161.2	496.2	163.1	528.1
Education of head								
No high school diploma	27.9	103.7	24.5	91.4	27.2	109.7	20.6	136.5
High school diploma	63.9	163.7	62.7	182.9	61.8	192.5	68.7	196.8
Some college	57.6	232.3	85.6	275.5	76.3	303.8	69.3	308.6
College degree	128.6	473.7	169.7	612.3	227.2	845.7	226.1	851.3
Race or ethnicity of respondent								
White non-Hispanic	94.3	308.7	111.0	391.1	129.6	518.7	140.7	561.8
Nonwhite or Hispanic	19.5	94.9	19.3	116.5	19.1	123.8	24.8	153.1
Current work status of head								
Working for someone else	60.3	168.4	61.2	194.8	69.3	240.1	67.2	268.5
Self-employed	191.8	862.8	288.0	1,071.3	375.2	1,340.6	335.6	1,423.2
Retired	99.9	277.2	131.0	356.5	120.4	479.2	139.8	469.0
Other not working	4.5	70.1	.1	85.8	.5	191.7	11.8	162.3
Region								
Northeast	102.0	308.9	109.3	351.3	98.3	480.0	161.7	569.1
Midwest	80.8	244.7	93.1	288.5	111.3	361.6	115.0	436.1
South	54.2	229.5	71.0	309.6	78.6	400.4	63.8	348.0
West	67.4	286.1	71.1	379.1	93.3	468.8	94.8	523.7
Housing status								
Owner	128.1	373.7	153.2	468.7	182.9	594.8	184.4	624.9
Renter or other	6.0	53.8	.9	50.4	.1	58.5	.0	54.1
Percentile of net worth								
Less than 25	1.2	−.2	.6	−2.1	.2	†	1.7	−1.4
25–49.9	34.7	37.6	37.9	41.6	43.4	47.0	43.6	47.1
50–74.9	117.1	122.6	139.7	149.1	166.8	176.6	170.7	185.4
75–89.9	272.3	293.6	357.7	372.6	458.2	478.6	506.8	526.7
90–100	836.7	766.7	1,039.1	2,244.2	1,386.6	2,936.1	1,430.1	3,114.2

†Less than 0.05 ($50).
Note: For questions on income, respondents were asked to base their answers on the calendar year preceding the interview. For questions on saving, respondents were asked to base their answers on the twelve months preceding the interview. Percentage distributions may not sum to 100 because of rounding. Dollars have been converted to 2004 values with the current-methods consumer price index for all urban consumers.

SOURCE: Brian K. Bucks, Arthur B. Kennickell, and Kevin B. Moore, "Table 3. Family Net Worth, by Selected Characteristics of Families, 1995–2004 Surveys," in "Recent Changes in U.S. Family Finances: Evidence from the 2001 and 2004 Survey of Consumer Finances," *Federal Reserve Bulletin*, vol. 92, February 2006, http://www.federalreserve.gov/pubs/oss/oss2/2004/bull0206.pdf (accessed June 10, 2008).

family income and net worth between the SCFs conducted in 2001 and 2004. Overall, the researchers find that average pretax family income decreased by 2.3% between 2001 and 2004. (Income values were adjusted for the effects of inflation.) Bucks, Kennickell, and Moore also analyze the median pretax family income. The median is the value at which half of the values are greater than the median and the other half are less than the median.

Between 2001 and 2004 the median pretax family income increased by 1.6%.

Table 8.5 shows family net worth by demographic characteristics for the 1995, 1998, 2001, and 2004 SCFs. Between 2001 and 2004 the median net worth of all families grew from $91,700 to $93,100, an increase of 1.5%. The mean (average) net worth grew from $421,500 to

$448,200, an increase of 6.3%. Bucks, Kennickell, and Moore note that the wealth increase was most pronounced for families in the middle-income range.

A variety of factors are cited for overall changes in wealth between 2001 and 2004. The most notable are:

- An increase in homeownership combined with strong growth in real estate appreciation (increase in value over time)

- A decrease in wages

- A decrease in stock ownership and investment income

- An increase in the amount of debt held relative to total assets

Bucks, Kennickell, and Moore indicate that average wages declined by 3.6% between 2001 and 2004. The median wage also decreased, by 6.2%. The researchers conclude that wealth growth over this period was weak, compared to strong growth experienced between 1992 and 1995 and between 1995 and 1998. Also, the wealth growth between 2001 and 2004 was not consistent across most demographic groups as it had been in the earlier periods.

Race

The mean net worth of white families in 2004 was $561,800, whereas for minority families it was $153,100. (See Table 8.5.) The median net worth of white families was $140,700, whereas for minority families it was $24,800.

According to Bucks, Kennickell, and Moore, wealth grew for both white and minority families between 2001 and 2004. In fact, the growth for all minorities grouped together outpaced the growth for white families. The average and median net worth of white families increased by 8.3% and 8.6%, respectively. By contrast, the average and median net worth of minority families increased by 23.7% and 29.8%, respectively.

However, Bucks, Kennickell, and Moore note that African-American families lagged behind other minorities in wealth growth. The median net worth of African-American families grew from $20,300 in 2001 to $20,400 in 2004, an increase of around 0.5%. The average net worth increased from $80,700 to $110,600 during this period, an increase of 37.1%. This suggests that only a small number of African-American families improved their net worth, and those families were at the top of the wealth class. By contrast, median and average net worth both increased by more than 8% for white families. This indicates that a greater number of white families improved their financial condition and that the gains were more evenly distributed among the wealth classes.

Other Demographics

The data in Table 8.5 indicate that families with the highest average net worth in 2004 had the following characteristics:

- A head of household between fifty-five and sixty-four years old

- A head of household with a college degree

- A self-employed head of household

- Living in the Northeast

- Owning a home

Comparison of data from 1995 and 2004 shows that all demographic groups improved their average net worth during this period. However, there are variations in median changes. For example, the mean net worth of families with a head of household younger than thirty-five increased from $53,200 in 1995 to $73,500 in 2004. (See Table 8.5.) Their median net worth, however, decreased from $14,800 to $14,200. The same trend is evident for families headed by a person with no high school diploma and for nonhomeowners. In each case, the mean net worth increased, but the median net worth decreased. Bucks, Kennickell, and Moore acknowledge that the reasons for this disparity in the growth of mean and median net worth are complex but attribute it to distributional changes within the demographic groups.

Nonfinancial Assets

Nonfinancial assets are large material items such as real estate, business-related machinery, and automobiles, as well as ownership in businesses. In 2004, 92.5% of American families held nonfinancial assets. (See Table 8.6.) The highest percentage of families (86.3%) owned at least one vehicle. A majority (69.1%) owned their primary residence. Smaller percentages owned other residential property (12.5%), had business equity (11.5%), held equity in a nonresidential property (8.3%), or held some other nonfinancial asset (7.8%). As expected, families with higher incomes were more likely to have nonfinancial assets.

Families in the lowest twentieth percentile of income, nonhomeowners, and families in which the head of household was not working were the least likely to hold nonfinancial assets. (See Table 8.6.) There was a notable difference among races: 95.8% of white families held nonfinancial assets in 2004, compared to 84% of minority families.

Financial Assets

According to Bucks, Kennickell, and Moore, 93.8% of all families held some type of financial asset in 2004. The most common were transaction accounts (checking, savings, money market deposit accounts, money market mutual funds, and call accounts at brokerages)—91.3%

TABLE 8.6

Family holdings of nonfinancial assets, 2004

Family characteristic	Vehicles	Primary residence	Other residential property	Equity in nonresidential property	Business equity	Other	Any nonfinancial asset	Any asset
				Percentage of families holding asset				
All families	**86.3**	**69.1**	**12.5**	**8.3**	**11.5**	**7.8**	**92.5**	**97.9**
Percentile of income								
Less than 20	65.0	40.3	3.6	2.7	3.7	3.9	76.4	92.2
20–39.9	85.3	57.0	6.9	3.8	6.7	4.4	92.0	97.8
40–59.9	91.6	71.5	10.0	7.6	9.5	7.5	96.7	99.8
60–79.9	95.3	83.1	14.0	10.6	12.0	10.4	98.4	100.0
80–89.9	95.9	91.8	19.3	12.8	16.0	8.3	99.1	99.8
90–100	93.1	94.7	37.2	20.8	34.7	16.7	99.3	100.0
Age of head (years)								
Less than 35	82.9	41.6	5.1	3.3	6.9	5.5	88.6	96.5
35–44	89.4	68.3	9.4	6.4	13.9	6.0	93.0	97.7
45–54	88.8	77.3	16.3	11.4	15.7	9.7	94.7	98.3
55–64	88.6	79.1	19.5	12.8	15.8	9.2	92.6	97.5
65–74	89.1	81.3	19.9	10.6	8.0	9.0	95.6	99.5
75 or more	76.9	85.2	9.7	7.7	5.3	8.5	92.5	99.6
Race or ethnicity of respondent								
White non-Hispanic	90.3	76.1	14.0	9.2	13.6	9.3	95.8	99.3
Nonwhite or Hispanic	76.1	50.8	8.9	5.8	5.9	3.8	84.0	94.4
Current work status of head								
Working for someone else	89.7	66.5	10.4	6.8	5.8	7.1	93.8	98.4
Self-employed	91.2	79.1	25.8	18.7	58.1	12.9	97.5	99.1
Retired	79.0	75.8	12.8	7.9	3.5	7.1	89.8	97.7
Other not working	66.9	40.0	5.4	*	6.9	6.4	76.3	89.6
Housing status								
Owner	92.3	100.0	15.7	11.0	14.7	9.2	100.0	100.0
Renter or other	73.0	—	5.4	2.4	4.3	4.6	75.9	93.3
Percentile of net worth								
Less than 25	69.8	15.2	*	*	*	2.9	73.7	91.7
25–49.9	89.2	71.2	4.9	4.1	5.6	5.4	97.5	100.0
50–74.9	92.0	93.4	12.7	8.3	11.2	7.8	99.0	100.0
75–89.9	95.2	96.2	23.1	15.1	19.9	12.3	99.8	100.0
90–100	93.1	96.9	45.6	28.8	40.8	18.8	99.9	100.0
				Median value of holdings for families holding asset (thousands of 2004 dollars)				
All families	**14.2**	**160.0**	**100.0**	**60.0**	**100.0**	**15.0**	**147.8**	**172.9**
Percentile of income								
Less than 20	4.5	70.0	33.0	11.0	30.0	4.5	22.4	17.0
20–39.9	7.9	100.0	65.0	30.0	30.0	7.5	71.1	78.3
40–59.9	13.1	135.0	55.0	36.0	62.5	10.0	131.2	154.4
60–79.9	19.8	175.0	100.0	47.0	150.0	10.0	197.2	289.4
80–89.9	25.8	225.0	98.0	60.0	100.0	17.5	281.8	458.5
90–100	33.0	450.0	268.3	189.0	350.0	50.0	651.2	1,157.7
Age of head (years)								
Less than 35	11.3	135.0	82.5	55.0	50.0	5.0	32.3	39.2
35–44	15.6	160.0	80.0	42.2	100.0	10.0	151.3	173.4
45–54	18.8	170.0	90.0	43.0	144.0	20.0	184.5	234.9
55–64	18.6	200.0	135.0	75.0	190.9	25.0	226.3	351.2
65–74	12.4	150.0	80.0	78.0	100.0	30.0	161.1	233.2
75 or more	8.4	125.0	150.0	85.8	80.3	11.0	137.1	185.2
Race or ethnicity of respondent								
White non-Hispanic	15.7	165.0	105.0	66.0	135.0	16.5	164.8	224.5
Nonwhite or Hispanic	9.8	130.0	80.0	30.0	66.7	10.0	64.1	59.6
Current work status of head								
Working for someone else	14.9	160.0	88.0	40.0	50.0	10.0	141.9	161.2
Self-employed	21.9	248.0	141.5	125.0	174.0	30.0	335.4	468.3
Retired	10.1	130.0	100.0	60.0	120.0	25.0	131.7	165.6
Other not working	10.7	130.0	86.0	*	25.0	20.0	60.0	30.3
Housing status								
Owner	17.5	160.0	100.0	62.0	122.8	17.5	201.6	289.9
Renter or other	7.2	—	80.0	56.0	50.0	8.0	8.4	12.2

TABLE 8.6

Family holdings of nonfinancial assets, 2004 [CONTINUED]

Family characteristic	Vehicles	Primary residence	Other residential property	Equity in nonresidential property	Business equity	Other	Any nonfinancial asset	Any asset
				Median value of holdings for families holding asset (thousands of 2004 dollars)				
Percentile of net worth								
Less than 25	5.6	65.0	*	*	*	3.0	7.4	7.7
25–49.9	11.9	85.0	25.6	14.9	17.5	6.0	72.4	84.5
50–74.9	17.4	159.3	65.0	25.0	55.0	10.0	188.1	257.3
75–89.9	22.6	250.0	100.0	73.9	150.0	25.0	360.8	600.2
90–100	30.6	450.0	325.0	250.0	527.4	80.0	907.7	1,572.6
Memo								
Mean value of holdings for families holding asset	20.1	246.8	267.3	298.1	765.5	66.6	366.3	538.4

*Ten or fewer observations.
—Not applicable.
Notes: For questions on income, respondents were asked to base their answers on the calendar year preceding the interview. For questions on saving, respondents were asked to base their answers on the twelve months preceding the interview.
Percentage distributions may not sum to 100 because of rounding. Dollars have been converted to 2004 values with the current-methods consumer price index for all urban consumers. The definition of vehicles is a broad one that includes cars, vans, sport-utility vehicles, trucks, motor homes, recreational vehicles, motorcycles, boats, airplanes, and helicopters. Of families owning any type of vehicle in 2004, 99.8 percent had a car, van, sport-utility vehicle, motorcycle, or truck. The remaining types of vehicle were held by 13.3 percent of families.

SOURCE: Brian K. Bucks, Arthur B. Kennickell, and Kevin B. Moore, "Table 8. Family Holdings of Nonfinancial Assets and of Any Asset, by Selected Characteristics of Families and Type of Asset, 2001 and 2004 Surveys. B. 2004 Survey of Consumer Finances," in "Recent Changes in U.S. Family Finances: Evidence from the 2001 and 2004 Survey of Consumer Finances," *Federal Reserve Bulletin*, vol. 92, February 2006, http://www.federalreserve.gov/pubs/oss/oss2/2004/bull0206.pdf (accessed June 10, 2008)

of families held these accounts. Nearly half of families (49.7%) had retirement accounts. Note that this category does not include Social Security benefits and certain employer-sponsored defined benefit plans. Nearly a quarter (24.2%) of families had cash value life insurance policies. Smaller percentages held stocks (20.7%), savings bonds (17.6%), pooled investment funds (15%), certificates of deposit (12.7%), and bonds (1.8%). Ten percent of families held financial assets of other types.

Overall, Bucks, Kennickell, and Moore note that families the most likely to hold financial assets were those in the highest income brackets, those with a head of household aged seventy-five or older, those with a self-employed head of household, and homeowners. Comparison among races indicates that 97.2% of white families held financial assets in 2004, compared to 85% of minority families. The largest difference lies in retirement accounts. More than half (56.1%) of white families had retirement accounts, compared to only 32.9% of minority families. Stock ownership also showed disparities. More than a quarter (25.5%) of white families owned stocks in 2004, compared to only 8% of minority families.

ANOTHER LOOK AT WEALTH DATA

In "Recent Trends in Household Wealth in the United States: Rising Debt and the Middle-Class Squeeze" (June 2007, http://www.levy.org/pubs/wp_502.pdf), Edward N. Wolff of Bard College and New York University examines the 2004 SCF data in relation to two other economic measures: debt to income ratio and debt to equity ratio. A debt to income ratio provides a measure of a household's

debt divided by its income. A debt to equity ratio measures a household's debt divided by its net worth.

Wolff calculates that in 2004 the debt to income ratio was 61.4% for the richest 1% of Americans and 141.2% for the middle class (defined as households with a net worth of $500 to $406,450). Thus, the middle class was burdened with a much higher debt to income ratio than the extremely wealthy. Likewise, the debt to equity ratio for the richest 1% of Americans was only 3.8% in 2004, compared to 61.6% for the middle class. Wolff believes the massive amount of indebtedness carried by middle-class households dramatically hampers their wealth growth rate.

WEALTH INEQUALITY: IS IT A PROBLEM?

Even though the data are clear that wealth inequality exists in the United States, there is contentious debate about whether or not this condition poses a problem to the economy and to society. A certain amount of inequality is built into a capitalist economy by its very nature. However, with wealth growing rapidly among the already richest 1% of Americans, but not among the lower classes, many economists worry that the perceived economic success of the 2000s may be just an illusion.

Wealth Inequality Seen as Harmful

The debate over wealth inequality has always been a politically partisan issue, with those on the right arguing that the market should be allowed to adjust itself with regard to wages and income and those on the left maintaining that widespread financial inequality causes many social and economic problems.

The Dollars & Sense Collective is a group of "left-thinking" scholars and authors who believe that income inequality is a serious problem with dire economic, political, and social consequences for the nation. Their views are presented in publications such as *Dollars & Sense: The Journal of Economic Justice*, a monthly journal, and *Wealth Inequality Reader* (2008). The latter includes essays by dozens of contributors on the scope and harmful effects of wealth inequality. The introduction notes, "The 1980s and 1990s were supposed to be economic good times, but the share of Americans with no wealth at all was larger in 2004 than it had been in 1983. The late-1990s economy gave a small boost to those at the bottom, but it didn't make up for the losses of the previous 15 years. The result: even after the 1990s—the most fabulous decade of economic growth in recent U.S. history—over a quarter of American households had less than $5,000 in assets."

Paul Krugman of Princeton University is an outspoken critic of wealth inequality in the United States. He explains his viewpoint at length in "For Richer" (*New York Times*, October 20, 2002). Krugman asserts that wage controls and other measures taken by the government during the Great Depression and World War II (1939–1945) created a broad and stable middle class in the United States. An abundance of high-paying unionized manufacturing jobs ensured that less-educated working-class people could maintain a standard of living similar to that of highly educated professionals. Krugman believes that changing social attitudes—a "new permissiveness"—have permitted wealth inequality to grow unchecked since the 1970s. He uses as an example the enormous growth in the salaries of chief executive officers (CEOs) of major corporations. He claims that ideas about corporate responsibility and financial prudence kept CEO salaries in check until the 1970s and 1980s, when a new societal attitude emerged that Krugman describes as "greed is good." In 1970 the top one-tenth of 1% of American taxpayers had average earnings that were seventy times as much as the average American. By 1998 the same segment had incomes that were three hundred times that of the average American. Yet, there has not been an uproar among the middle and lower classes about wealth inequality.

Krugman believes policy makers perpetuate wealth inequality in the United States and that the United States is becoming a plutocracy (government by the wealthy). He concludes that "as the gap between the rich and the rest of the population grows, economic policy increasingly caters to the interests of the elite, while public services for the population at large—above all, public education—are starved of resources. As policy increasingly favors the interests of the rich and neglects the interests of the general population, income disparities grow even wider."

Wealth Inequality Seen as Not Harmful

On the other side of this issue are those who believe that wealth inequality does not pose a problem to the U.S. economy or social system. This viewpoint is generally associated with conservative political thinking, which generally holds that market forces must be allowed to adjust themselves without government interference. One idea that is regularly expressed by politicians in this camp is that "what's good for the rich is good for the rest of us." This philosophy was espoused by President Ronald Reagan (1911–2004), who championed a trickle-down economic policy—economic actions (such as tax cuts beneficial to the wealthy) that encourage greater investment in business growth, thus, increasing employment, wages, and other benefits to those in the middle and lower classes.

In "Rich Man, Poor Man: How to Think about Income Inequality" (*National Review*, June 16, 2003), Kevin A. Hassett argues that income inequality is not harmful to the United States. He rebuts many of the criticisms leveled against income inequality. In fact, Hassett asserts that evidence shows that income inequality in extremely poor undeveloped countries probably limits economic growth, but not so in wealthy developed countries, where economies and income inequality grow together.

Hassett believes that unease over wealth inequality is driven by social views on the "basic justice" of society, but he argues that there are similarly compelling arguments against taking from the rich to benefit the poor. Hassett states, "In the real world, differences emerge between citizens because of both luck and choices. Virtually every circumstance is a mixture of these two cases. This distinction is important, because it makes it difficult if not impossible to conceive of scenarios where justice clearly supports forceful redistribution." Also, Hassett notes that taking resources from the rich limits their ability and incentive to start and grow businesses, which will ultimately hurt American workers even more. He concludes that on a global scale, nations emphasizing free-market capitalism (such as the United States) have done a better job of raising the standard of living of their poor than nations in which socialist views have encouraged a more equitable distribution of wealth.

Public Opinion on Wealth Distribution

As part of the *Gallup Poll Social Series: Economy & Personal Finance* (April 2008, http://brain.gallup.com/documents/questionnaire.aspx?STUDY=P0804015), pollsters asked Americans to answer two questions about wealth distribution in the United States. The first question asked: "Do you feel that the distribution of money and wealth in this country today is fair, or do you feel that the money and wealth in this country should be more evenly distributed among a larger percentage of the people?" More than two-thirds (68%) of respondents said the nation's money and wealth should be more evenly distributed. Only 27% felt the current distribution "is fair."

In the second question, Gallup asked: "Do you think our government should or should not redistribute wealth by heavy taxes on the rich?" A slim majority (51%) agreed that the government should redistribute wealth via heavy taxes on the rich. Forty-three percent disagreed with this approach.

CHAPTER 9
THE ROLE OF THE GOVERNMENT

In general, the art of government consists in taking as much money as possible from one party of the citizens to give to the other.

—Voltaire, *Dictionnaire Philosophique* (1764)

The government has many roles in the U.S. economy. Like other businesses, the government spends and makes money, consumes goods and services, and employs people. Federal, state, and local governments raise funds directly through taxes and fees. They often borrow money from the public by selling securities, such as bonds. A bond is an investment in which people loan money to the government for a specified time and interest rate. Governments also disburse money via contracts with businesses or through social programs that benefit the public.

Finally, the federal government is a manipulator of the U.S. economy. It influences macroeconomic factors, such as inflation and unemployment, through fiscal policy and monetary policy. Fiscal policy revolves around spending and taxation. Monetary policy is concerned with the amount of money in circulation and operation of the nation's central banking system.

FUNDING GOVERNMENT SERVICES

Governments are responsible for providing services that individuals cannot effectively provide for themselves, such as military defense, fire and police departments, roads, education, social services, and environmental protection. Some government entities also provide public utilities, such as water, sewage treatment, or electricity. To generate the revenue necessary to provide services, governments collect taxes and fees and charge for many services they provide to the public. If these revenues are not sufficient to fund desired programs, governments borrow money.

Taxation

Even before the United States became an independent nation, taxes were a significant issue for Americans. The Stamp Act of 1765 was the first tax imposed specifically on the North American colonies by the British Parliament and was strongly resisted by the colonists, who maintained that only representative legislatures in each colony possessed the right to impose taxes. The view that "taxation without representation" was tyranny contributed to the opposition to British rule that led to the Revolutionary War (1775–1783). Of course, it was necessary for the newly independent colonies to establish taxes of their own. As Benjamin Franklin (1706–1790) wrote, "In this world nothing can be said to be certain, except death and taxes" (November 13, 1789), and over the next two centuries a complex taxation code was developed at the federal, state, and local levels.

The most common taxes levied by federal, state, and local governments are:

- Income taxes—charged on wages, salaries, and tips
- Payroll taxes—Social Security insurance and unemployment compensation, which are paid by employers and withdrawn from payroll checks
- Property taxes—levied on the value of property owned, usually real estate
- Capital gains taxes—charged on the profit from the sale of an asset such as stock or real estate
- Corporate taxes—levied on the profits of a corporation
- Estate taxes—charged against the assets of a deceased person
- Excise taxes—collected at the time something is sold or when a good is imported
- Wealth taxes—levied on the value of assets rather than on the income they produce

Taxes are broadly defined as being either direct or indirect. Direct taxes (such as income taxes) are paid by the entity on whom the tax is being levied. Indirect taxes are passed on from the responsible party to someone else. Examples of indirect taxes include business property taxes, gasoline taxes, and sales taxes, which are levied on businesses but passed on to consumers via increased prices.

When individuals with higher incomes pay a higher percentage of a tax, it is called a progressive tax; when those with lower incomes pay a larger percentage of their income, a tax is considered regressive. The federal income tax is an example of a progressive tax, because individuals with higher incomes are subject to higher tax rates. Sales and excise taxes are regressive, because the same tax applies to all consumers regardless of income, so less prosperous individuals pay a higher percentage of their income.

Borrowing against the Future

Like many members of the public, government entities sometimes spend more than they make. When cash revenues from taxes, fees, and other sources are not sufficient to cover spending, money must be borrowed. One method used by government to borrow money is the selling of securities, such as bonds, to the public. A bond is basically an IOU that a government body writes to a buyer. The buyer pays money up front in exchange for the IOU, which is redeemable at some point in the future (the maturity date) for the amount of the original loan plus interest. In addition, the federal government has the ability to write itself IOUs—to spend money now that it expects to make in the future.

U.S. government bodies borrow money because they are optimistic that future revenues will cover the IOUs they have written. This optimism is based in part on the power that governments have to tax their citizens and control the cost of provided government services. Even though tax increases and cuts in services can be enacted to raise money, these actions have political and economic repercussions. Politicians who wish to remain in office are reluctant to displease their constituents. Furthermore, the more citizens pay in taxes, the less money they will have to spend in the marketplace or invest in private business, thereby hurting the overall economy. As a result, governments must weigh their need to borrow against the future likely consequences of paying back the loan.

LOCAL GOVERNMENTS

The U.S. Census Bureau performs a comprehensive Census of Government every five years; the most recent was conducted in 2007 (http://www.census.gov/govs/www/cog2007.html). In between the censuses, annual surveys are

FIGURE 9.1

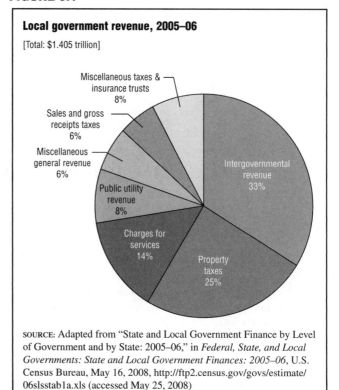

Local government revenue, 2005–06

[Total: $1.405 trillion]

- Miscellaneous taxes & insurance trusts 8%
- Sales and gross receipts taxes 6%
- Miscellaneous general revenue 6%
- Public utility revenue 8%
- Charges for services 14%
- Intergovernmental revenue 33%
- Property taxes 25%

SOURCE: Adapted from "State and Local Government Finance by Level of Government and by State: 2005–06," in *Federal, State, and Local Governments: State and Local Government Finances: 2005–06*, U.S. Census Bureau, May 16, 2008, http://ftp2.census.gov/govs/estimate/06slsstab1a.xls (accessed May 25, 2008)

conducted to collect certain data on government finances and employment.

The 2007 Census of Government found 89,476 local government units in operation. These units are comprised of counties, municipalities, townships, school districts, and special districts. Special district governments usually perform a single function, such as flood control or water supply. For example, Florida is divided into five water management districts, each of which is responsible for managing and protecting water resources and balancing the water needs of other government units within its jurisdiction.

Local Revenues

The latest survey data for local government revenues were compiled between 2005 and 2006. Local governments took in just over $1.4 trillion that year. (See Figure 9.1.) Nearly three-fourths of the money came from only three sources: intergovernmental revenue (33%), property taxes (25%), and charges for services (14%). Intergovernmental revenue consists of funds transferred to local governments from the federal and state governments. State funds accounted for the vast majority of intergovernmental transfers between 2005 and 2006.

Taxes, particularly property taxes, are an important source of revenue for many local governments. Property taxes accounted for a fourth of all revenue between 2005 and 2006 and were the largest single source of self-generated money. (See Figure 9.1.) Consumption taxes were also collected on sales and gross receipts. This includes selective taxes levied against particular goods, such as motor fuels, alcoholic beverages, and tobacco products. Miscellaneous taxes include personal and corporate income taxes, motor vehicle license taxes, and a wide variety of other taxes.

The revenue included in "charges for services" comes from many local sources, including hospitals, sewage treatment facilities, solid waste management, parks and recreation areas, airports, and educational facilities (e.g., the sale of school lunches). (See Figure 9.1.)

Other revenue sources for local governments are public utilities, miscellaneous general revenue, and insurance trusts. (See Figure 9.1.) Public utilities primarily supply electricity, water, natural gas, and public transportation (such as buses and trains). Miscellaneous general revenue comes from a variety of sources, including interest payments and the sale of public property. Insurance trusts are monies collected from the paychecks of local government employees to pay for worker programs, such as retirement benefits.

PROPERTY TAXES. A property tax is tax levied on the value of land, buildings, businesses, or personal property, including business equipment and automobiles. The U.S. Department of the Treasury explains that property taxes in the United States date back to the Massachusetts Bay Colony in 1646 and that the separate states began imposing property taxes soon after declaring independence from Britain. A property tax is an example of an ad valorem tax. Ad valorem is a Latin phrase meaning "according to the value."

Property taxes are generally levied annually and calculated by multiplying the property value by an assessment ratio to obtain a taxable value. Assessment ratios can vary from less than 0.1 (less than 10%) to more than 1.0 (greater than 100%). The calculated taxable value is multiplied by a tax rate typically expressed in tax dollars per hundred or thousand dollars of value. For example, a home valued at $150,000 in an area with an assessment ratio of 0.5 (50%) would have a taxable value of $75,000. Assuming a tax rate of $3 per $1,000 of value, the property tax would be three times $75, or $225. Tax rates based on $1,000 of value are also known as millage rates.

Government entities at the local and sometimes state level determine the tax rate and the assessment ratio for their area. If permitted by their constituents, governments may choose to increase these values to raise additional revenue. Because real estate generally increases in value over time, property taxes can increase each year even if the tax rate and the assessment ratio remain constant.

Local Expenditures

Local governments spent nearly $1.4 trillion on annual expenses between 2005 and 2006. (See Figure 9.2.) Education was the largest single component, accounting for $525 billion and encompassing about 37% of the total. Spending on public health, welfare, and hospitals; utilities; environmental and housing concerns; and public safety (e.g., police and fire) each accounted for roughly 10% of the total.

According to the Census Bureau (May 16, 2008, http:// ftp2.census.gov/govs/estimate/06slsstab1a.xls), salaries and wages for local government employees amounted to $518.1 billion, or 37% of the total expenditures between 2005 and 2006.

The Census Bureau (March 5, 2007, http://ftp2.census .gov/govs/apes/06locus.txt) estimates that in March 2006 local governments employed the equivalent of 11.9 million full-time employees. The payroll for that month was nearly $43.9 billion. Education positions were the single largest component, accounting for 6.9 million employees and $24.3 billion in payroll (more than half of employee numbers and payroll). The second largest component consisted of police, fire, and corrections officers. Nearly 1.4 million of them were employed by local governments and accounted for $6.3 billion of monthly payroll.

STATE GOVERNMENTS

State Revenues

According to the Census Bureau, state governments had revenues of nearly $1.8 trillion between 2005 and 2006. (See Figure 9.3.) Intergovernmental revenue (funds from the federal government) accounted for almost one-fourth (24%) of the total. Insurance trusts were the largest source of self-generated revenue for states, accounting for 21% of the total. Other major sources of revenue included sales taxes (19%) and individual income taxes (14%). Charges for services, miscellaneous general revenue, and miscellaneous taxes (such as property taxes) each accounted for 9% or less of the total.

In February 2008 the Census Bureau released detailed data on state tax collections for 2007. Each of the fifty states is ranked in Table 9.1 by total tax collected. In general, the largest and most populous states collected the most taxes. Four states—California, New York, Texas, and Florida—accounted for 38% of all taxes collected in 2007.

STATE SALES TAXES. Sales taxes are a major source of revenue for state governments. (See Figure 9.3.) The Federation of Tax Administrators (FTA) is a nonprofit organization that provides research services for the tax administrators of all fifty states. According to the FTA, in "State Sales Tax Rates" (January 1, 2008, http://www.taxadmin .org/fta/rate/sales.html), forty-five states and the District of Columbia assessed sales taxes. As of January 2008, the five states without a sales tax were Alaska, Delaware, Montana, New Hampshire, and Oregon. The state sales tax rates ranged from a low of 2.9% in Colorado to 7% and greater in California, Mississippi, New Jersey, Rhode Island, and Tennessee. Nearly all states exempted prescription drugs and food from sales taxes.

FIGURE 9.2

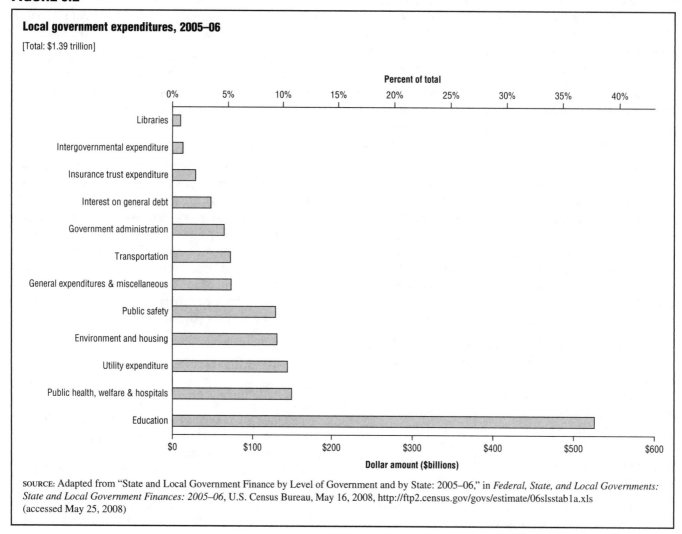

Local government expenditures, 2005–06

[Total: $1.39 trillion]

SOURCE: Adapted from "State and Local Government Finance by Level of Government and by State: 2005–06," in *Federal, State, and Local Governments: State and Local Government Finances: 2005–06*, U.S. Census Bureau, May 16, 2008, http://ftp2.census.gov/govs/estimate/06slsstab1a.xls (accessed May 25, 2008).

STATE INCOME TAXES. In "State Individual Income Taxes" (January 1, 2008, http://www.taxadmin.org/fta/rate/ind_inc.html), the FTA provides information on state income tax rates. As of January 2008, forty-three states and the District of Columbia imposed income taxes. The states that did not tax income were Alaska, Florida, Nevada, South Dakota, Texas, Washington, and Wyoming. Two additional states, Tennessee and New Hampshire, taxed only personal income derived from dividends and interest.

According to the FTA, several states imposed a single rate for all income levels, including Colorado (4.6%), Illinois (3%), Indiana (3.4%), Massachusetts (5.3%), Michigan (4.4%), Pennsylvania (3.1%), and Rhode Island (25% of federal tax liability). Many states have devised tax codes based on multiple income brackets. Overall, tax rates varied from a low of 0.4% in Iowa to a high of 9.5% in Vermont.

State Expenditures

The Census Bureau reports that state governments had expenditures of nearly $1.6 trillion between 2005 and 2006. (See Figure 9.4.) About $428 billion (28%) of this total was in the form of transfers to other govern-

ments, such as local governments within the state. The remainder was devoted to spending priorities at the state level. Public welfare and social services composed the single largest expense at $407 billion, accounting for 26% of all money expended. Education and libraries accounted for the second largest category of expenditures at $202 billion, or 13% of the total. State spending on education is primarily for higher education, such as colleges and universities. Payments from insurance trusts amounted to 11% of state spending. All other expenditures each accounted for 6% or less of state spending.

The Census Bureau (March 5, 2007, http://ftp2.census.gov/govs/apes/06stus.txt) estimates that in March 2006 state governments employed the equivalent of 4.3 million full-time employees. The payroll for that month was nearly $16.8 billion. Education positions were the single largest component, accounting for 1.7 million employees and $6.9 billion in payroll. The second largest contingent consisted of corrections officers. Nearly half a million of them were employed by state governments in March 2006, accounting for $1.7 billion of monthly payroll.

FIGURE 9.3

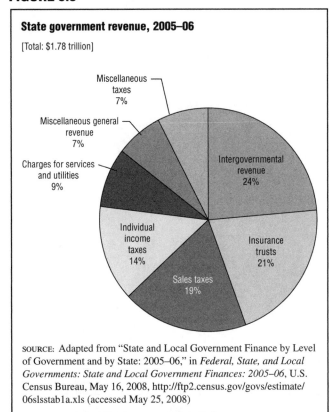

State government revenue, 2005–06

[Total: $1.78 trillion]

- Miscellaneous taxes 7%
- Miscellaneous general revenue 7%
- Charges for services and utilities 9%
- Individual income taxes 14%
- Sales taxes 19%
- Insurance trusts 21%
- Intergovernmental revenue 24%

SOURCE: Adapted from "State and Local Government Finance by Level of Government and by State: 2005–06," in *Federal, State, and Local Governments: State and Local Government Finances: 2005–06*, U.S. Census Bureau, May 16, 2008, http://ftp2.census.gov/govs/estimate/06slsstab1a.xls (accessed May 25, 2008)

FEDERAL GOVERNMENT

For accounting purposes, the federal government operates on a fiscal year (FY) that begins in October and runs through the end of September. Thus, FY 2009 covers the period of October 1, 2008, through September 30, 2009. Each year by the first Monday in February the U.S. president must present a proposed budget to the U.S. House of Representatives. This is the amount of money that the president estimates will be required to operate the federal government during the next fiscal year.

It can take several months for the House to debate, negotiate, and approve a final budget. The budget must also be approved by the U.S. Senate. This entire process can take many months, and sometimes longer than a year. This means that the federal government can be well into (or beyond) a fiscal year before knowing the exact amount of its budget for that year.

Detailed data on the finances of the federal government are maintained by the Office of Management and Budget (OMB), an executive office of the U.S. president. The OMB assists the president in preparing the federal budget and supervises budget administration. Information on the FY 2009 budget is available at http://www.whitehouse.gov/omb/budget/fy2009/. Budget documents include historical tables that provide annual data on federal government receipts, outlays, debt, and employment dating back to 1940 or earlier. The FY 2009 budget includes

TABLE 9.1

States ranked by total state taxes, 2007

[Amount in thousands]

Rank	State	Total tax Amount
	United States	750,290,885
1	California	114,736,981
2	New York	63,161,582
3	Texas	40,314,714
4	Florida	35,738,291
5	Pennsylvania	30,837,657
6	Illinois	29,516,656
7	New Jersey	29,106,788
8	Ohio	24,810,567
9	Michigan	23,848,753
10	North Carolina	22,612,798
11	Massachusetts	20,663,664
12	Virginia	18,972,392
13	Georgia	18,636,905
14	Minnesota	17,780,164
15	Washington	17,692,767
16	Maryland	15,094,183
17	Wisconsin	14,482,624
18	Indiana	14,098,233
19	Connecticut	12,847,554
20	Arizona	12,396,587
21	Tennessee	11,344,998
22	Louisiana	10,863,502
23	Missouri	10,704,834
24	Kentucky	9,895,207
25	Colorado	9,205,912
26	Oklahoma	8,906,320
27	Alabama	8,868,314
28	South Carolina	8,688,935
29	Oregon	7,742,862
30	Arkansas	7,391,778
31	Kansas	6,893,359
32	Iowa	6,469,752
33	Mississippi	6,394,513
34	Nevada	6,304,753
35	Utah	5,889,423
36	New Mexico	5,205,322
37	Hawaii	5,093,842
38	West Virginia	4,654,213
39	Nebraska	4,071,032
40	Maine	3,581,680
41	Idaho	3,536,574
42	Alaska	3,442,930
43	Delaware	2,905,905
44	Rhode Island	2,766,046
45	Vermont	2,558,806
46	Montana	2,319,992
47	New Hampshire	2,175,057
48	Wyoming	2,025,090
49	North Dakota	1,782,990
50	South Dakota	1,257,084

SOURCE: "States Ranked by Total State Taxes: 2007," in *Federal, State, and Local Governments: 2005 State Government Tax Collections*, U.S. Department of Commerce, U.S. Census Bureau, February 29, 2008, http://www.census.gov/govs/statetax/07staxrank.html (accessed May 24, 2008)

final values for years through 2007 and estimates for 2008 through 2013.

Federal Revenues

The federal government had revenues (receipts) of $2.5 trillion in 2007. (See Figure 9.5.) Individual income taxes were the largest single component, amounting to $1.2 trillion, or 47% of the total. The second largest source

FIGURE 9.4

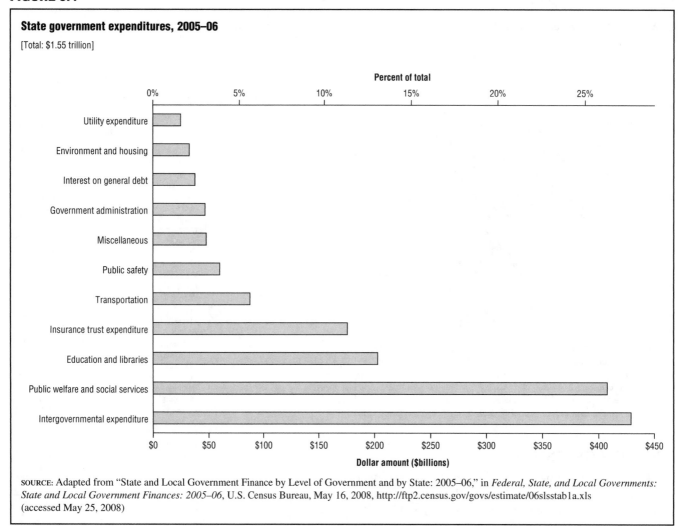

State government expenditures, 2005–06

[Total: $1.55 trillion]

SOURCE: Adapted from "State and Local Government Finance by Level of Government and by State: 2005–06," in *Federal, State, and Local Governments: State and Local Government Finances: 2005–06*, U.S. Census Bureau, May 16, 2008, http://ftp2.census.gov/govs/estimate/06slsstab1a.xls (accessed May 25, 2008)

of revenue was social insurance and retirement receipts, at $873 billion, or 34% of the total. Corporation income taxes accounted for another 13%, followed by other revenue at 4% and excise taxes at 3%.

TAXES ON INCOME. The federal income tax was authorized in 1913 with ratification of the Sixteenth Amendment to the U.S. Constitution: "The Congress shall have power to lay and collect taxes on incomes, from whatever source derived, without apportionment among the several states, and without regard to any census or enumeration." In the United States tax rates are approved by Congress and signed into law by the president; the Internal Revenue Service (IRS), a bureau of the Department of the Treasury, enforces the tax codes and collects tax payments, which are due each year on April 15.

The percentage of an individual's income that he or she pays in federal tax is based on his or her income level, which determines the individual's tax bracket. Tax brackets change as Congress modifies the tax codes, but individuals with higher incomes are always taxed at a higher rate than individuals with lower incomes. Through

a variety of tax credits and deductions, individuals can lower the amount of income on which taxes are calculated, thereby lowering the amount of tax they pay.

The federal tax on corporate income has been in effect since 1909. Because corporations are owned, and individuals derive income from them, the potential exists for "double taxation," that is, the same income taxed twice, once as corporate income and, when the profits have been distributed to shareholders, again as individual income. To reduce the effects of double taxation, various credits and deductions have been enacted throughout the years to allow income to pass through a corporation without being taxed until it reaches the individual. Credits and depreciation schedules reduce the amount of revenue subject to tax.

SOCIAL INSURANCE AND RETIREMENT RECEIPTS. Social insurance and retirement receipts are collected to fund specific programs for people who are retired, disabled, unemployed, or poor. The primary programs are Social Security and Medicare. Social Security provides funds to most workers who retire or become disabled. It

FIGURE 9.5

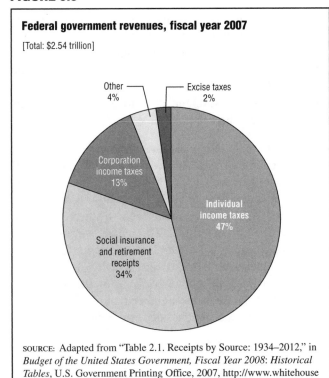

Federal government revenues, fiscal year 2007

[Total: $2.54 trillion]

SOURCE: Adapted from "Table 2.1. Receipts by Source: 1934–2012," in *Budget of the United States Government, Fiscal Year 2008: Historical Tables*, U.S. Government Printing Office, 2007, http://www.whitehouse.gov/omb/budget/fy2008/pdf/hist.pdf (accessed May 27, 2008)

also pays money to the survivors of workers who die. Medicare is a health insurance program for poor people.

As of 2008, the federal government collected money to pay for these two programs as follows:

• Social Security—a tax of 12.4% on earned annual income up to $102,000. In other words, people who earn more than the annual limit pay the tax on $102,000, no matter how much they earn.

• Medicare—a tax of 2.9% on earned annual income. No income limit.

These taxes are known as payroll taxes, because they are assessed based on the amounts that businesses pay their workers. Half of the tax (6.2% for Social Security plus 1.45% for Medicare) is paid by wage earners and is deducted from their paychecks; the other half is paid directly by employers. Self-employed people pay the entire tax bill but can deduct half of it as a business expense when they file income taxes.

Unemployment insurance is a joint federal-state program almost entirely funded by employers. Employers that meet certain criteria (regarding number of employees and amount of payroll) pay both state and federal unemployment taxes.

EXCISE TAXES AND OTHER RECEIPTS. Sales and excise taxes are considered taxes on consumption. Even though there is no federal sales tax, the federal government does levy excise taxes on items such as airplane tickets, gasoline, alcoholic

beverages, firearms, and cigarettes. Excise taxes on certain commodities are often hypothecated, meaning they are used to pay for a related government service. For example, fuel taxes are typically used to pay for road and bridge construction or public transportation, or a cigarette excise may go to cover government-supported health-care programs. Excise taxes can be intended to generate revenue or to discourage use of the taxed product (as in high cigarette taxes that raise the per-pack cost in an attempt to discourage smoking).

The "other" category in Figure 9.5 includes estate and gift taxes and customs duties and fees. Estate and gift taxes are taxes on wealth. Estate taxes are levied against a person's estate after that person dies; gift taxes are levied against the giver while the giver is alive. Estate and gift taxes only apply to amounts over specified limits. According to the IRS (May 1, 2008, http://www.irs.gov/businesses/small/article/0,,id=164871,00.html), as of 2008 only total taxable estates and lifetime gifts exceeding $1 million actually had to pay estate and gift taxes.

Customs duties are taxes charged on goods imported into the United States. The taxes vary by product and by exporting nation.

Federal Spending

According to the OMB, the federal government spent nearly $2.8 trillion during FY 2007. (See Table 9.2.) The OMB breaks down expenditures into broad categories called superfunctions and narrower categories called functions. Overall, human resources were the largest expenditure for the federal government, accounting for 61% of spending during 2007. The largest single component of federal spending was for the Social Security program, which accounted for 20% of expenditures. Social Security was followed by Medicare and income security (both at 13%), and health (9%).

According to the Census Bureau (June 28, 2007, http://ftp2.census.gov/govs/apes/06fedfun.pdf), the federal government employed 2.7 million civilian (nonmilitary) employees as of December 2006. The civilian payroll for that month was nearly $13.9 billion. The largest contingent of workers (over 772,000 people) worked for the U.S. Postal Service. It accounted for 28% of civilian employees and 26% of the total payroll. The next largest workforce was employed in national defense and international relations (more than 698,000 employees). This workforce accounted for 19% of the total payroll.

The U.S. Department of Defense reports in *Financial Summary Tables* (February 2008, http://www.defenselink.mil/comptroller/defbudget/fy2009/fy2009_summary_tables_whole.pdf) that it employed nearly 1.4 million military personnel on full-time active duty at the end of FY 2007. The Department of Defense had outlays of nearly $129 billion for all military personnel (active and reserve duty) for that year.

TABLE 9.2

Federal government outlays, fiscal year 2007

[Billions of dollars]

	Amount	Percent of net total by super function	Percent of net total by super function or function
National defense	572	20%	20%
Human resources	1,759	61%	
Education, training, employment, and social services	94		3%
Health	269		9%
Medicare	372		13%
Income security	365		13%
Social security	587		20%
Veterans benefits and services	72		3%
Physical resources	144	5%	
Energy	1.8		0.06%
Natural resources and environment	35		1%
Commerce and housing credit	0.2		0.01%
Transportation	75		3%
Community and regional development	33		1%
Net interest	239	8%	8%
Other functions	152	5%	
International affairs	35		1.2%
General science, space and technology	25		0.9%
Agriculture	20		0.7%
Administration of justice	45		1.6%
General government	19		0.7%
Allowances	7		
Undistributed offsetting receipts	−81		
Total, federal outlays	2,784	100$	100$

SOURCE: Adapted from "Table 3.1. Outlays by Superfunction and Function: 1940–2012," in *Budget of the United States Government, Fiscal Year 2008: Historical Tables*, U.S. Government Printing Office, 2007, http://www.whitehouse.gov/omb/budget/fy2008/pdf/hist.pdf (accessed May 27, 2008)

Federal Deficits and Surpluses

If the government spends less money than it takes in during a fiscal year, the difference is known as a budget surplus. Likewise, if spending is higher than revenues, the difference is called a budget deficit. A balanced budget occurs when spending and revenue are the same.

Figure 9.6 shows the annual surplus or deficit from 1900 to 2012 as reported in the OMB's FY 2008 budget (years 2007 to 2012 are estimated). In general, the federal government had a balanced budget for more than half of the twentieth century, excluding slight deficits that occurred around World War I (1914–1918) and World War II (1939–1945). Beginning in 1970 the United States had an annual deficit for nearly three decades. The years 1998 through 2002 had budget surpluses. In 2000 the surplus reached a record $236 billion. Budget deficits returned between 2003 and 2007 and are forecast by the OMB for 2008 through 2011. In 2004 the federal deficit reached a record high of nearly $413 billion and then began to shrink. The OMB predicts that budget deficits will continue to shrink through 2011 and that a budget surplus of $61 billion will occur in 2012.

National Debt

Whenever the federal government has a budget deficit, the Department of the Treasury must borrow money to cover the difference. The total amount of money that the Treasury has borrowed over the years is known as the federal debt, or more commonly the national debt. Budget surpluses cause the debt to go down, whereas deficits increase the debt.

The national debt was low until the early 1940s, when it jogged upward in response to World War II government spending. (See Figure 9.7.) Over the next three decades the debt increased at a slow pace. During the late 1970s the national debt began a steep climb that has continued into the 2000s. The budget surpluses from 1998 through 2002 had a slight dampening effect on the growth of the debt but did not actually decrease the amount of debt. The budget deficits of the years that followed sent the debt into another rapid incline. By the end of FY 2007, the national debt stood at $9 trillion.

BORROWED MONEY AND IOUS. The national debt has two components: money that the federal government has borrowed from the public and money that the federal government has loaned itself. The public loans money to the federal government by buying federal bonds and other securities. The government borrows the money with a promise to pay it back with interest after a set term. Some of the most common federal securities sold to the public are Treasury bills, Treasury notes, Treasury bonds, and savings bonds. These vary in value, interest paid, and set terms. Public investors include individuals and businesses (both domestic and foreign) and state and local governments.

The federal government also borrows from itself. This is debt owed by one Treasury account to another. Most of the so-called internal debt involves federal trust funds. For example, if a trust fund takes in more revenue in a year than is paid out, it loans the extra money to another federal account. In exchange, the loaning trust fund receives an interest-bearing security (basically an IOU) that is redeemable in the future from the Treasury. In *Federal Debt and the Commitments of Federal Trust Funds* (May 6, 2003, http://www.cbo.gov/ftpdocs/39xx/doc3948/10-25-LongRangeBrief4.pdf), the Congressional Budget Office (CBO) explains this accounting procedure in simple terms. The CBO sums up the situation by stating that "what is in the trust funds is simply the government's promise to pay itself back at some time in the future."

On June 19, 2008, the Department of the Treasury (http://www.treasurydirect.gov/govt/reports/pd/mspd/2008/opds062008.pdf) reported that the national debt was nearly $9.5 trillion, broken down as follows:

• Owed to the public—$5.3 trillion (56% of the total)

• Intragovernmental—$4.2 trillion (44% of the total)

FIGURE 9.6

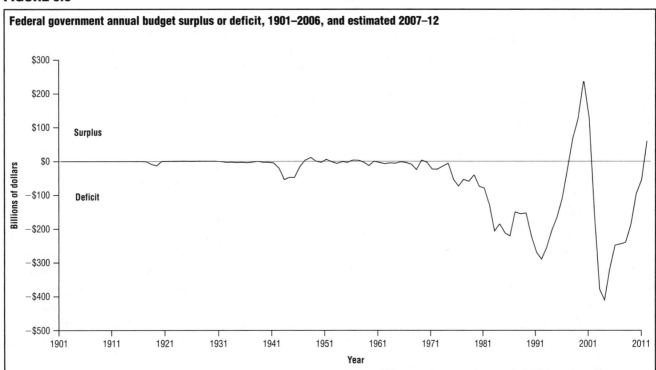

Federal government annual budget surplus or deficit, 1901–2006, and estimated 2007–12

SOURCE: Adapted from "Table 1.1. Summary of Receipts, Outlays, and Surpluses or Deficits (−): 1789–2012," in *Budget of the United States Government, Fiscal Year 2008: Historical Tables*, U.S. Government Printing Office, 2007, http://www.white house.gov/omb/budget/fy2008/pdf/hist.pdf (accessed May 27, 2008)

FIGURE 9.7

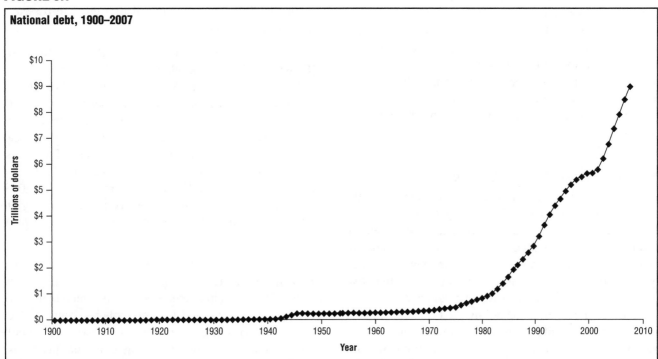

National debt, 1900–2007

SOURCE: Adapted from "Historical Debt Outstanding—Annual: 1900–1949," "Historical Debt Outstanding—Annual:1950–1999," and "Historical Debt Outstanding—Annual: 2000–2007," in *Public Debt Reports*, U.S. Department of the Treasury, Bureau of the Public Debt, March 14, 2007–January 31, 2008, http://www.treasurydirect.gov/govt/reports/pd/histdebt (accessed May 27, 2008)

According to the Department of the Treasury, in "The Debt to the Penny and Who Holds It" (July 2008, http://www.treasurydirect.gov/NP/BPDLogin?application=np), the portion of the national debt that the government owes to itself has grown substantially since the 1990s. In 1997 intragovernmental debt made up 30% of the total debt.

Over the following decade the intragovernmental debt grew to account for more than 40% of the total debt.

AS A PERCENTAGE OF THE GDP. Economists often discuss the national debt in terms of its percentage of the gross domestic product (GDP; the total market value of final goods and services produced within an economy in a given year), because a debt amount alone does not provide a complete picture of the effect of that debt on the one who owes it. According to the Central Intelligence Agency (CIA), in *World Factbook* (July 15, 2008, https://www.cia.gov/library/publications/the-world-factbook/rankorder/2186rank.html), in 2007 the U.S. national debt made up an estimated 60.8% of the nation's GDP in 2007.

INTERNATIONAL COMPARISON. In *World Factbook*, the CIA ranks nations of the world in descending order of national debt as a percentage of GDP in 2007. The United States ranked twenty-sixth on this list, behind industrialized nations including Japan (195.5%), Italy (104%), Singapore (101.2%), Greece (89.7%), Belgium (84.9%), Israel (80.6%), Norway (75.1%), Canada (68.5%), France (64%), and Germany (63.2%). By comparison, the United Kingdom had a national debt to GDP ratio of 43%, Spain was at 35.9%, China was at 18.4%, and Australia was at 15.4%.

THE BURDEN ON THE ECONOMY. The national debt represents a twofold burden on the U.S. economy. The debt owed to the public imposes a current burden. The federal government pays out interest to investors, and these interest payments are funded by current taxpayers. The debt that the federal government owes to itself is a future burden. At some point in the future the securities issued for intragovernmental debt must be redeemed for cash. The government will have to raise these funds by raising taxes, reducing spending, and/or borrowing more money from the public.

PUBLIC INVESTMENT AND TAXES

To fund itself, the federal government uses the money of its constituents. The buying of federal securities, such as bonds, represents a voluntary investment in government by the public. Federal securities are considered a safe low-risk investment because they are backed by an entity that has been in existence for more than two hundred years and has a proven track record of fiscal soundness. However, money invested in government securities is not available for private investment. In general, private investments are seen as more stimulating for the economy because they provide direct funds for growth, such as the building of new factories and the hiring of new workers. Public (government) investment may or may not have a stimulating effect on the economy, depending on how the funds are spent.

Taxes represent an involuntary investment by the public in government. The effect of taxes on the economy is a source of never-ending debate in U.S. politics. Taxing personal income decreases the spending power of the individual; people have less money to invest in private enterprise or to use to consume goods and services. Limited taxation is favored by those who believe that workers and companies with more available money to spend will participate to a greater extent in the economy. This, they say, will lead to economic growth. Others observe that cutting taxes without severely reducing government spending leads to large budget deficits and undermines the government programs that provide a social safety net to the disadvantaged.

The Bush Tax Cuts

Historically, the Republican Party has advocated smaller government and lower taxes. The Economic Growth and Tax Relief and Reconciliation Act (EGTRRA) of 2001 was initiated by the first administration of George W. Bush (1946–) and is commonly referred to as the "Bush tax cuts." The EGTRRA instituted a series of tax rate reductions and incentive measures to be phased in over several years. Included in the law were increases in income tax credits for families with children and reductions in estate, gift, and generation-skipping transfer taxes (a special tax on property transfers from grandparents to their grandchildren), but it did not address business taxes. It also called for reductions in the tax brackets. The EGTRRA was designed to expire on January 1, 2011, unless additional measures are passed to extend its provisions.

The Jobs and Growth Tax Relief Reconciliation Act (JGTRRA) of 2003 accelerated implementation of the EGTRRA, reduced taxes on capital gains and dividends, and increased deductions for property depreciation. Additional measures were accelerated or added through the Working Families Tax Relief Act of 2004, the American Jobs Creation Act of 2004, the Tax Increase Prevention and Reconciliation Act of 2005, the Pension Protection Act of 2006, and the Economic Stimulus Act of 2008. The latter included a one-time tax rebate for eligible Americans of up to $600 per qualifying adult and $300 per qualifying child.

TAX CUT ADVOCATES. President Bush was reelected in 2004, and he pressed Congress to make the provisions of the EGTRRA permanent as a way to stimulate the U.S. economy. Bush asserted that his policies would reduce poverty by lowering taxes for low- and lower-middle income families. In addition, he asserted that tax breaks benefit families by helping them reduce their debt.

In the press release "Treasury Releases Papers on Anniversary of President's 2003 Tax Relief" (May 28, 2008, http://www.ustreas.gov/press/releases/hp999.htm), the Department of the Treasury announces the issuing of two reports in May 2008 that highlighted "the benefits to American families and businesses from the tax relief enacted over the last seven years." According to the first report, *Topics Related to the President's Tax Relief* (http://www.treasury.gov/press/releases/reports/president _taxrelief_topics_0508.pdf), the tax cuts have made the individual income tax "highly progressive." As proof, the Treasury cites data indicating that in 2005 the top 1% of taxpayers paid 39.4%, the top 5% paid 59.7%, and the top 50% paid 96.9% of all individual income taxes. In the second report, *Tax Relief in 2001 through 2011* (http:// www.treasury.gov/press/releases/reports/taxrelief_20012011 _052708.pdf), the Treasury gives examples of the tax increases that will affect American families if the Bush tax cuts are allowed to expire. For example, the Treasury predicts that a family of four with one income earner making $40,000 per year in 2007 dollars will experience a tax increase of $2,345 in 2011.

TAX CUT CRITICS. Critics of President Bush's tax policy point out that changes in the tax structure unfairly shift the burden from corporations and wealthy individuals to low- and middle-class wage earners, that tax cuts already instituted have erased the federal surplus built up in the late 1990s, and that further tax cuts will lead to unacceptable increases in government debt.

Lori Montgomery examines in "As Candidates Warm to Bush Tax Cuts, Economists Warn of Long-Term Effect" (*Washington Post*, March 28, 2008) the effects of the Bush tax cuts and the opinions of economists who oppose continuing the cuts past their expiration date. Montgomery notes that the tax cuts are projected to save U.S. taxpayers $1.6 trillion by the time they expire. However, the economist Alan Viard states the tax cuts "are neither sustainable nor beneficial" unless the federal government makes enormous cuts in government spending, a scenario unlikely to occur. The economist Jason Furman complains "if you cut taxes without cutting spending, you're just shifting taxes to the future."

Tax Burden

The amount of tax an individual or family pays to the government, including his or her income, payroll, excise, and other taxes, is known as his or her tax burden. In *Tax Rates and Tax Burdens in the District of Columbia—A Nationwide Comparison: 2006* (November 2007, http://www.taxadmin .org/fta/rate/DC_tax_burden_2006.pdf), Natwar M. Gandhi, the chief financial officer of the District of Columbia, focuses on the tax burden in fifty-one large U.S. cities. Gandhi estimates that an American family of three with an annual income of $50,000 paid an average of 8.7% of its income in state and local taxes in 2006, including $2,153 in property taxes, $1,265 in state or local income taxes, $943 in sales taxes, and $250 in automobile taxes. At the $75,000 income level, American families paid an average of $6,649 in state and local taxes, or 8.9% of their income in 2006. The average tax burden for families with higher incomes was 8.5% for an income of $100,000 and 8.4% for an income of $150,000.

In *Who Pays Taxes and Who Receives Government Spending? An Analysis of Federal, State, and Local Tax and Spending Distributions, 1991–2004* (March 2007, http://www.taxfoundation.org/files/wp1.pdf), Andrew Chamberlain and Gerald Prante of the Tax Foundation, a nonpartisan tax research organization, split American taxpayers into five quintiles based on household income and estimate each quintile's tax burden as a percentage of income. The bottom quintile (i.e., the taxpaying household in the bottom 20% of the income range) had a tax burden rate of 4.3%. This compares to 9.6% and 14.8% for the second and third quintiles from the bottom and 22.4% for the second quintile from the top. The top quintile had a tax burden rate of 48.8%.

Chamberlain and Prante note that even though the U.S. tax system is progressive, the country's overall fiscal system is even more progressive when federal, state, and local government spending distributions are taken into account. The researchers indicate that households in the bottom quintile of income received approximately $8.21 in government spending for every dollar of taxes paid during 2004. Middle-class households received $1.30 for every tax dollar spent, and households in the top quintile received $0.41 for every tax dollar spent. Chamberlain and Prante conclude that "the current practice of judging the fairness of policy based on tax distributions alone is clearly inadequate."

International Comparisons

Even though Americans commonly complain about the amount of taxes they pay, the overall tax burden in the United States is generally lower than it is in other advanced economies. The Organization for Economic Cooperation and Development (OECD) compares in *Tax Administration in OECD and Selected Non-OECD Countries: Comparative Information Series: 2006* (February 2007, http://www .oecd.org/dataoecd/37/56/38093382.pdf) the tax burdens of various nations as of 2003. According to the OECD, the tax burden as a percentage of the GDP in the United States was 25.6%, which compared favorably to nations such as the United Kingdom (35.6%), Canada (33.8%), Germany (35.5%), France (43.4%), and Sweden (50.6%), and was only slightly higher than Korea and Japan (both at 25.3%).

THE FUTURE OF SOCIAL SECURITY AND MEDICARE

Social Security and Medicare are two of the most expensive programs operated by the federal government. (See Table 9.2.) Together, they accounted for $952 billion of spending in 2007, or 34% of total expenditures.

Signing Social Security into law on August 14, 1935, President Franklin D. Roosevelt (1882–1945; July 3, 2008, http://www.fdrlibrary.marist.edu/odssast.html) said, "We can never insure one hundred percent of the population against one hundred percent of the hazards and vicissitudes of life, but we have tried to frame a law which will give some measure of protection to the average citizen and to his family against the loss of a job and against poverty-ridden old age."

As part of his war on poverty, President Lyndon B. Johnson (1908–1973) signed into law the Social Security Amendments of 1965, which included a new program called Medicare to provide health insurance for the elderly.

The program conditions and requirements have been changed many times over the succeeding decades. As of 2008, people born in 1929 or later qualify for retirement benefits once they have worked for ten years. Benefit amounts are based on wage history; thus, higher-paid workers will have higher retirement benefits than lower-paid workers. The Social Security Administration (SSA) indicates in "Retirement Benefits by Year of Birth" (May 5, 2008, http://www.socialsecurity.gov/retire2/agereduction.htm) the age at which full benefits can be paid:

- People born in or before 1937—age sixty-five

- People born between 1938 and 1959—sliding age scale ranging from sixty-five and two months to sixty-six and ten months

- People born in 1960 and later—age sixty-seven

People who have worked for at least ten years are eligible for permanently reduced retirement benefits starting at age sixty-two. Benefits for widows, widowers, and family members have varying age requirements and other conditions that must be met. Medicare coverage begins at age sixty-five for everyone except for certain disabled people who can qualify earlier.

Since their inception, the Social Security and Medicare programs have been a source of partisan contention and debate. Much of the debate has centered on how the programs should be funded and the role of government in social welfare. In recent years, attention has turned to concerns about how the nation can afford these programs in the future as the population ages and as the number of earners contributing to the plans decreases.

Fewer Contributors, More Beneficiaries

Figure 9.8 shows the percentage of the U.S. population aged sixty-five and older from 2000 to 2008 and projected through 2050. A huge increase in the aged population is expected to take place during the late 2010s and 2020s because of the baby boom that followed World War II. However, as these workers retire, there will be fewer workers contributing to the plan, because succeeding generations have been smaller due to declin-

FIGURE 9.8

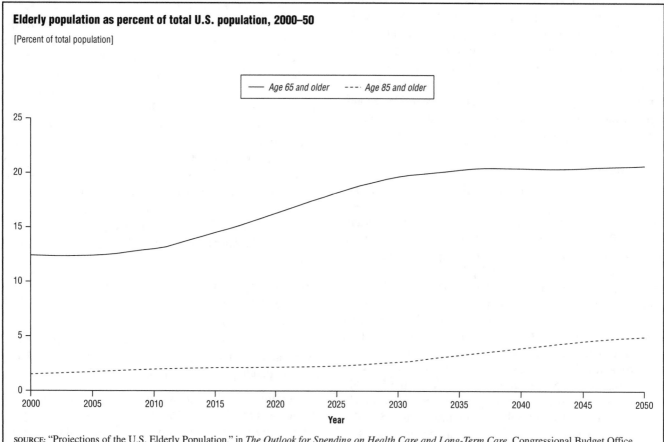

Elderly population as percent of total U.S. population, 2000–50

[Percent of total population]

— Age 65 and older   - - - Age 85 and older

SOURCE: "Projections of the U.S. Elderly Population," in *The Outlook for Spending on Health Care and Long-Term Care,* Congressional Budget Office, February 24, 2008, http://www.cbo.gov/ftpdocs/89xx/doc8995/02-24-2008-NGA.pdf (accessed April 9, 2008)

The American Economy

FIGURE 9.9

Actual and projected number of workers contributing to Social Security system per beneficiary, 1960–2080

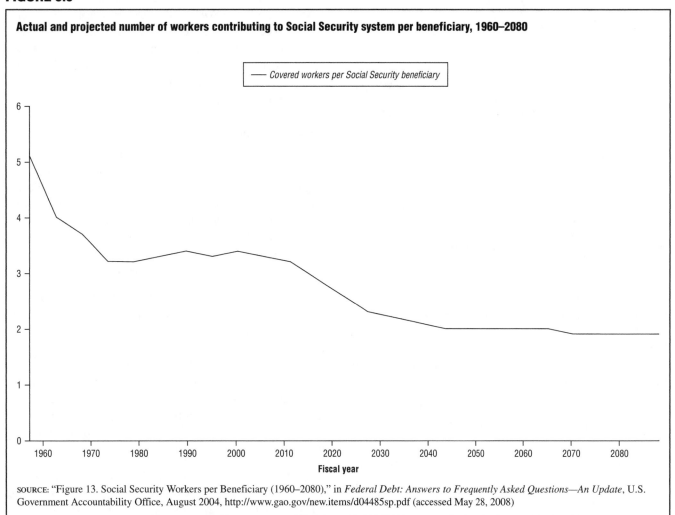

SOURCE: "Figure 13. Social Security Workers per Beneficiary (1960–2080)," in *Federal Debt: Answers to Frequently Asked Questions—An Update*, U.S. Government Accountability Office, August 2004, http://www.gao.gov/new.items/d04485sp.pdf (accessed May 28, 2008)

ing birth rates. At the same time, life expectancies have been increasing, meaning that elderly people are living longer past retirement age and collecting benefits for more years.

The U.S. Government Accountability Office (GAO) estimates in *Federal Debt: Answers to Frequently Asked Questions—An Update* (August 2004, http://www.gao .gov/new.items/d04485sp.pdf) the number of workers contributing to Social Security per beneficiary. In 1960 there were approximately five workers per beneficiary. (See Figure 9.9.) By 2000 this number had dropped to 3.3 workers. The GAO estimates that by 2060 there will be about two workers contributing for each beneficiary. This is expected to put unprecedented stresses on the Social Security system.

Funding Social Security

In *The 2008 Annual Report of the Board of Trustees of the Federal Old-Age and Survivors Insurance and Federal Disability Insurance Trust Funds* (March 25, 2008, http://www.ssaonline.us/OACT/TR/TR08/tr08.pdf),

an annual report on the status of the Social Security trust funds—Old-Age and Survivors Insurance (OASI) and Disability Insurance (DI), the Social Security Board of Trustees notes that approximately 163 million people had earnings covered by Social Security during 2007. Together, the OASI and DI trust funds had revenues of $785 billion, of which nearly 84% came from payroll taxes. The remaining 16% was from interest earnings and taxes assessed on benefits. Approximately $585 billion was paid in benefits to forty-eight million people as follows:

• Thirty-four million retirees and their dependents

• Nine million survivors of deceased workers

• Six million disabled workers and their dependents

The trustees project that tax revenues will be less than program costs beginning in 2017. (See Table 9.3.) At that point the trust funds will be used to pay the shortfall so that payments to beneficiaries can continue at expected levels. The trust funds will be exhausted in 2041, and over the following four decades the program's

TABLE 9.3

Key dates for the Social Security and Medicare trust funds, April 2008

	Key dates for the trust funds			
	OASI	DI	OASDI	HI
First year outgo exceeds income excluding interest	2018	2005	2017	2008
First year outgo exceeds income including interest	2028	2012	2027	2010
Year trust funds are exhausted	2042	2025	2041	2019

OASI = Old Age Survivors Insurance.
DI = Disability Insurance.
OASDI = Old Age, Survivors, and Disability Insurance.
HI = Health Insurance.

SOURCE: "Key Dates for the Trust Funds," in *A Summary of the 2007 Annual Social Security and Medicare Trust Fund Reports*, Social Security Administration, April 22, 2008, http://www.ssa.gov/OACT/TRSUM/index.html (accessed May 28, 2008)

annual income will fund approximately 75% of the benefits currently available to beneficiaries. Accessing the trust funds will put pressure on the federal budget, as the federal government has often borrowed money from the trust funds to pay for other programs but will no longer be able to do so.

In total, the trustees estimate that the Social Security program will be short by $4.3 trillion over a seventy-five-year period.

FIXING THE PROBLEM. How best to prepare for future shortfalls in Social Security is a fiercely debated issue within the federal government. During early 2005 President Bush campaigned for significant reform of the Social Security program, including allowing younger workers to opt out of the Social Security plan and establish their own retirement savings accounts. This came to be known as the privatization of Social Security.

Democrats in Congress did not accept that a radical reform of the program was necessary to recover the shortfall, as the actual deficit over a seventy-five-year period, according to the Social Security Board of Trustees, in the *2008 Annual Report*, was expected to be about 2%. In other words, the payroll tax for Social Security would need to be increased by 2% to make up the difference. Democrats have suggested that such a sum could also be recouped by, for example, removing the cap on income subject to FICA taxes (those mandated by the Federal Insurance Contribution Act), but President Bush has adamantly dismissed any alternatives that could be construed as a tax increase.

In addition, the president's plan to privatize Social Security has been opposed by influential seniors groups, including the AARP (formerly the American Association of Retired Persons), a special interest group for people over age fifty. In "Frequently Asked Questions about Strengthening Social Security" (2008, http://www.aarp.org/money/

social_security/frequently_asked_questions_about_social_security.html), the AARP advocates increasing the income limit subject to Social Security withholding. As of 2008, the limit was $102,000; it has been raised many times over the years. The AARP also encourages the federal government to invest trust fund assets differently so as to reap higher rates of return.

Funding Medicare

The Social Security Board of Trustees notes in the *2008 Annual Report* that Hospital Insurance (HI), the largest Medicare trust fund, took in $224 billion during 2007. The vast majority of this money was from payroll taxes. The remainder came from interest earnings, taxes on benefits, beneficiary premiums, and other sources. The HI trust fund pays hospital benefits (known as Part A under Medicare) to all beneficiaries.

The trustees note that the Medicare HI trust fund faces a shortfall much sooner than the OASI and DI funds. Benefits to be paid out will exceed income (including interest) as early as 2010. The HI trust fund is expected to be exhausted by 2019. Immediately after exhaustion, tax revenues will be sufficient to pay only 78% of HI costs. That number will drop to 30% by 2082. The HI trust fund faces extreme funding problems in future decades because technological advances are expected to dramatically increase health-care costs in the United States.

The Medicare Supplementary Medical Insurance (SMI) trust fund had revenues of $238 billion during 2007. SMI covers the costs of physician services (Part B) and prescription drugs (Part D). Coverage under Parts B and D is optional and requires payment of monthly premiums. These are subtracted from the beneficiaries' Social Security checks. Part D coverage is relatively new, having been added to the Medicare program in late 2003. In 2005 the SMI trust fund was financed largely by revenues from the general fund and supplemented with beneficiary premiums and interest earnings. Because SMI is not dependent on payroll taxes, it is not expected to experience the same kind of shortfalls facing the OASI, DI, and HI trust funds. It is, however, projected to put increasing pressure on the general fund because of rising health-care costs.

FIXING THE PROBLEM. The pending shortfalls in the Medicare HI trust fund have received far less national attention than the problems facing the OASI and DI trust funds. In his 2003 State of the Union address (http://www.whitehouse.gov/news/releases/2003/01/20030128-19.html), President Bush spoke about the need for health care reform, particularly in Medicare. The president called Medicare "the binding commitment of a caring society." However, concrete reform measures have not been forthcoming. Medicare reform is likely to require politically unpopular actions, such as raising taxes and/or reducing benefits.

FEDERAL GOVERNMENT MANIPULATION OF MACROECONOMICS

The federal government plays a role in the national economy as a tax collector, spender, and employer. Federal policy makers also engage in purposeful manipulation of the U.S. economy at the macroeconomic level—for example, by influencing supply and demand factors. This was not always the case. Before the 1930s the government mostly maintained a hands-off approach to macroeconomic affairs—a tradition dating back to the founding of the nation. The ravages of the Great Depression brought a level of desperation (e.g., the unemployment rate was as high as 25%) that encouraged leaders to attempt to influence macroeconomic factors. Even though these efforts were largely futile at soothing deep economic depression, they accustomed a generation of Americans to the idea of government interference in economic affairs.

When immense federal spending during World War II helped end the Great Depression, policy makers believed they had discovered a new solution, a government solution, for economic downturns. Government efforts to manage macroeconomic factors became a routine matter over the following decades. These manipulations are commonly divided into two categories, known as fiscal policy and monetary policy.

Fiscal Policy

The word *fiscal* is derived from the Latin term *fiscalis*, meaning "treasury." It is believed that a fiscalis was originally a woven basket in which money was kept. In modern English, the word *fiscal* has become synonymous with the word *financial*. The federal government's fiscal policy is concerned with the collection and spending of public money so as to influence macroeconomic affairs. Examples of fiscal policy include:

- Increasing government spending to spur businesses to produce more and hire more, lowering the unemployment rate

- Increasing taxes to pull money out of the hands of consumers; this can lower excessive demand that is driving high inflation rates

- Decreasing taxes to put more money in the hands of consumers to increase demand and consequently increase supply (production)

These examples illustrate optimistic outcomes. In reality, the actions of fiscal policy can have complicated (and unforeseen) effects on the U.S. economy. The situation described in the first example can backfire if production does not grow fast enough to satisfy consumer demand. The result will be rising prices and high inflation rates. Likewise, tax increases and decreases can have unexpected and undesirable consequences.

The relationships between the major macroeconomic factors—unemployment, inflation, and supply and demand—are complex and difficult to keep in balance.

Fiscal policy is strongly associated with the economist John Maynard Keynes (1883–1946) and is a cornerstone of Keynesian economics.

Monetary Policy

Monetary policy is concerned with influencing the supply of money and credit and the demand for them to achieve specific economic goals. The actions of monetary policy are not as direct and obvious as the tax and spend activities associated with fiscal policy. Monetary changes are achieved indirectly through the nation's banking system. The following are some results of monetary policy changes:

- An increase in the amount of money that banks can loan to the public. This leads to greater borrowing, which puts more money into the hands of consumers, increasing the demand for goods and services.

- A decrease in the amount of money that banks can loan to the public. This leads to less borrowing, which slows the growth of the money supply and dampens demand, which can reduce high inflation rates.

- Lower interest rates on loans. This encourages borrowing, which increases the money supply and consumer demand.

- Higher interest rates on loans. This discourages people from borrowing more money, which slows the growth of the money supply and can reduce high inflation rates.

Just as in fiscal policy, it is difficult to achieve the exact results desired. An oversupply of money and credit will aggravate price inflation if production cannot meet increased consumer demand. Likewise, an undersupply can lower consumer demand too much and stifle economic growth. The challenge for the federal government is deciding when, and by how much, money supply and credit availability should be changed to maintain a healthy economy. These decisions and manipulations are made by the Federal Reserve, the nation's central bank.

THE FEDERAL RESERVE SYSTEM. In 1913 Congress passed the Federal Reserve Act to form the nation's central bank. The Federal Reserve System was granted power to manipulate the money supply—the total amount of coins and paper currency in circulation, along with all holdings at banks, credit unions, and other financial institutions.

The Federal Reserve includes a seven-member board of governors headquartered in Washington, D.C., and twelve Reserve Banks located in major cities around the country: Boston, New York City, Philadelphia, Cleveland, Richmond, Atlanta, Chicago, St. Louis, Minneapolis, Kansas City, Dallas, and San Francisco.

In *The Federal Reserve System: Purposes and Functions* (June 2005, http://www.federalreserve.gov/pf/pdf/pf_complete.pdf), the Federal Reserve explains that it uses three techniques to indirectly achieve "maximum employment, stable prices, and moderate long-term interest rates":

- Open market operations—the Federal Reserve buys and sells government securities on the financial markets. The resulting money transfers ultimately lower or raise the amount of money that banks have available to loan to the public and the associated interest rates.

- Discount rate adjustments—the Federal Reserve raises or lowers the discount rate. This is the rate that it charges banks for short-term loans. In response, the banks adjust the federal funds rate, the rate they charge each other for loans. Then the banks adjust the prime rate, the interest rate they charge their best customers (typically large corporations). In the end, these adjustments affect the interest rates paid by the general public on mortgages, car loans, credit cards, and so on.

- Reserve requirement adjustments—the Federal Reserve raises or lowers the reserve requirement, the amount of readily available money that banks must have to operate. Each bank's reserve requirement is based on a percentage of the total amount of money that customers have deposited at that bank. Money above the reserve requirement can be loaned out by the banks. Changes in the reserve requirement influence bank decisions about loans to the public.

CHAPTER 10
INTERNATIONAL TRADE AND THE UNITED STATES' PLACE IN THE GLOBAL ECONOMY

Those who have money go abroad in the world.

—Chinese proverb

Technology has made it easier to go abroad in the world. U.S. companies can sell their goods and services on a global market. Likewise, U.S. consumers can purchase merchandise made around the world—and they do so in large numbers. Global trade is driven by the same forces that control the U.S. market: supply and demand. However, there is the added complication of many very different national governments trying to exert influence over trade and market factors in their favor. The U.S. economy is preeminent in the global economy when it comes to national production. Yet, the United States buys far more from foreign lands than it sells to them. Economists disagree about whether this trade imbalance is a good or bad thing for the nation.

THE UNITED STATES' PLACE IN THE GLOBAL ECONOMY

According to the Central Intelligence Agency (CIA), in *World Factbook* (June 13, 2008, https://www.cia.gov/library/publications/the-world-factbook/rankorder/2001rank.html), the international gross domestic product (GDP) was $65.8 trillion in 2007. (See Table 10.1.) The United States had the largest economy of any single nation ($13.9 trillion), followed by China ($7 trillion), Japan ($4.4 trillion), and India ($3 trillion). The combined nations of the European Union (EU) had a gross domestic product (GDP; the total market value of final goods and services produced within an economy in a given year) of $14.5 trillion, putting the EU in a position above the United States in terms of economic strength. The GDP values in Table 10.1 were calculated based on purchasing power parity. This is an accounting method useful for comparing different economies. The CIA explains that each non-U.S. GDP listed in Table 10.1 was calculated by valuing that economy's goods and services at the prices prevailing in the United States.

How the United States Compares

The United States' rise as the global economic leader has resulted from a combination of four factors: geographical, political, social, and financial. The United States has also been fortunate, in that it escaped the ravages of two world wars that severely damaged the industrial infrastructure of other nations. In general, the United States' dominance is attributed to its wealth in natural resources, a motivated and educated labor force, many technological innovations, and a sociopolitical climate conducive to economic growth.

NATURAL RESOURCES. Natural resources are commodities that can be taken from the environment and either used in the manufacture of other products or sold in their original form. Forestry, fishing, and mining are classified as natural resources industries. Natural resources are considered either renewable or nonrenewable. Renewable resources are those that can be replanted or restocked (such as trees and fish), whereas nonrenewable resources, such as minerals, cannot be replaced once they become depleted. A country's natural resources can affect the overall health of its economy. According to the CIA, in *World Factbook* (July 15, 2008, https://www.cia.gov/library/publications/the-world-factbook/geos/us.html#Geo), the United States is the third largest country in the world (after Russia and Canada), at 3.8 million square miles (9.8 million sq km). The United States has direct access to two oceans; many rivers and waterways; coal, oil, and mineral deposits; fertile soil for farming; and many heavily forested areas, all of which make it one of the richest geographical regions on the planet.

LABOR. The highly skilled and well-trained U.S. labor force is one of the most important elements of the United States' economic success. The U.S. Department of Labor's Bureau of Labor Statistics (BLS) indicates in the press release "Employment Situation Summary" (July 3, 2008, http://www.bls.gov/news.release/empsit.nr0.htm) that in

TABLE 10.1

Gross domestic product (purchasing power parity), world and 25 wealthiest countries, estimated 2007

Rank	Country	GDP (purchasing power parity)
1	World	$65,820,000,000,000
2	European Union	$14,450,000,000,000
3	United States	$13,860,000,000,000
4	China	$ 7,043,000,000,000
5	Japan	$ 4,417,000,000,000
6	India	$ 2,965,000,000,000
7	Germany	$ 2,833,000,000,000
8	United Kingdom	$ 2,147,000,000,000
9	Russia	$ 2,076,000,000,000
10	France	$ 2,067,000,000,000
11	Brazil	$ 1,838,000,000,000
12	Italy	$ 1,800,000,000,000
13	Spain	$ 1,362,000,000,000
14	Mexico	$ 1,353,000,000,000
15	Canada	$ 1,274,000,000,000
16	Korea, South	$ 1,206,000,000,000
17	Iran	$ 852,600,000,000
18	Indonesia	$ 845,600,000,000
19	Australia	$ 766,800,000,000
20	Taiwan	$ 690,100,000,000
21	Turkey	$ 667,700,000,000
22	Netherlands	$ 638,900,000,000
23	Poland	$ 624,600,000,000
24	Saudi Arabia	$ 572,200,000,000
25	Argentina	$ 523,700,000,000
26	Thailand	$ 519,900,000,000

Note: All data were estimated in 2007.

SOURCE: Adapted from "Rank Order—GDP (Purchasing Power Parity)," in *The World Factbook*, Central Intelligence Agency, June 13, 2008, https://www.cia.gov/library/publications/the-world-factbook/rankorder/ 2001rank .html (accessed June 13, 2008)

June 2008 the civilian labor force consisted of 154.4 million employees. The BLS also measures the productivity of American workers using the ratio of output of goods and services to labor hours devoted to producing that output. According to the BLS, in the press release "Productivity and Costs, First Quarter 2008 Revised" (June 4, 2008, http://www.bls.gov/news.release/prod2.nr0.htm), productivity of the nonfarm business sector increased by 2.6% in the first quarter of 2008 and had experienced an annual average increase of 2.7% from 2000 to 2006.

TECHNOLOGY. U.S. companies have long been at the forefront of technological innovation, pioneering developments such as electricity, factory assembly lines, and computer software. These new technologies have increased both worker productivity and business efficiency, which, in turn, allow companies to deliver goods and services at lower costs to consumers, thereby stimulating spending and boosting the economy. At the same time, advances in technology can affect the job market. New technologies lead to more jobs as workers are needed to design, manufacture, and service them. By contrast, such advances can also cause job losses, as increased efficiency streamlines processes so that fewer employees are needed.

SOCIOPOLITICAL ENVIRONMENT. The sociopolitical environment of the United States has played a major role in the nation's rise to dominance in the global economy. Even though people argue about the proper role of government in the nation's economic affairs, the relatively free market–based system that has developed in the United States has proved to be conducive to economic growth.

GLOBAL AND U.S. TRADE

The World Trade Organization (WTO) states in *International Trade Statistics 2007* (2007, http://www.wto.org/english/res_e/statis_e/its2007_e/its2007_e.pdf) that world trade was more than $14 trillion in 2006. The value of merchandise trade was $11.5 trillion, and trade in commercial services was $2.8 trillion. Manufactured products accounted for more than 70% of the value of trade in merchandise. The two single largest sectors in commercial services were travel and transportation, accounting for 27% and 26%, respectively, of the total value of that category. Overall, the WTO reports that the value of worldwide trade increased by 8% between 2005 and 2006.

According to the WTO, the United States was the world's leading importer of goods in 2006, accounting for $1.9 trillion in imports, or 15.5% of the world total. Finishing out the top-five list of importers were Germany, China, the United Kingdom, and Japan. The United States was the second largest exporter of goods, ranking behind Germany. U.S. exports amounted to over $1 billion in 2006, accounting for 8.6% of world merchandise exports. Other nations in the top five were China, Japan, and France. The United States was the top exporter and importer of commercial services in 2006, with $307.8 billion in imports and $388.8 billion in exports. U.S. trade accounted for more than 11% of the world total in both imports and exports of commercial services.

U.S. Trade in Goods

Table 10.2 provides a breakdown of goods imported and exported by the United States in 2004, 2005, and 2006. Two different totals are given—a total using a balance of payments basis and a total using a census basis. These values represent different accounting methods used by the Bureau of Economic Analysis (BEA) and the U.S. Census Bureau, respectively, to track international trade of goods.

IMPORTED GOODS. Nearly $1.9 trillion in goods was imported into the United States in 2006. (See Table 10.2.) The industrial supplies category had the most imports, accounting for $601.9 billion of the total. According to the BEA, in *U.S. International Trade in Goods and Services, Annual Revision for 2006* (June 8, 2007, http://www.bea.gov/newsreleases/international/trade/2007/pdf/trad1307 .pdf), crude oil was the largest component in this category, accounting for more than one-third of industrial supply imports. Nearly $217 billion in crude oil was imported

TABLE 10.2

Imports and exports of goods by principal end-use category, 2004–06

[In millions of dollars. Details may not equal totals due to seasonal adjustment and rounding.]

Period	Total balance of payments basis	Net adjustments	Total Census basis[a]	End-use commodity category					
				Foods, feeds, beverages	Industrial supplies[b]	Capital goods	Automotive vehicles, etc.	Consumer goods	Other goods
Exports									
2004									
Jan.–Dec.	807,516	−11,259	818,775	56,570	203,910	331,441	89,213	103,238	34,404
2005									
Jan.–Dec.	894,631	−11,347	905,978	58,955	233,045	362,342	98,578	116,093	36,964
2006									
Jan.–Dec.	1,023,109	−13,525	1,036,635	65,962	276,045	413,894	107,161	129,982	43,589
Imports									
2004									
Jan.–Dec.	1,477,094	7,390	1,469,704	62,143	412,772	343,582	228,163	372,938	50,106
2005									
Jan.–Dec.	1,681,780	8,325	1,673,455	68,094	523,771	379,334	239,487	407,196	55,572
2006									
Jan.–Dec.	1,861,380	7,442	1,853,938	74,938	601,988	418,271	256,660	442,595	59,487

[a]Detailed data are presented, on a Census basis.
[b]Includes petroleum and petroleum products.

SOURCE: Adapted from "Exhibit 5. Exports of Goods by Principal End-Use Category," and "Exhibit 5a. Imports of Goods by Principal End-Use Category," in *U.S. International Trade in Goods and Services, Annual Revision for 2006*, U.S. Department of Commerce, Bureau of Economic Analysis, June 8, 2007, http://www.bea.gov/newsreleases/international/trade/2007/pdf/trad1307.pdf (accessed May 28, 2008)

into the United States in 2006. Other industrial supply imports included petroleum products ($44.2 billion), natural gas ($28.3 billion), and fuel oil ($27.1 billion). The top nonfuel import in this category was iron and steel mill products ($22.4 billion).

Consumer goods accounted for $442.6 billion of U.S. imports in 2006. (See Table 10.2.) This category includes a wide variety of household, sporting, and personal use items. The BEA indicates that pharmaceutical preparations were the largest single component of this category, accounting for $64.4 billion of the total. They were followed by miscellaneous household goods ($51.9 billion), apparel and household goods made of cotton ($48.7 billion), televisions and video cassette recorders ($35.9 billion), and apparel and textile goods—nonwool or cotton ($31.1 billion).

The United States imported $418.3 billion in capital goods in 2006. (See Table 10.2.) Capital goods are items such as machinery, equipment, apparatuses, engines, machine parts, aircraft, tractors, telecommunication devices, computers and computer accessories, and similar goods (excluding automotive vehicles and parts). According to the BEA, the largest value components were computer accessories ($67.6 billion), telecommunications equipment ($40.3 billion), computers ($33.8 billion), electric apparatuses ($33.6 billion), and miscellaneous industrial machines ($29.1 billion).

Nearly $257 billion in automotive vehicles, parts, and engines were imported in 2006. (See Table 10.2.) The BEA states that foods, feeds, and beverages accounted for $74.9 billion in imports, with fish and seafood making up the largest percentage by value ($13.2 billion). This was followed by miscellaneous foods ($7.9 billion); wine, beer, and related products ($7.8 billion); fruits and frozen juices ($7.5 billion); and meat products ($7.4 billion).

Other goods imported into the United States during 2006 had a value of $59.5 billion. (See Table 10.2.)

EXPORTED GOODS. The United States exported over $1 trillion worth of goods in 2006. (See Table 10.2.) The largest category of exports was capital goods, totaling $413.9 billion. In *U.S. International Trade in Goods and Services*, the BEA notes that semiconductors were the top export in this category, accounting for $52.4 billion in capital good exports. Other top exports included civilian aircraft ($40.8 billion), computer accessories ($36 billion), miscellaneous industrial machines ($32.7 billion), and electric apparatuses ($29.8 billion).

Just over $276 billion in industrial supplies were exported in 2006. (See Table 10.2.) According to the BEA, organic chemicals accounted for $27.1 billion of the total, followed by plastic materials ($25.1 billion), miscellaneous industrial supplies ($18.9 billion), miscellaneous chemicals ($18.6 billion), and fuel oil ($12.1 billion).

FIGURE 10.1

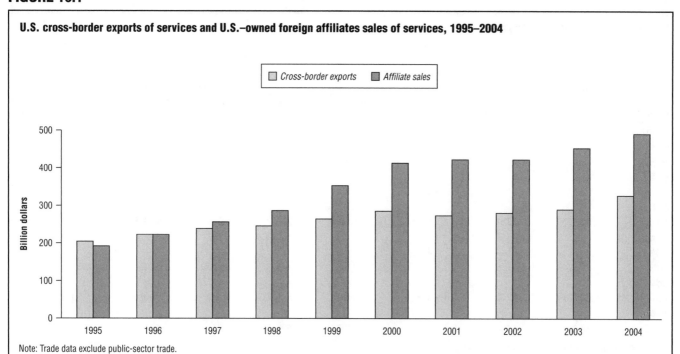

U.S. cross-border exports of services and U.S.–owned foreign affiliates sales of services, 1995–2004

Note: Trade data exclude public-sector trade.

Beginning in 1999, sales data for foreign affiliates of U.S. parent firms were reported under a new industry classification system, which resulted in a net gain in transactions reported for such affiliates reclassified in service industries in contrast to a net loss in transactions reported for such affiliates reclassified in goods industries.

SOURCE: "Figure 2.1. U.S. Cross-Border Exports of Services and U.S.–Owned Foreign Affiliates Sales of Services, 1995–2004," in *Recent Trends in U.S. Services Trade: 2007 Annual Report*, U.S. International Trade Commission, June 2007, http://hotdocs.usitc.gov/docs/Pubs/332/Pub3925.pdf (accessed May 28, 2008)

The value of exported consumer goods was $129.9 billion in 2006. (See Table 10.2.) The BEA explains that pharmaceutical preparations were the largest component at $30.9 billion. Other top exports in this category included miscellaneous household goods ($14.1 billion); gem diamonds ($9.9 billion); toys, games, and sporting goods ($9 billion); and toiletries and cosmetics ($6.8 billion).

U.S. exports of automotive vehicles, engines, and parts totaled $107.2 billion in 2006. (See Table 10.2.) The sum for exported foods, feeds, and beverages was $65.9 billion. The BEA indicates that corn accounted for $8.2 billion of the total, followed by meat and poultry ($7.8 billion), soybeans and miscellaneous foods ($7.3 billion each), and fruits and frozen juices ($5.6 billion).

Other goods exported by the United States during 2006 totaled $43.6 billion. (See Table 10.2.)

U.S. Trade in Services

According to the Census Bureau, in *U.S. International Trade in Goods and Services, May 2008* (July 11, 2008, http://www.census.gov/foreign-trade/Press-Release/current_press_release/ft900.pdf), U.S. businesses sold $497.2 billion worth of services in 2007. American consumers paid for $378.1 billion in foreign-provided services. Specific major types of imported services include travel ($76.2 billion), other transportation ($67.1 billion), and direct defense expenditures ($32.8 billion). However, the largest category

of imported services was "other private services" ($144.4 billion). This category includes business, professional, and technical services; insurance services; and financial services. Major exported services in 2007 were "other private services" ($223.4 billion), travel ($96.7 billion), and royalties and license fees ($82.6 billion).

The service export values do not completely show the United States' business presence in foreign lands. Increasingly, U.S. companies operate affiliate offices abroad, and their sales of services have become an important factor in U.S. trade. This growth is shown in Figure 10.1, which tracks the value of U.S. exports of services and the sales of services by U.S.-owned foreign affiliates from 1995 to 2004.

In 2004 sales of services by U.S.-owned foreign affiliates totaled $490 billion, up from less than $200 billion in 1995. According to the U.S. International Trade Commission, in *Recent Trends in U.S. Services Trade: 2007 Annual Report* (June 2007, http://hotdocs.usitc.gov/docs/Pubs/332/Pub3925.pdf), the industries accounting for the largest shares of foreign affiliate sales of services during 2004 were insurance (17.4%), computer systems design (9.1%), utilities (6.8%), telecommunications (6.6%), and transportation and warehousing (6.4%). The major locations of these affiliates were in the United Kingdom (which accounted for nearly a fourth of all foreign locations), Japan, Canada, and various European countries. Taken as a whole, Europe accounted for more than half of all foreign locations for U.S.-owned affiliates.

U.S. Trading Partners

In "Top Trading Partners: Total Trade, Exports, Imports" (February 14, 2008, http://www.census.gov/foreign-trade/statistics/highlights/top/top0712.html), the Census Bureau tracks the total imports and exports of goods to and from the United States on a monthly and yearly basis. In 2007 the United States' top-ten trading partners and the value of goods traded with them were:

- Canada—$562 billion
- China—$386.7 billion
- Mexico—$347.3 billion
- Japan—$208.1 billion
- Germany—$144 billion
- United Kingdom—$107.2 billion
- South Korea—$82.3 billion
- France—$69 billion
- Taiwan—$64.7 billion
- Netherlands—$51.4 billion

Together, these ten countries accounted for nearly two-thirds of all U.S. trade value during 2007.

U.S. TRADE BALANCE

The difference between exports and imports over a specific time period is known as the balance of trade (exports − imports = balance of trade). A positive balance of trade is called a surplus. This is a situation in which the value of exports is greater than the value of imports. A negative balance of trade is called a deficit. This occurs when the value of imports exceeds the value of exports.

The United States has had a trade deficit for goods every year since 1976, with record levels reached in the 2000s. (See Figure 10.2.) In 2007 there was a trade surplus of $107 billion for services. In other words, the value of exported services exceeded the value of imported services

FIGURE 10.2

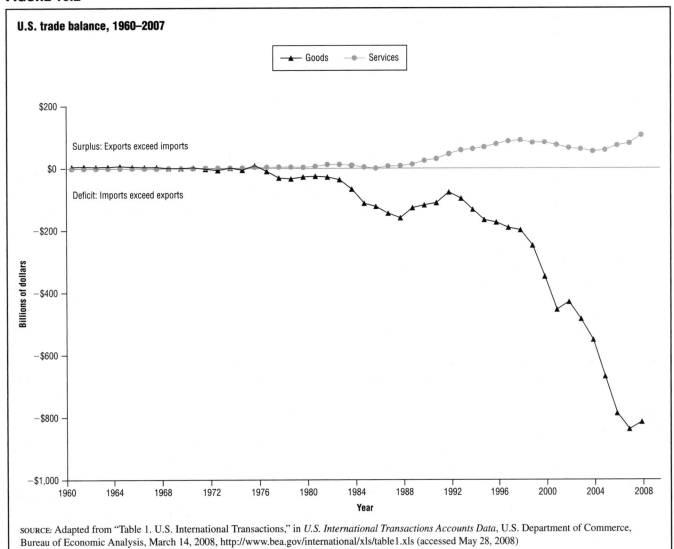

U.S. trade balance, 1960–2007

SOURCE: Adapted from "Table 1. U.S. International Transactions," in *U.S. International Transactions Accounts Data*, U.S. Department of Commerce, Bureau of Economic Analysis, March 14, 2008, http://www.bea.gov/international/xls/table1.xls (accessed May 28, 2008)

FIGURE 10.3

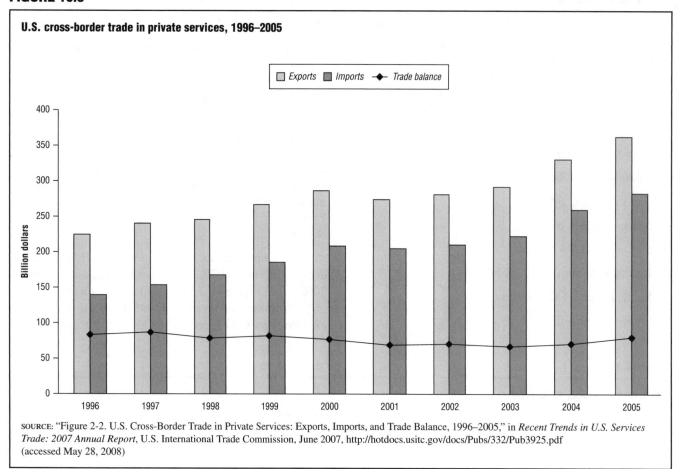

U.S. cross-border trade in private services, 1996–2005

SOURCE: "Figure 2-2. U.S. Cross-Border Trade in Private Services: Exports, Imports, and Trade Balance, 1996–2005," in *Recent Trends in U.S. Services Trade: 2007 Annual Report*, U.S. International Trade Commission, June 2007, http://hotdocs.usitc.gov/docs/Pubs/332/Pub3925.pdf (accessed May 28, 2008)

by $107 billion. This surplus was more than offset by an enormous trade deficit of $815 billion for goods. In other words, the value of imported goods was $815 billion greater than the value of exported goods. Even though the trade deficit in goods was down slightly in 2007, it is still high by historical standards.

The historical trade balance in services has been quite different. It has grown from mildly negative numbers during the 1960s to more than $100 billion in the last half of the first decade of the 2000s. From 1996 to 2005 the service trade balance has varied only slightly, even as imports and exports have increased. (See Figure 10.3.)

The Trade Deficit and the U.S. Dollar

The trade deficit is directly linked to the value of the U.S. dollar on foreign exchange markets. A dollar can be exchanged for equivalent amounts of any other foreign currency. The exchange rate for any given foreign currency at any given time depends on many complex economic factors, and exchange rates can vary widely over time.

When the U.S. dollar weakens compared to a foreign currency, it means that each dollar buys less of the foreign currency than it did before. Consequently, each dollar buys less goods from that nation. By contrast, each unit of the foreign currency is now worth more in U.S.

dollars and has more purchasing power of American goods. For example, when the dollar weakens compared to the Japanese yen, Japanese goods cost more to Americans, but American goods become cheaper for Japanese consumers. As a result, imports from Japan to the United States are likely to decrease, whereas exports from the United States to Japan will probably increase.

Likewise, when the dollar strengthens, it buys more foreign currency (and more foreign goods) than it did before. Thus, a stronger dollar is associated with higher imports into the United States and fewer exports to foreign lands.

Many economists believe the reduced U.S. trade deficit in goods during the late 1980s and early 1990s was associated with a rapid weakening of the dollar that occurred at the same time. The trade deficit reduction is evidenced as an upward spike in the bottom line in Figure 10.2 during this period. The trade deficit grew increasingly larger each year between 1980 and 1987 and then suddenly reversed its path for several years. During this time Americans were importing fewer foreign goods than before, because foreign goods suddenly cost more.

Cédric Tille, Nicolas Stoffels, and Olga Gorbachev indicate in "To What Extent Does Productivity Drive the

TABLE 10.3

Foreign holdings of U.S. securities, selected years 1994–2007

[Billions of dollars]

Type of security	Dec. 1994	Mar. 2000	June 2002	June 2003	June 2004	June 2005	June 2006	June 2007
Long-term securities	**1,244**	**3,558**	**3,926**	**4,503**	**5,431**	**6,262**	**7,162**	**9,136**
Equities*	398	1,709	1,395	1,564	1,930	2,144	2,430	3,130
Debt	846	1,849	2,531	2,939	3,501	4,118	4,733	6,007
U.S. Treasury	464	884	908	1,116	1,426	1,599	1,727	1,965
U.S. agency	107	261	492	586	619	791	984	1304
Corporate	276	703	1,130	1,236	1,455	1,729	2,021	2,738
Short-term debt	**n.a.**	**n.a.**	**412**	**475**	**588**	**602**	**615**	**635**
U.S. Treasury	n.a.	n.a.	232	269	317	284	253	229
U.S. agency	n.a.	n.a.	88	97	124	150	147	109
Corporate	n.a.	n.a.	92	110	147	168	215	297
Total long-term and short-term	**n.a.**	**n.a.**	**4,338**	**4,979**	**6,019**	**6,864**	**7,778**	**9,772**

n.a. Not available.
*"Equities" includes both common and preferred stock as well as all types of investment company shares, such as open-end, closed-end, and money market mutual funds.
Note: Components may not sum to totals because of rounding.

SOURCE: "Table 1. Foreign Holdings of U.S. Securities, by Type of Security, as of Selected Survey Dates," in *Report on Foreign Portfolio Holdings of U.S. Securities as of June 30, 2007*, U.S. Treasury Department, the Federal Reserve Bank of New York, and the Board of Governors of the Federal Reserve System, April 2008, http://www.treas.gov/tic/shl2007r.pdf (accessed May 29, 2008)

Dollar?" (*Current Issues in Economics and Finance*, vol. 7, no. 8, August 2001) that the dollar appreciated by 5.8% against the euro and by 4.8% against the yen on an average annual basis during the late 1990s. The relatively strong dollar made foreign goods cheaper for Americans and American goods more expensive for other countries, and unsurprisingly this period coincided with ballooning growth in the U.S. trade deficit. (See Figure 10.2.)

In the early 2000s the value of the dollar began to drop compared to foreign currencies. In contrast to conventional economic wisdom, the U.S. trade deficit continued to grow even as the dollar weakened. This contradiction is examined by Peter S. Goodman and Nell Henderson in "Dollar at 20-Month Low against the Euro" (*Washington Post*, November 29, 2006). Goodman and Henderson note that other factors allowed the U.S. trade deficit to grow as the dollar was shrinking—primarily huge buys of U.S. government securities by the governments of China and Japan. However, dollar value changes can take many months to several years to be reflected in the U.S. trade balance. Goodman and Henderson's observation proved to be prophetic as the growth in the U.S. trade deficit was less dramatic between 2005 and 2006 and actually decreased between 2006 and 2007. (See Figure 10.2.)

The Trade Deficit and the Flow of Capital

When Americans buy more foreign goods, more dollars flow into the foreign exchange markets. This provides greater opportunities for foreigners to invest in U.S. financial instruments, such as stocks, bonds, and Treasury bills. These purchases are tracked by the federal government in what is called the capital account. As of June 30, 2007,

foreign holdings of U.S. securities totaled $9.7 trillion. (See Table 10.3.) The vast majority of the holdings ($9.1 trillion) consisted of long-term securities (securities with maturity time more than one year). A much smaller value ($635 billion) of short-term debt was in foreign hands.

The U.S. Department of the Treasury states in the press release "Report on U.S. Portfolio Holdings of Foreign Securities at End-Year 2006" (November 30, 2007, http://www.ustreas.gov/press/releases/hp705.htm) that in November 2007 U.S. holdings of foreign securities totaled nearly $6 trillion at the end of 2006. This value was up from $4.6 trillion reported at year-end 2005.

Is the Trade Deficit Good or Bad?

The United States' enormous trade deficit is a subject of great debate among economists and politicians. Some believe the deficit is bad for the U.S. economy, particularly the country's manufacturing sector, and that steps should be taken by the government to correct the imbalance. Others contend the deficit is a natural consequence of a strong U.S. economy and should not be an issue of concern.

In "The U.S. Trade Deficit: Causes, Consequences, and Cures" (January 25, 2008, http://italy.usembassy.gov/pdf/other/RL31032.pdf), Craig K. Elwell of the Congressional Research Service outlines the perceived good and bad effects of a large trade deficit. Elwell notes that the U.S. trade deficit reached $811.5 billion in 2006 and grew by $20 billion from the year before. This growth was driven by an increase in import purchases by Americans.

As noted earlier, there is a direct link between the trade deficit and the flow of capital. As Americans buy more foreign goods, foreigners have more money to invest in U.S. financial instruments (e.g., stocks, bonds, and Treasury notes). On the plus side, these investments indicate strong foreign confidence in the security and future growth of the U.S. economy. Also, much of the money flowing into the country has been invested in productive capital—that is, invested in growing U.S. industry. However, in many cases these purchases represent debt obligations that the United States will have to pay in the future. In essence, the United States is becoming indebted to foreign nations. Elwell states that "borrowing from abroad allows the United States to live better today, but the payback must mean some decrement to the rate of advance of U.S. living standards in the future."

In a broader sense, large capital inflows demonstrate that Americans prefer spending their money on foreign imports rather than investing it in domestic financial instruments. Put simply, Americans prefer spending to saving. Elwell points out that the opposite is true in most other nations with healthy economies. In those countries people prefer saving (by investing in U.S. financial instruments), to buying American goods. Elwell notes, "So long as domestic saving in the United States falls short of domestic investment and an inflow of foreign saving is available to fill all or part of the gap, the United States will run a trade deficit."

Many critics of the trade deficit claim it hurts the U.S. economy overall, particularly by raising unemployment. Elwell disputes this claim, explaining that the dramatic growth of the trade deficit during the 1990s and 2000s has coincided with a generally healthy U.S. economy and relatively low unemployment rates. However, Elwell acknowledges that extensive foreign imports have hurt some U.S. manufacturing industries, particularly textiles, apparel, and steel.

TRADE AGREEMENTS

The U.S. government has long been part of free trade agreements with other individual countries (known as bilateral agreements) and with groups of countries (known as trading blocs). The U.S. bilateral free trade agreements in force, pending, or in negotiations as of May 2008 are listed in Table 10.4.

In this context, free trade means the ability to buy and sell goods across international borders with a minimum of tariffs or other interferences. Tariffs (import taxes) are fees charged by a country to import goods into that country. Figure 10.4 shows the average U.S. tariff as a percent charged on imported goods from 1930 through 2005. U.S. tariffs were relatively high during the early 1930s but decreased dramatically over the following decades.

Priorities regarding trade policy have shifted over the years according to the state of the economy. During the

TABLE 10.4

U.S. bilateral trade agreement status, 2008

Free-trade agreements (FTAs) pending Congressional approval
- Colombia
- Panama
- Republic of Korea

FTAs in force
- Israel
- NAFTA—North American Free Trade Agreement (Canada & Mexico)
- Jordan
- Chile
- Singapore
- Australia
- Morocco
- Bahrain
- DR-CAFTA—Dominican Republic-Central America Free Trade Agreement (Costa Rica*, Dominican Republic, El Salvador, Guatemala, Honduras, & Nicaragua)

FTAs pending implementation
- Peru
- Oman

Other FTA negotiations
- Malaysia
- Thailand
- SACU—Southern African Customs Union
- United Arab Emirates

*Approved by Costa Rican national referendum in October 2007; pending legislative approval.

SOURCE: Adapted from "Bilateral Trade Agreements," in *Bilateral Trade Agreements*, U.S. Treasury Department, Office of the United States Trade Representative, 2008, http://www.ustr.gov/Trade_Agreements/Bilateral/Section_Index.html (accessed May 29, 2008)

FIGURE 10.4

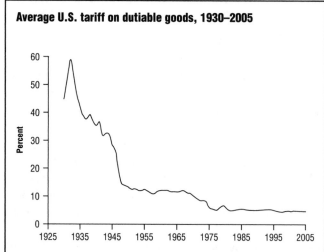

Average U.S. tariff on dutiable goods, 1930–2005

SOURCE: "Chart 7-1. Average U.S. Tariff on Dutiable Goods, 1930–2005," in *Economic Report of the President*, U.S. Government Printing Office, February 2006, http://www.gpoaccess.gov/eop/2006/2006_erp.pdf (accessed May 29, 2008)

recession of the late 1970s, U.S. producers called for the government to institute measures—such as high tariffs—to protect them from international competition. During the growth period of the 1980s, however, the focus of companies turned to their own international expansion, and by the 1990s a push for free trade had gained increased momentum.

According to Bruce Arnold of the Congressional Budget Office, in *The Pros and Cons of Pursuing Free-Trade Agreements* (July 31, 2003, http://www.cbo.gov/showdoc.cfm?index=4458&sequence=0), opponents to trading blocs argue that when countries with strong economies—such as the United States, Japan, and the countries of the EU—negotiate agreements, smaller nations with developing economies are left at an unfair disadvantage because they are excluded from the favorable terms of the agreement.

North American Free Trade Agreement

The United States, Canada, and Mexico implemented the North American Free Trade Agreement (NAFTA) on January 1, 1994. A primary objective of NAFTA has been the complete elimination of barriers to trade among the three signing countries. Many tariffs were dropped immediately, and others were scheduled to be phased out over time. Agricultural products were an integral part of NAFTA and had some of the longest phase-out schedules. All agricultural provisions of NAFTA were implemented by January 2008.

NAFTA has had a positive effect on the marketability of goods among the participating nations. The efficient production of goods that are exported from one country to another keeps pricing fair and competitive as nations produce and export the goods for which they already have.

However, there has been concern that importing goods from other countries could cause the loss of jobs in the United States. In "The High Price of 'Free' Trade" (November 17, 2003, http://www.epinet.org/content.cfm/briefingpapers_bp147), Robert E. Scott of the Economic Policy Institute estimates that by 2002, 879,280 U.S. jobs—mostly high-paying manufacturing industry positions—were displaced as a result of NAFTA's removal of trade barriers.

Until 2002, workers displaced because of NAFTA were eligible for the NAFTA Transitional Adjustment Assistance program, administered by the Department of Labor's Employment and Training Administration (ETA; January 12, 2006, http://www.doleta.gov/tradeact/nafta_taa.cfm), which offered "rapid and early response to the threat of unemployment and the opportunity to receive reemployment assistance, including job search assistance, retraining and income support while in training, to enhance and ease the transition to a new job." The ETA (November 15, 2004, http://www.doleta.gov/tradeact/nafta_certs.cfm) estimates that by 2004, 525,407 workers had received help through the program. Because of the impact on U.S. employment, free trade agreements such as NAFTA remain controversial.

The European Union

In 1957 six European countries signed the Treaty of Rome, establishing the European Economic Community.

In 1992 the Maastrict Treaty was signed, officially establishing the EU. After centuries of war, leaders of European countries hoped that by engaging in commerce they could create long-term stability and enforce the rule of law in cooperative democratic societies. The EU, which is one of the most important trading partners of the United States, expanded in 2004 from fifteen nations to twenty-five, creating the largest trading bloc in history.

The Delegation of the European Commission to the United States (May 12, 2008, http://www.eurunion.org/eu/index.php?option=com_content&task=view&id=57&Itemid=51) states that as of May 2008 the EU consisted of twenty-seven countries: Austria, Belgium, Bulgaria, Cyprus, the Czech Republic, Denmark, Estonia, Finland, France, Germany, Greece, Hungary, Ireland, Italy, Latvia, Lithuania, Luxembourg, Malta, the Netherlands, Poland, Portugal, Romania, Slovakia, Slovenia, Spain, Sweden, and the United Kingdom. Candidate countries for admission to the EU in the future included Croatia, the former Yugoslav Republic of Macedonia, and Turkey.

General Agreement on Tariffs and Trade and the WTO

One of the most important trade agreements is the General Agreement on Tariffs and Trade (GATT), which was first signed by the United States and twenty-two other countries in 1947. This agreement dealt primarily with industrial products and marked a trend toward the increasing globalization of the world economy. The agreement reduced tariffs, removed other obstacles to international trade, and clarified rules surrounding barriers to free trade. Agriculture was for the most part kept out of the initial negotiations. By the end of the 1980s, more than one hundred countries had ratified the GATT.

A series of GATT negotiations that concluded in 1994 created the WTO, which replaced GATT and now functions as the principal international body charged with administering rules for trade among member countries. The new agreements covered a range of topics, including agriculture, food safety, animal and plant health regulations, technical standards (testing and certification), import licensing procedures, trade in services, intellectual property rights (including trade in counterfeit goods), as well as rules and procedures for settling disputes. As of May 2008, the WTO (http://www.wto.org/english/theWTO_e/whatis_e/tif_e/org6_e.htm) consisted of 152 member countries, including the United States.

THE INTERNATIONAL MONETARY FUND

At the United Nations (UN) Monetary and Financial Conference—more commonly known as the Bretton Woods conference because it took place in Bretton Woods, New Hampshire—in July 1944, the forty-five countries fighting on the side of the Allied forces in World War II (1939–1945) negotiated the creation of the International Monetary Fund

(IMF), a global financial system. The IMF extends short-term loans to members experiencing economic instability. As a condition of receiving its credit assistance, the IMF requires the debtor country to enact significant reform of its economic structure, and often of its political structure as well, eliminating corruption and establishing effective institutions such as courts. The conditions for being granted a loan can include drastic cuts in government spending; privatizing government-owned enterprises, such as railroads and utilities; establishing higher interest rates; increasing taxes; and eliminating subsidies on necessities such as food and fuel.

Critics maintain that the austerity demanded by the IMF can have devastating social consequences, including severe unemployment, crippling price increases in the cost of basic goods, and political instability resulting from widespread dissatisfaction. As of June 2008, the IMF (http://www.imf.org/external/about.htm) included 185 member countries, including the United States.

THE WORLD BANK

At the same conference that created the IMF in July 1944, the International Bank for Reconstruction and Development (IBRD) was established. The IBRD and the International Development Association (IDA) are commonly known as the World Bank. The World Bank is not a bank in the traditional sense of the word but an agency of the UN. The World Bank works to combat world poverty by providing low-interest loans, interest-free credit, and grants to developing countries. As of June 2008, the World Bank (http://web.worldbank.org/) noted that the IBRD and IDA included 185 and 167 member countries, respectively.

In its early days, the World Bank often participated in large projects such as dam building. In the twenty-first century, it supports the efforts of governments in developing countries to build schools and health centers, provide water and electricity, fight disease, and protect the environment. It is one of the world's largest sources of development assistance. The World Bank notes in *Annual Report 2007* (2007, http://go.worldbank.org/A2QP25LQX0) that since 1944 it has provided $433 billion in loans to developing countries worldwide.

GLOBALIZATION AND THE ANTIGLOBALIZATION MOVEMENT

The move toward global free trade, or globalization, has generated intense controversy. Proponents maintain that globalization can improve living standards throughout the world. Their arguments include the following:

- Countries and regions will become more productive by concentrating on industries in which they have a natural advantage and trading with other nations for goods in which they do not have an advantage.

- Multinational corporations will be able to realize economies of scale—that is, operate more economically because they are buying in bulk, selling to a much larger market, and utilizing a much larger labor pool. This will increase productivity and lead to greater prosperity.

- Free trade will lead to faster growth in developing countries.

- Increased incomes and the development of job-related skills among the citizens of poorer nations will foster the spread of information, education, and, ultimately, democracy.

Critics of globalization point out the negative effects that multinational corporations have on people in the developing world. They argue that most of the profits from free trade flow to the United States and other industrialized countries; that local industries can be destroyed by competition from wealthier nations, causing widespread unemployment and social disruption; that centuries of cultural tradition can be quickly obliterated by the influence of international companies; and that multinational corporations often impinge on national sovereignty to protect their profits.

Critics also note that the free trade policies are often applied unfairly, as the United States insists that other countries open their markets to American goods at the same time that it protects its own producers from competition. For example, the U.S. government has established many tariffs and regulations that raise the prices of imported food products, denying poor farmers in the developing world access to the lucrative U.S. market. In addition, opponents of globalization point out that the spread of multinational corporations can be detrimental to workers in industrialized nations by exporting high-paying jobs to countries with lower labor costs, and that international competition in the labor market could actually lead to lower living standards in the industrialized world.

The antiglobalization movement is not an organized group but an umbrella term for many independent organizations that oppose the pursuit of corporate profits at the expense of social justice in the developing world. These groups often protest the actions of organizations such as the WTO, the IMF, and the World Bank for their perceived bias toward corporations and wealthy nations. In 1999 a WTO conference in Seattle, Washington, drew more than forty thousand protestors in a massive demonstration that generated intense media attention and completely overshadowed the meeting itself.

SANCTIONS

The United States has used economic and trade sanctions (stopping some or all forms of financial transactions and trade with a country) as a political tool against countries that are thought to violate human rights, tolerate drug trafficking, support terrorism, and produce or store weapons of mass destruction. Sanctions are enforced by the Department of the Treasury's Office of Foreign Assets Control (OFAC). As of June 2008, the OFAC (http://www.ustreas.gov/offices/enforcement/ofac/faq/answer.shtml#9) listed economic and/or trade sanctions against the following countries: the Balkans, Belarus, Burma, Côte d'Ivoire (Ivory Coast), Cuba, Democratic Republic of the Congo, Iran, Iraq, the former Liberian regime of Charles Taylor, North Korea, Sierra Leone, Sudan, Syria, and Zimbabwe.

The Trade Act of 1974 allowed the United States to impose sanctions on countries with unfair trade policies. The Jackson-Vanik amendment to this legislation barred the president from granting favorable trade status to countries that limited emigration, and required annual certification for communist countries, including China. This amendment was repealed in 2000, marking a major step in the restoration of relations between China and the United States. The Chinese market presents an enormous opportunity for U.S. exports, but it has remained difficult to penetrate by U.S. exporters. On December 11, 2001, China was admitted as a member of the WTO.

THE CHANGING FACE OF FREE TRADE
Trade Promotion Authority

President George W. Bush (1946–) signed the Trade Act of 2002 in August 2002. The act gave the president Trade Promotion Authority (TPA), under which international trade agreements were subject to an up-or-down vote, but not amendment, in Congress. The TPA was designed to promote freer trade by giving other countries confidence that the agreements they negotiated with U.S. diplomats would not be subject to changes and renegotiation when they are submitted to Congress for ratification.

The TPA expired in 2007 and was not renewed amid concerns about its effectiveness. In *An Analysis of Free Trade Agreements and Congressional and Private Sector Consultations under Trade Promotion Authority* (November 2007, http://www.gao.gov/new.items/d0859.pdf), the U.S. Government Accountability Office (GAO) summarizes its investigation of the TPA. The GAO explains that the TPA was administered by the Office of the U.S. Trade Representative (USTR). The TPA required specific procedural steps, such as meetings between the USTR and congressional committees with jurisdiction over trade matters. The GAO finds that during the five-year period that the TPA was in effect, 1,605 of these meetings took place. Even though congressional committee staff reported that the USTR provided "good information" in these meetings, many staff members were frustrated by their lack of opportunity to provide input to the USTR.

The GAO notes that such procedural problems need to be fixed if the TPA is to be reimplemented.

Regarding the overall success of the TPA, the GAO finds that seventeen free trade agreements (FTAs) with forty-seven countries were pursued under the TPA process. Six of these agreements were approved and went into force. Negotiations for an additional four agreements were concluded. The GAO concludes that the number of agreements reached under the TPA was relatively small and notes that "most economic studies find the gains for the United States of the completed FTAs to be relatively small compared with the overall U.S. economy."

Parity in Labor Standards and Environmental Laws

Discrepancies in labor and environmental regulations among trading nations have formed another barrier to free trade. The administration of President Bill Clinton (1946–) pushed to impose the same labor and environmental standards on trading nations that the United States imposes on itself. The move was designed to discourage trading partners from exploiting workers and abusing the environment to keep capital costs lower and prices down, thus making their goods and services more competitive than U.S. goods in the global market. Before NAFTA was signed, the United States insisted on assurances from Canada and Mexico that they would enforce labor and environmental laws before ratifying the agreement.

Intellectual Property

Technological advancements have posed new challenges to world trade. As private-sector investment in information technology continues, world economies are becoming even more interconnected. Proponents of free trade, including the United States, have pushed for more protection of intellectual property rights, abuse of which poses a major barrier to world trade. As defined by the UN in the Convention Establishing the World Intellectual Property Organization (May 25, 2007, http://www.wipo.int/treaties/en/convention/trtdocs_wo029.html), which was signed on July 14, 1967, and amended on September 28, 1979, intellectual property includes:

- Literary, artistic, and scientific works

- Performances of performing artists, phonograms, and broadcasts

- Inventions in all fields of human endeavor

- Scientific discoveries

- Industrial designs

- Trademarks, service marks, and commercial names and designations

- Protection against unfair competition and all other rights resulting from intellectual activity in the industrial, scientific, literary, or artistic fields

WORLD INTELLECTUAL PROPERTY ORGANIZATION.
Challenges for the international community include establishing minimum standards for protecting intellectual property rights and procedures for enforcement and dispute resolution. These challenges are not new. The World Intellectual Property Organization (WIPO) explains in "Major Events 1883 to 2002" (July 4, 2007, http://www.wipo.int/treaties/en/general/) that as early as 1883, with the fourteen-member Paris Union for the Protection of Industrial Property, states recognized the special nature of creative works, including inventions, trademarks, and industrial designs. Soon afterward, in 1886, the Berne Union for the Protection of Literary and Artistic Works extended the model of international protection to copyrighted works such as novels, short stories, poems, plays, songs, operas, musicals, sonatas, drawings, paintings, sculptures, and architectural works.

In 1893 the Paris Union and the Berne Union combined to form the United International Bureaus for the Protection of Intellectual Property, which maintained its headquarters in Berne, Switzerland. This organization eventually evolved into the WIPO, located in Geneva, Switzerland, which carries out a program designed to:

- Harmonize national intellectual property legislation and procedures

- Provide services for international applications for industrial property rights

- Exchange intellectual property information

- Provide legal and technical assistance to developing and other countries

- Facilitate the resolution of private intellectual property disputes

- Marshal information technology as a tool for storing, accessing, and using valuable intellectual property information

As of October 2007, the WIPO (http://www.wipo.int/members/en/) included 184 member nations, including the United States.

FEDERAL INITIATIVES: FOCUS ON KNOCKOFFS AND COUNTERFEIT PRODUCTS. Knockoffs (or counterfeit goods) are copies of legitimate goods sold in the marketplace. In the past, knockoffs were primarily imitations of select items with upscale brand names, such as designer purses or watches. They appealed to some consumers who wanted to pay low prices for inferior-quality merchandise that could masquerade as expensive brand-name items. Purchases were usually conducted by street or back-alley vendors in large cities. In recent years the knockoff industry has greatly matured, spreading its scope to include many different consumer goods that can be purchased (knowingly or unknowingly) in a wide variety of markets.

During the early 2000s the U.S. government stepped up its campaign against the manufacture, distribution, and sale of knockoffs. In March 2004 the U.S. attorney general John D. Ashcroft (1942–) established an Intellectual Property Task Force within the U.S. Department of Justice. The task force published recommendations calling for greater focus on criminal prosecution both at home and abroad, additional regulatory measures, and enhanced public education about the negative impact of intellectual property crime on the U.S. economy. Later that year, the U.S. Department of Commerce launched the Strategy Targeting Organized Piracy initiative to link together many agencies engaged in the protection of intellectual property rights.

In March 2006 President Bush signed the Stop Counterfeiting in Manufactured Goods Act to strengthen federal laws and expand the tools available to law enforcement agencies to combat goods counterfeiting. The action was driven by growing evidence that knockoffs pose a serious problem to the U.S. and global economies, public safety, and even national security. According to the article "Hezbollah Pushes Prada?" (CNNMoney.com, March 26, 2005), in 2005 law enforcement officials testified before the U.S. Senate Homeland Security Subcommittee that international terrorist groups were involved in the knockoff trade in the United States to raise money for their organizations.

Officials note that knockoffs have moved out of back allies and into mainstream American markets. The U.S. Chamber of Commerce warns in *What Are Counterfeiting and Piracy Costing the American Economy?* (2005, http://www.uschamber.com/) that "fakes are infiltrating the supply chain and making their way into legitimate retail outlets." The organization cites a number of events in which consumers were harmed by defective knockoffs, including counterfeit batteries sold at retail stores. Furthermore, it reports that knockoffs cost U.S. businesses $200 billion to $250 billion in lost sales in 2004. Global losses were estimated at around $500 billion.

In the press release "May Is National Electrical Safety Month: CPSC Warns of Dangerous Counterfeit Electrical Products" (May 9, 2007, http://www.cpsc.gov/cpscpub/prerel/prhtml07/07185.html), the U.S. Consumer Product Safety Commission notes that as of May 2007 it had recalled a total of more than one million counterfeit electrical products, including defective cell phone batteries, circuit breakers, and extension cords. The agency states that "many counterfeit products are made in China." Maureen Fan reports in "China's Olympic Turnabout on Knockoffs" (*Washington Post*, June 13, 2008) that in June 2008 Chinese authorities had begun a massive crackdown on counterfeiters in preparation for the summer Olympic Games, which were scheduled for August 2008. Fan notes that "for years, China has been known as the leading exporter of fake goods." Chinese